The Heroes of Treća Gimnazija

The Heroes of Treća Gimnazija

A War School in Sarajevo, 1992–1995

David M. Berman

ROWMAN & LITTLEFIELD PUBLISHERS, INC.
Lanham • Boulder • New York • Oxford

ROWMAN & LITTLEFIELD PUBLISHERS, INC.

Published in the United States of America
by Rowman & Littlefield Publishers, Inc.
4720 Boston Way, Lanham, Maryland 20706
www.rowmanlittlefield.com

12 Hid's Copse Road, Cumnor Hill, Oxford OX2 9JJ, England

British Library Cataloguing in Publication Information Available

Library of Congress Cataloging-in-Publication Data

Berman, David M.
    The heroes of Treća Gimnazija : a war school in Sarajevo, 1992–1995 / David M.
Berman.
        p. cm.
    Includes bibliographical references and index.
    ISBN 0-8476-9567-0 (alk. paper) — ISBN 0-8476-9568-9 (pbk. : alk. paper)
        1. Yugoslav War, 1991–1995—Education and the war. 2. Treća gimnazija 3.
Yugoslav War, 1991–1995—Bosnia and Hercegovina—Sarajevo. 4. Sarajevo (Bosnia
and Hercegovina)—History. I. Title: Heroes of 3. Gimnazija. II. Title.

DR1313.7.E38 B47 2001
373.49742—dc21

                                                                        2001020454
Printed in the United States of America

♾™ The paper used in this publication meets the minimum requirements of American
National Standard for Information Sciences—Permanence of Paper for Printed Library
Materials, ANSI/NISO Z39.48-1992.

To the Teachers and Students
of Treća Gimnazija

Contents

Tables

Notes on Pronunciation

c = *ts* as in cats

ć = *tj* (soft) as in tune

č = *ch* (hard) as in chamber

đ = *j* (soft) as in bridge

dž = *j* (hard) as in jet

j = *y* as in yes

lj = *lli* as in million

š = *sh* as in show

ž = *s* as in pleasure

Notes on Orthography and Terminology

Throughout the narrative, and in both the text citations and reference list, I have adhered to the traditional Serbo–Croatian orthographic style. In this regard, all Serbo–Croatian references and terms, with the exception of proper names, are marked by capitalization of the first word only, as in, for example, *Prva gimnazija*. Thus the reference, *Ratna škola mjesne zajednice Avdo Hodžić*, is marked by the capitalization of the first word, *Ratna*, with the succeeding words in small letters, *škola mjesne zajednice*. Because *Avdo Hodžić* is a proper name, both *Avdo* and *Hodžić* are capitalized. When these terms or references are used in English, however, all terms or references are capitalized, as in, for example, the First Gymnasium, or the Avdo Hodžić Local Community War School.

I have made one exception to the rule, however, in the case of *Treća Gimnazija*, the Third Gymnasium, which is, of course, the subject of the book. I have chosen to refer to the school by the Serbo–Croatian terminology because that is how I have come to know the school and, in this regard, I have used the Serbo–Croatian name in the English format during the course of the narrative and have capitalized both words. When the school is cited as a reference, however, I have reverted to the Serbo–Croatian orthography, as in *Treća gimnazija*, consistent with all other Serbo–Croatian references.

Finally, the language here is identified as Serbo–Croatian, although references in the text sometimes identify the language as Bosnian which is, of course, a result of the breakup of the Socialist Federal Republic of Yugoslavia and the establishment of Bosnia and Herzegovina as an independent state. Although texts and grammar books for the Bosnian language now appear in Sarajevo bookstores, the languages are, for the most part, one and the same.

Foreword

As a former student of Treća Gimnazija, it is a great honor for me to write this preface. While I was a student, I could never imagine I would once write a foreword for a book dedicated to my high school, let alone the foreword for a book that describes it as a "war school." When I was a student there, World War II was just a distant memory of my father who, as a member of a Sarajevo's Sephardic Jewish community, had escaped death in Nazi concentration camps by joining the antifascist partisans. The members of my generation were taught to believe that the war would not happen ever again. And we deeply believed it.

Carrying all these nice memories from my school days in Treća Gimnazija, memories of endless laughs and the fun that we had—playing soccer in the backyard, holding hands and strolling down Wilson Promenade with my high school sweetheart, I was deeply saddened and horrified when I first saw on CNN the mortar round hit the bench on Wilson Promenade where I had stolen my first kisses, windows of the chemistry lab smashing in the blast, walls of my classroom pierced with bullets.

While my generation of Treća Gimnazija students was stealing kisses and exchanging laughs on their way to and from school, the 1992–1995 generation was dodging snipers and hiding themselves from the firefights on the frontline that cut through the city, right in front of the school building. Together with other citizens of Bosnia and Herzegovina and its capital Sarajevo, the teachers and students of Treća Gimnazija have endured unprecedented suffering during the war, 1992–1995, the kind of suffering that earned them the title of heroes and martyrs. What I feel compelled to say is that their heroic experience should have and would have been avoided had the West been willing to intervene militarily in Bosnia and Herzegovina in 1992 in order to put a stop to Milošević's policy of ethnic cleansing.

But the West did not intervene and the destruction of a uniquely tolerant multiethnic, multicultural, and multireligious society in Bosnia and Herzegovina lasted for another three and one-half years. Centuries of peaceful coexistence of the Muslims, Catholics, Orthodox Christians, and Jews of Sarajevo, epitomized by the fact that their largest places of worship are all placed in the city center and within walking distance from one another—was suddenly made irrelevant due to the so-called political reality, and when the 1995 Dayton Agreement was signed, it was done by dividing Bosnia into two ethnically based entities. It took a couple of years more and, unfortunately, 250,000 deaths, before the West finally decided to put a stop to Milošević's genocidal policy by militarily intervening in the Balkans.

It was already 1999 when Western leaders openly compared Milošević to Adolf Hitler, the comparison that Sarajevans were painfully aware of during more than a thousand days of siege that their city went through during the Bosnian war. Faced with the impossible task of unraveling the tightly interwoven fabric of a centuries-old multiethnic and multicultural city, the Bosnian Serb Army, backed by Milošević's regime, placed a medieval siege around Sarajevo exposing its citizens to starvation and death from shelling and sniping for more than three and one-half years—the longest siege in the history of modern warfare.

The entire city was thus turned into a concentration camp before the eyes of the modern world, which once vowed not to allow that to happen ever again. The foreign media and other foreign nationals who were allowed entrance to that "camp" were often amazed by the unbreakable spirit of Sarajevo's citizens, the spirit that was also reflected in the fact that the schools and other public institutions were functioning throughout the siege. For those foreigners who were allowed to get in and out of the city at their free will, this may look like an act of heroism. But for those who knew they would be detained and possibly killed once they tried to pass the Bosnian Serb checkpoints surrounding the city, this was simply life happening until and despite inescapable death. Since their besiegers solved for them the ultimate dilemma, "to be or not to be," clearly hoping for the latter, the answer to the question, "to teach or not to teach," was relatively easy.

The teachers and students of Treća Gimnazija, together with other Sarajevans, were left with nothing but their strong will to survive. In order to survive they had to go out of their apartments and search for food and water. They knew very well that they may lose their life or a limb whenever they did it since, as they sarcastically used to say during the siege, "everyone of us has a mortar round that awaits him/her." That awaiting mortar round could easily hit them (and often did) in their own apartments. Therefore, those who stayed inside and those who ventured outside were equally close to death.

Sarajevans understood that the crucial difference between those who kept themselves useful and busy and went to work during the siege, and those who remained hiding in the cellars, lay in the fact that the former refused to succumb to the wishes of their besiegers and reduce themselves solely to inhuman-like creatures with survivalist instincts. That's why the streets of Sarajevo were full of people despite constant sniping and shelling. That's why the schools were open and functioning. When the Bosnian Serb Army besieged and occupied Grbavica, carving the dividing line right through the tissue of cohesive, inner city communities, the teachers and students of Sarajevo schools were first among those who courageously crossed the line of danger, going out of their shelters and back to work and study. By deciding to do that despite constant shelling and sniping from the enemy lines, they openly rebelled against the idea of the siege and division of the city.

For their spirit and will to live was simply stronger than death itself. And that's the most important lesson the readers of this book can learn from the teachers and students of Treća Gimnazija: When the enemy threatens to kill an entire city, all its citizens can do is to try to live their lives as best as they can, for their lives are the only weapon they have in the fight against evil.

There are many other lessons that can be drawn from the recent war in Bosnia. The organization of war schools is just one of them. Professor Berman deserves full credit for his effort to pass it onto us through this book. As for the rest of the world, the lesson it should have finally learned from the Bosnian war is to adhere to its post–World War II grand promise and prevent genocide and ethnic cleansing from happening *ever again*. This lesson should finally be learned so that the memories of all new generations of Treća Gimnazija can once again be as happy and joyful as mine was.

—Sven Alkalaj,
Ambassador of Bosnia and Herzegovina
to the United States, 1994–2000

◆◆◆◆◆◆◆◆◆◆◆◆◆◆◆◆◆◆◆◆◆◆

During the war, on 1 May 1993, I began working as the director of Treća Gimnazija. I was handed down an inadequate school that lacked basic necessities, and I had to deal with these problems myself. Most of the teachers had left the city, and the original school facility was taken over by the Bosnian Army. At that time, some war schools operated, while my role consisted of opening new punkts, finding adequate teachers, and taking care of the school archives. I had to do all of those things while having in mind the importance of providing a safe environment for the students and their teachers. Thank God, I did not make many mistakes.

Besides my intended goals, I also focused on a higher one and that was creating a multiethnic group of teachers who would cooperate and work towards establishing friendly relationships. The current war situation destroyed that bond among people, the bond that was created based upon both common and different things that made this country so special. Despite that, we were able to cooperate and work with all our hearts and produce excellent results in upbringing and education.

During the toughest periods of the war, we managed our war school successfully, making it one of the best gimnazija in Sarajevo. All the helpful hands from friendly people all over the world opened their doors. All of a sudden we found ourselves on the world platform. First in 1995, the Swedes started to help, then the Danes, the Germans, and later on in 1998 came an agreement with the United States through USAID. To the United States, we owe the reconstruction of our school, while to the city of Stockholm we owe the equipping of the interior. The highlight of Treća Gimnazija was the visit by President Bill Clinton, Secretary of State Madeleine Albright, and various others diplomats, on 30 July 1999. That will be one of the dearest memories of our Treća Gimnazija.

The reconstruction of the school is a beautiful work of art that was made possible by our numerous friends all over the world and by Sarajevo Canton. The heroes of Treća Gimnazija have received their highest reward for all of the suffering that they endured and the courage that they showed during the years of war (1992–1995). I would like to thank everybody, and thank Mr. David Berman, who wrote this book about us. That is how the facts will be preserved from being forgotten.

—Emina Avdagić,
School Director, Treća Gimnazija

Preface

First and foremost, I wish to thank the teachers, administrators, and students of Treća Gimnazija for their assistance with my research. Emina Avdagić, the school director, Avdo Hajdo, the assistant school director, and Mirko Marinović, the school director who preceded Professor Avdagić, were particularly helpful to me. Professor Avdagić provided me with a copy of the *Školski ljetopis* (*School Annual*) of Treća Gimnazija for the war years, 1992–1995, upon my initial visit to the school, and thus provided me with the documentary basis for my research. In addition to providing me with numerous other documents, she also responded to my unending requests for information. Perhaps most importantly, she allowed me access to the teachers and students without which the research could not have been accomplished. Professor Hajdo also responded to my numerous requests for information and, in addition, gave me a walking tour of the Avdo Hodžić Local Community where he served as coordinator of the Avdo Hodžić Local Community War School under the administration of Treća Gimnazija. This firsthand view of the storefronts and basements that served as war school classrooms provided a visual perspective on schooling under siege in Sarajevo. Although now the school director of the Comprehensive Wood–Forestry Secondary School (Mješovita srednja drvna-šumarska škola), Professor Marinović also answered numerous questions for me concerning his entries in the *School Annual* as both school director and assistant school director of Treća Gimnazija during the war years. In addition, he provided me with papers presented at the *Školstvo u ratnim uslovima* Symposium, the "Schooling in War Conditions" Symposium, held on 18 April 1994, in the midst of the 1993–1994 war school year, which provided a wider perspective of war schools throughout Sarajevo. Without the assistance of all three Treća Gimnazija school administrators, this work simply could not have been accomplished.

In what is now the Ministry of Education, Science and Information (Ministarstvo obrazovanja, nauke i informisanja) of Sarajevo Canton, I would like to thank Minister Safet Halilović and Deputy Minister Ismet Salihbegović for their support of my research in the schools under their administration. I would especially like to thank Safija Rašidović, the associate for education, for without her assistance, I would still be stranded in the offices of the Ministry of Education drinking Turkish coffee. To this day, I remember her grabbing me by the arm, dragging me onto a bus along Maršala Tita Street, and taking me out to Hrasno to meet with the faculty of Treća Gimnazija. She has continued to provide me with her assistance to this day by contacting schools, arranging appointments, and providing all sorts of information, and I am deeply indebted to her.

I also wish to thank Adis Pitić who, in 1998, worked in the Ministry of Education, and today works as a computer analyst for the Danish Refugee Council. Adis befriended me during my regular visits to the Ministry in the spring and summer of 1998 while I was a visiting scholar at the Faculty of Philosophy of the University of Sarajevo. During the war, Adis was not in a classroom but on the frontline, first at Goražde and later with the Bosnian Army's 104th Motorized Brigade at Stup and Nedžarići, where he was severely wounded in the defense of Sarajevo. I know the terrain of Sarajevo quite well because of Adis, and our tours of the urban battlefields of Grbavica, Hrasno, Azići, and Otes have proved invaluable to me in understanding what Kemal Kurspahić refers to as "the 'geography' of murder" as a backdrop to the story of schooling under siege (1997:173).

In what is now the Ministry of Education, Science, Culture and Sport (Ministarstvo obrazovanja, nauke, kulture i sporta) of the Federation of Bosnia and Herzegovina, I would like to thank Minister Fahrudin Rizvanbegović and especially, Deputy Minister Abdulah Jabučar, for their support of my research in the schools of the federation. The opportunity to visit schools throughout Bosnia has provided me with a clearer picture of schooling in Sarajevo for this particular book. It is clear from such visits that there are many stories of schooling during the years of the war yet to be told, from places like Goražde, for example, or the Sarajevo suburb of Dobrinja. So, given the support of the Ministry of Education, perhaps this book on a war school in Sarajevo will serve as the prelude to forthcoming books on other schools throughout the country. Such stories of schooling during wartime conditions are certainly there to be told.

Two educators who worked at the Pedagogical Institute of Sarajevo during the war deserve special thanks. Melita Sultanović, pedagogy advisor, and Hajrija-Šahza Jahić now at the Pedagogical Academy, were two of a very few educators at this level who remained in the city and continued their work during the early months of the siege. These two educators were certainly not *podrumski ljudi* (cellar people), those people who remained in their basements when there was serious work to be done "to normalize the lives of children living in totally impossible circumstances" (Jahić, 1996:11). Both were involved in the reconstruction and reorganization of the educational system, but perhaps their most notable contribution was the development of the prototype war school, the Bjelave School, for example, that set the stage for the development of war schools throughout the city. In addition, both proved especially helpful to me in developing a picture of schooling throughout Sarajevo beyond the level of the individual school. I also wish to thank Professor Sultanović for providing me with documents based upon her work in the development of local community war schools that were otherwise unavailable to me.

I wish to thank Professor Zvonimir Radeljković of the Department of English Language and Literature, Faculty of Philosophy, University of Sarajevo, whom I first met during the siege, and who invited me back to the Faculty as a visiting scholar. Two years later, I returned as a visiting scholar to the Faculty of Philosophy once again under an academic exchange program between the University of Pittsburgh and the University of Sarajevo, but now in the Department of Pedagogy thanks to the invitation of Professor Miljenko Brkić. The academic exchange was accomplished primarily through the efforts of Mirjana Mavrak, the higher assistant in the Department of Pedagogy, who served as my host during my time at the Faculty. I cannot count the ways Mirjana assisted me well above and beyond the call, from assistance with translations to assistance in daily efforts at the University. Her greatest endeavors on my behalf, however, placed me in contact with educators throughout the city who were involved in the reconstruction and reorganization of the schools. Through Mirjana's efforts, I gained not only a wider perspective of schooling throughout Sarajevo but a greater appreciation of the work of dedicated Sarajevo educators. For Mirjana's efforts, I am deeply indebted. Professor Adila Pašalić-Kreso of the Faculty of Philosophy has been especially supportive of my research as well and has proved to be a valuable colleague to me during my continuing efforts to conduct research on Bosnian schools. To reciprocate the academic exchange program with the University of Sarajevo that I initiated in 1998, Professor Kreso came to the University of Pittsburgh as a visiting scholar under the auspices of the Russian and East European Studies (REES) Program during May and June 2000.

From the REES Program at the University of Pittsburgh, I wish to thank, first and foremost, Robert Hayden, director, and Robert Donnorummo, assistant director, for their wholehearted support of my research efforts. This support was especially beneficial upon the realization of the academic exchange between the University of Pittsburgh and the University of Sarajevo that resulted in an extended stay in Bosnia during the spring and summer of 1998. Eileen O'Malley, the administrative assistant for REES, was especially helpful to me with all kinds of administrative matters during my visits to the area, and Maja Budovalčev, graduate student and REES secretary from Kikinda in the Federal Republic of Yugoslavia, helped me with numerous translations. Milica Bakić-Hayden was most helpful with tutoring sessions in the language and with translation assistance, and she continues to assist me when I call on her for additional advice. The support of REES was especially appreciated considering my status as a latecomer to the region, which began with a United Nations Children's Fund (UNICEF) education project during the Bosnian war, but no one ever held this against me and I was accepted as one of their own. The University Center for International Studies (UCIS) provided additional support for my research through a Hewlett International Studies Grant, and the School of Education provided support with a Faculty Small Grant Research Award.

While any number of individuals assisted me with any number of translations, Jasmina Hadžić served as the primary translator of the *School Annual*. Jasmina now works for the World Bank located on what is today Hamdije Kreševljakovića Street but, during the war, referred to as Dobrovoljačka Street, where the administrative offices of Treća Gimnazija were located in the Comprehensive Agricultural, Veterinarian, and Food Secondary School nearby. I simply could not have written this book without Jasmina's efforts, and we hope one day to bring her to the University of Pittsburgh to continue her studies. In Sarajevo, I also wish to thank Dragan Golubović, the librarian at what was once the Soroš Media Center, who assisted me beyond measure with documents and newspapers from the Center collections. Dragan has continued to assist me to this day with my research efforts.

I wish to thank Ibrahim (Ibro) Sejfović, a recent graduate of the Pennsylvania State University, who worked at the University of Pittsburgh in the REES Program during the summer of 1999. Ibro assisted me with the translation of numerous documents but, during the siege, he lived in Dobrinja where he was critically wounded by a mortar round on 17 August 1993. Ibro and his family eventually emigrated to Pittsburgh where he received therapy at a local rehabilitation institute. The friend-

ship of the Sejfović family enabled me to live in Dobrinja upon my return to Sarajevo to continue my research. In this regard, I wish to thank
Ibro's relatives, Bojana Burlović and her daughters Maja and Sanja who
attend the Skender Kulenović Elementary School in Dobrinja. I also wish
to thank Vojislav Andrić for his kindness and for hosting me in his Ciglane home during the spring of 1998, and Dr. Jozo Stijepić and his family for their kindness and for hosting me in their home in Bjelave during
the spring and summer of 1996.

Perry Lingman, the rector of the Office of Educational Administration of the City of Stockholm, Sweden, deserves special mention. I first
met Perry at the Treća Gimnazija masked ball where he was an honored
guest that evening. No single individual has worked as long and as hard
as Perry to assist the Treća Gimnazija community in the reconstruction
of its school buildings. His dedication to the task at hand has been truly
remarkable over the years, and he deserves special recognition here in a
book about the school that he so ably assisted. I am indebted to him for
sharing with me his work during a particularly difficult time, as well as
for his photographs of the school.

Finally, I wish to thank the many teachers and students of Treća
Gimnazija who provided me with firsthand accounts of teaching and
learning in the war schools of Sarajevo in general and Treća Gimnazija
in particular. Although the experience of the siege was often emotionally
difficult for them to recall, these teachers and students assisted me with
interviews and translations throughout the course of my research. There
were teachers such as Gordana Roljić who walked from her home in
Mojmilo many dangerous kilometers across the city to teach her classes,
and there were teachers like Behija Jakić who taught in the stairway
schools of Dobrinja amidst the siege within a siege. These teachers were
the heroes of Treća Gimnazija.

And there were students such as Jasmin Kulovac who deserve personal mention as well. At the time Jasmin would have entered the first
year of high school during the fall of 1992, he was on the frontlines as a
defender of the besieged enclave of Žepa in eastern Bosnia. For the better part of the next four years, "instead of carrying a pencil," writes Jasmin, "in my hands I held a gun" (1999). When Žepa fell to the enemy in
August 1995, just after the fall of Srebrenica, Jasmin was captured and,
in handcuffs, witnessed the execution of eight other friends and soldiers
who were captured with him. The only survivor of the execution squad,
Jasmin celebrated his eighteenth birthday in a Rogatica prison where he
spent the next five months in solitary confinement until a prisoner exchange following the Dayton Accords. Eighteen years of age, and one

week out of an enemy prison, Jasmin began his first year of high school four years late at Treća Gimnazija, the one school that would still accept him as just another student. True to his spirit and perseverance, he completed his schooling with high honors and is now a student at the Faculty of Criminal Studies of the University of Sarajevo. I am indebted to Jasmin for sharing with me his story of life at Treća Gimnazija and his childhood in Žepa, and for sharing his courage and heroism as well, without intending to do so.

I am indebted to all of these men and women for their assistance with this book. Indeed, their dedication, their perseverance, and their courage are the mark of "everyday heroes" who fought the war against their people in basement classrooms with books and pencils and on city streets with audacity and defiance. Even today, four years after the Dayton Accords, "the war still exists in the souls of the students, in the souls of the teachers," said Hajrija-Šahza Jahić in words to me during a recent conversation. "The war is still there" (1999). Indeed, considering that "the war still exists in the souls" of students and teachers alike, the difficulty of talking about the past to an outsider such as myself is something that I deeply appreciate. It is not very easy to recall the close encounters with rockets and mortars that whistled through the night sky or the loss of loved ones who were cut down by snipers. Thus wrote Ehlimana Hrapović, another of those Treća Gimnazija students, and whose brother was one of those cut down, "the departure of some dear and close people from this world left an incurable wound in the heart and soul. The wound is the symbol of the town, of the generation. A single look back is enough to feel the pain from that wound" (1994). This book could not have been written without the assistance of the students and teachers of Treća Gimnazija who were forced to look back to the siege of their town in response to my questions and who no doubt felt the searing pain from that wound. These *Sarajlije* shared something of their lives with me at a time when Sarajevo was under siege and when Bosnia was in flames. This is the story of "the heroes of Treća Gimnazija," the students who asserted their right to their education and the teachers who answered their call during the siege of Sarajevo. In the words of Belma Huskić, one of those students:

> This is a story about war. The truth and reality to me. Someone might think I am lying. I can tell it to my family abroad, and they can say: "We know what you must be going through," but they don't. They can not even feel a premonition of it, because they were taught from the same history books as I was. (1995)

CZECH REP.

SLOVAKIA

UKRAINE

Moravia

Donau

Inn

Vienna● ●Bratislava

●Salzburg

AUSTRIA

Budapest●

HUNGARY

●Graz

CARINTHIA
Mt. *Cahorce* ●Klagenfurt ●Maribor
Triglav ●Bled
L. *Bohinj* SLOVENIA *Drava* Szeged● ●Arad
Celje● Subotica● *Mures*
Ljubljana● *Sava* ROMANIA
Trieste● ●Sezana ●Zagreb *Drava* VOJVODINA
Piran● CROATIA Novi Sad● *Danube*
●Rijeka ●Pakrac Vukovar●
Cetingrad● ●Jasenovac KRAJINA Belgrade●
Otoka● ●Bosanski Novi Zupanje● YUGOSLAVIA
Bihać● ●Banja Luka *Bosna* SERBIA
Sanski● Most ●Tuzla
Bosanska Krupa Zvornik●
Danube
Zadar● DINARIC BOSNIA Srebrenica● *Drina*
Knin● ●Livno Sarajevo● ●Žepa *Morava*
●Ancona ALPS Pale● Niš●
Split● Goražde●
●Mostar

A d r i a t i c   S e a

MONTENEGRO
Dubrovnik● ●Cetinje Priština● ●Sofia
Herceg-Novi● Podgorica● KOSOVO BULGARIA
Prizren●
L. *Scutari* Skopje●
●Shkodër *Vardar*

I T A L Y
●Bari MACEDONIA
Tiranë● ALBANIA
Durrës● L. *Ohrid*
Naples● Elbasan● L. *Prespa*
●Brindisi GREECE
Taranto● Vlorë● Thessaloniki●

Gjirokastra● *Aegean
Sea*

0   100   200   *Ionian
Sea*
miles

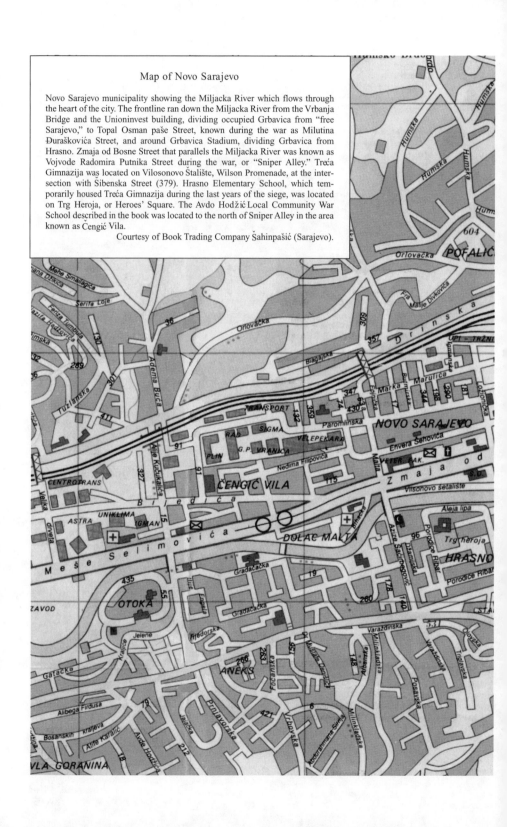

Map of Novo Sarajevo

Novo Sarajevo municipality showing the Miljacka River which flows through the heart of the city. The frontline ran down the Miljacka River from the Vrbanja Bridge and the Unioninvest building, dividing occupied Grbavica from "free Sarajevo," to Topal Osman paše Street, known during the war as Milutina Đuraškovića Street, and around Grbavica Stadium, dividing Grbavica from Hrasno. Zmaja od Bosne Street that parallels the Miljacka River was known as Vojvode Radomira Putnika Street during the war, or "Sniper Alley." Treća Gimnazija was located on Vilosonovo Štalište, Wilson Promenade, at the intersection with Šibenska Street (379). Hrasno Elementary School, which temporarily housed Treća Gimnazija during the last years of the siege, was located on Trg Heroja, or Heroes' Square. The Avdo Hodžić Local Community War School described in the book was located to the north of Sniper Alley in the area known as Čengić Vila.

Courtesy of Book Trading Company Šahinpašić (Sarajevo).

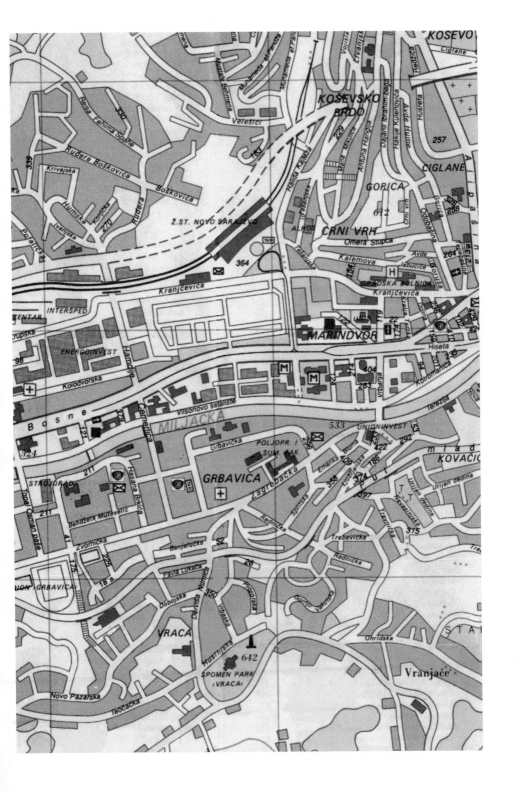

I došlo neko tuđe vrijeme
I došlo neko tuđe vrijeme,
I rat.
Ubili moje roditelje
Srušili moju kuću
Oteli moju zemlju
Promijenili moj jezik.

S' prijateljem ne znam šta je bilo
Jer se moj prijatelj podijelio na troje
I ne vidim više svog prijatelja
Jer nemam tri oka
I ne znam više svog prijatelja
Jer ne umijem sa razlomcima

◆◆◆◆◆◆◆◆◆◆◆◆◆◆◆◆◆◆◆◆◆◆

And some foreign time came
And some foreign time came,
And war.
Killed my parents
Destroyed my home
Took my country
Changed my language.

I don't know what happened to my friend
Because my friend divided himself in three
And I don't see my friend anymore
Because I don't have three eyes
And I don't know my friend anymore
Because I don't understand fractions

—Mirzeta Memišević,
student of Treća Gimnazija

Chapter One

On Baking Bread, Building a Palace, and Doing Research On the War Schools of Sarajevo

Zrno po Zrno Pogača
Kamen po Kamen Palača
—Traditional Bosnian Proverb

The Battle of the Mind

The city of Sarajevo represents a special case. Subject to a classic military siege of a sort one had not expected to see in the late twentieth century, Sarajevo has been the victim of non-stop bombardment by artillery for almost 22 months. . . . Access to the city remains essentially closed and a blockade has been imposed on all commodities including the most essential necessities of life. (UNICEF, 1994:I)

After almost four savage years under classic military siege, Sarajevo came up for breath to experience an interlude of relative peace. "The vocabulary of a high school pupil is too poor for describing and interpreting Peace at this moment of its coming," wrote Zgodić Ensar, a fourth-year student at Treća Gimnazija. "For me, peace is everything that is not war" (1996). "For me, peace is something to be respected," wrote Dino Ćatović, another fourth-year student. "Peace is the mother with a child in her own house. Peace is a man with both legs. Peace is a child who has not lost a parent, or his eyes. Peace is a house that did not burn. Peace is a whole city that has not been bombed. That is peace for me" (1996).

In a city that has been bombed into oblivion, and where peace is measured by the absence of war, the story of the war schools of Sarajevo can now be constructed from the stark, eyewitness accounts of schooling amidst the horror and carnage of the siege. In this regard, the antiseptic tone of the United Nations Children's Fund (UNICEF) situation analysis fails in translation in much the same way that the United Nations Protection Force (UNPROFOR) failed to protect the *Sarajlije*, the Sarajevans, from the butchers in the hills above the city. Perhaps Sarajevo as "a special case" might be better understood as "the sense of being inside a killing jar," in the words of one eyewitness, a "slaughter in slow motion" (Rieff, 1996:124, 120), over four years of siege warfare.

In phrases thick with merciless imagery, the *Saralije* themselves clarify what it means to be "the victim of non-stop bombardment by artillery" over almost four years of the siege. "Every child in Sarajevo is affected by war trauma," offered one clinical psychologist (Jevdević, 1996). "Those who haven't seen brains on the asphalt don't know what war is," offered one teacher (Dmitrović, 1996). "Probably no one in the USA has seen children's brains on the asphalt," offered one student. "I still want to wake up and say, 'This was an awful nightmare' and continue with my life as a sixteen-year-old girl. *Nema Vode, Nema Hljeba—Crkni (Umri)*," Lejla Polimac said to me. "No Water, No Bread—Drop Dead" (1996).

Indeed, war creates new images and new terminology to somehow describe the horror and the slaughter. "Sarajevo is the city of the future and of the life in the post-cataclysm," reads the FAMA *Sarajevo Survival Guide*, in mockery of contemporary travel books. The Sarajevo guidebook "was written at the site where one civilisation was dismantled . . . and where another one had to be born, the one of the 21st century. It is the picture of civilisation that emerges out of the cataclysm" (Prstojević, 1993:89, 1). Thus my own students at the Faculty of Philosophy of the University of Sarajevo, where I was a visiting scholar in 1996, gave me a book of Sarajevo at the end of our seminar, which they signed in cryptic fashion: "This is where West and East have halted."

The reality of the nightmare of Sarajevo evokes the surrealism of a postmodern war where biblical siege warfare is conducted with twentieth-century weaponry to lay waste to a modern European city which, only eight years before, hosted the 1984 Winter Olympics as a symbol of peace and brotherhood among nations. "One of the cruellest aspects of this extraordinarily cruel war is the blend of sophisticated technology and primitive brutality," writes Nada Conić in the translator's preface to *Sarajevo Days, Sarajevo Nights*, by Elma Softić (1996), noting the surrealistic nature of it all. "Bosnia can watch its own destruction on television. How can Elma, who has been both a student and a teacher of philosophy, survive the absurdity of such a situation?" (1996:6). This "new kind of conflict, like that in Sarajevo," writes Martin van Creveld, is marked by the blurring of military and civilian "in which armies and peoples become indistinguishable," where "states are replaced by militias or other informal—often tribal groupings. These new wars tend to be very bloody because there is no distinction between armies and peoples, so everybody who gets in the way gets killed" (Cohen, 1995:1–8). Writing at the onset of the breakup of Yugoslavia, and one year prior to the siege of Sarajevo, van Creveld suggested that such low-intensity conflict "will become a much more direct experience for civilians [who] will be affected . . . as immediate participants, targets, and victims." He further suggested that practices that had previously been considered "uncivilized, such as capturing civilians and even entire communities for ransom are almost certain to make a comeback" (1991:203).

In fact, the citizens of Sarajevo became participants, targets, and victims of siege warfare that held the entire population of what remained of the city, which they referred to as "free Sarajevo," for ransom. Viewed in this light, the story of the siege of Sarajevo may be told in terms of the adaptation of the *Sarajlije* to survive under the most savage and surreal of conditions. Thus at an Ombudsman Roundtable in Sarajevo on "Children with Special Needs," Milanka Miković of the Department of Social Work, Faculty of Political Science, University of Sarajevo, stated in no uncertain terms that the war in Bosnia was "a war against civilians" and that "mostly the victims were children." In this regard, she echoed the words of a number of participants and clarified her charge in the following manner. "If to everything mentioned we add the fact, evident from our close reality, personified in the offering of assistance for our very survival, with a priority to help the children, humanitarian organizations sent medication and food for babies which were given to children and adults, with a due expiration date, or children and old people of Sarajevo and Bosnia were given cookies three decades old, then we have the right to ask ourselves whether this was an experiment perpetrated on our children and all other generations" (1998:51–52). The surrealism of it all was such that *Sarajlije* could only wonder whether this was not some sort of experiment to determine whether a

modern" European city could survive under siege in the twentieth century while the outside world provided Bisquick supplies some thirty
years old to ease the starvation. In his book on *The Fall of Yugoslavia*,
Misha Glenny connects the military reality with the insanity of it all:

> When fighting broke out around Sarajevo in earnest on the weekend of
> 4 and 5 April 1992, the third Bosnian war had begun. . . . The first war
> involved Serbs and Croats; the second was between Serbs and Mos-
> lems; the third war, although as cruel as the other two, pitted Serb ir-
> regulars, largely culled from the surrounding peasantry together with
> JNA [*Jugoslovenska Narodna Armija* or Yugoslavian Peoples' Army]
> and its awesome arsenal of heavy artillery against the sophisticated, ur-
> ban dwellers of Sarajevo and other major towns. . . . The battle for
> Sarajevo was launched by Karadžić doubtless for strategic reasons, but
> if successful it would signal a victory for the primitive and irrational
> over the civilized and rational. (1994:171)

The incongruity not to mention the insanity here is that the son of Radovan Karadžić himself, the political leader of the Republika Srpska, the
Serbian Republic, was a student at Treća Gimnazija, the very same
school attended by Zgodić Ensar, who wrote of peace as everything that
is not war. In fact, the younger Karadžić graduated from Treća Gimnazija at the end of the 1991–1992 school year that was abbreviated by
his father whose command for Bosnian Serb forces to assault the city
saw the destruction of the very school from which he graduated.

The struggle between the primitive and irrational versus the civilized
and rational suggests that perhaps the underlying story of the battle for
Sarajevo, told in educational terms, becomes a story of "the battle of the
mind" for the students and teachers in the war schools of the city. "In the
aftermath of another brutal war a half-century ago, Robert King Hall, an
American education officer in the Civil Information and Education Section of the Allied Occupation of Japan, wrote an article entitled, "The
Battle of the Mind: American Educational Policy in Germany and Japan" (1948). Hall wrote, "Thoughtful people realized that the military
victory marked only a phase in a far more basic conflict, one involving
economic, psychological, and diplomatic pressures, and one which
would ultimately be determined on that most intangible yet fundamental
of battlegrounds—the mind of the defeated peoples" (1948:59). Hall's
perspective is particularly relevant here and suggests that the military
battle for Sarajevo was "a phase in a far more basic conflict" to be determined "on that most intangible yet fundamental of battlegrounds," not

for the mind of the defeated peoples but, in this case, to determine whether these peoples would be defeated.

The nature of this battleground is expressed by Slavenka Drakulić in her afterword to Dževad Karahasan's book, *Sarajevo, Exodus of a City* (1994). Drakulić wrote that "the city of Sarajevo became a sort of concentration camp, which one could enter only with the greatest difficulty, and from which one could hardly get out. In besieged Sarajevo people lived and starved, lost hope, and got killed at random." Although there is no systematic attempt to explore this idea in greater depth, Drakulić notes one particular similarity between the besieged city and the concentration camps. "Both Sarajevo under siege and Auschwitz represent a closed system, with their own set of rules and patterns of human behavior. And every closed system where people get killed and one is uncertain about the future, produces a certain kind of psychology that is not easy to understand" (1994:114). Drakulić speaks to the manner in which people living inside "a closed system," in other words, a besieged city, develop their own patterns of behavior and their own world view in order to survive extreme conditions. In a letter to me about life under siege, Mujo Musagić, the editor of the journal, *Prosvjetni list* (Educational Gazette), attempted to explain the mindset of the people of besieged Sarajevo and the location of the war school phenomena within this mindset. I will offer passages from his letter here in some detail:

> The psychology of people in the besieged cities, in which tens of people were dying each day, and sometimes thousands of different caliber projectiles were falling, was trying to establish a "normal" life. Those people wished, at least in their illusions, to form a more ordinary environment that resembled a normal way of life, because only in that way could they have the desire to survive.
>
> Life in the besieged cities was equal to that in the concentration camps. The long-term siege was destroying the last spark of life in people, of hope for a possible solution, optimism. So stage shows were performed, art galleries were opened, poetry forums and musical shows were organized; even a "Miss Besieged Sarajevo" competition was organized.
>
> That's how we come to "war schools." They were also a part of the normal illusions of life, although we can't take away their numerous functions. Children did learn, teachers did hold classes, the educational process did take place on the basis of a reduced program written by the Ministry of Education. However, my impression is, the most important value of schools during the war can't be measured by numbers and sta-

tistics but, as I would put it in words, it can be measured by *the value of the significance of life.* . . .

There are many reasons why this aspect of "war school" research should be given special attention. For sure, the war schools in Bosnia and Herzegovina played a part in defending this country and its people. The war schools offered an additional sense of normal life to children and adults; they offered strength and the belief that it is possible to survive the impossible conditions of hunger, thirst, wounding and dying. Even fighters with guns in their hands believed that there was a sense in fighting when they knew that their children were attending so-called classes. . . . Even the children concluded that peace and normal life would come because they were taught everything they would need in peacetime and normal conditions. Therefore, everyone "took advantage" . . . of the belief in the possible return of peace and normal life. But sometimes during the long, war-camp life, hope and belief that peace and normal life would return, is equal to normal life itself. (1998)

Mujo Musagić speaks of the desperation of people living under siege and their efforts to assume the illusion of normality "because only in that way could they have the desire to survive." Should there be any doubt as to the nature of this psychological battleground, we have only to witness the imagery employed by the enemy, seen in the words of Ratko Mladić, the Bosnian Serb military commander, overheard on military frequency on 27 May 1992, the day of the Breadline Massacre, while directing the bombardment of Sarajevo. The "brain" metaphor so pronounced in the words of the *Sarajlije* during the siege is seen in perhaps its most chilling form in the words of General Mladić, here recalled by Zoran Bečić, who also speaks of the desperate struggle to survive:

"Stretch their brains," he said. Remember that? Back then, even when I listened to a recording of that command, I couldn't possibly figure out what he meant. I think that today, almost two years later, I understand what he had in mind, what he meant to do, and what he finally did. . . . Now, I have finally begun to understand what Mladic meant when he said to his commanders: "Stretch their brains!" There is nothing here any more, no memories, nothing to remember, and nothing to hope for. And every time I think we've reached rock bottom, that it's the limit, that it couldn't be any worse, a new layer opens up, a new chasm, a new dimension of pain and suffering. And you can even go beyond that, into a still deeper, darker, and more horrifying abyss. The worst thing is that we have suffered and survived all that. I hate survival. I no longer want to survive and I am desperate because of it. (Dizdarević, 1994:65–66)

Set against the backdrop of the enemy military commander who employed the imagery of *razvlačenje pameti* (stretching the brain) while his artillery pounded Sarajevo, Hajrija-Šahza Jahić, of the Pedagogical Institute in Sarajevo at that time, asks: "What can one say about teachers in wartime?" Her response is that the educational system could never "have functioned without the teachers, who were thus in *the frontline in the fight against the aggressor*" [my emphasis] (1996:27). Thus writes Abdulah Jabučar, the deputy minister of education of the Republic during the war, "provinces, municipalities, and particularly schools, as well as teachers, have to be maximally engaged and try to find all possible ways of successfully educating the children. That is '*the second battle line*' [my emphasis], and our victory as well as the final liberation of Bosnia and Herzegovina depends on it" (1994:5). Indeed, the imagery of the military battle for the country is employed by student and teacher alike to describe the psychological battle to preserve the illusion of normality and the logistical battle to reconstruct an educational system under siege. This imagery suggests that "the battle of the mind" became a form of patriotic resistance against the enemy expressed in the very terminology of the "war schools" of Sarajevo. In my view, the educators of Sarajevo took it upon themselves, with virtually no outside assistance, to reconstruct an educational system "on that most intangible yet fundamental of battlegrounds" in order to create what they perceived as their own frontline in the defense of the besieged city. In the words of Mujo Musagić, "That's how we come to 'war schools'" (1998).

In academic terms, this research is a case study of a war school in Sarajevo during the siege, the chronicle of Treća Gimnazija, the Third Gymnasium (hereafter, Treća Gimnazija), also referred to as the Third Grammar School. One of twenty-nine secondary schools in the city at the onset of the siege, Treća Gimnazija was the third of five *gimnazija*, or academic secondary schools whose purpose was to prepare students for the university. The story of Treća Gimnazija is recorded here within the background of schooling throughout the besieged city under what was then the administration of the City Secretariat for Education, Science, Culture and Physical Culture (Gradski sekretarijat za obrazovanje, nauku, kulturu i fizičku kulturu) at the beginning of the war, and what is today the Ministry of Education, Science, and Information (Ministarstvo obrazovanja, nauke i informisanja) of Sarajevo Canton. Much of this story was recorded in the pages of the *Školski ljetopis* (*School Annual*) of Treća Gimnazija (hereafter, *School Annual*), where regular entries by school administrators provide the documentary record of schooling. In this regard, perhaps this essay is the story of all Sarajevo schools during the period between 1992 and 1995 which, as the educational institutions of the fledgling Bosnian republic, became principal targets of the military forces besieging the city.

In more human terms, this essay is the story of the teachers and students of Treća Gimnazija, the students who asserted their right to their education and the teachers who answered their call as they waged their own personal "battle of the mind" in the battle for Sarajevo. The sense of this struggle, of the tenacity and the desperation, of the nature of this battleground, is captured by Amira Prcić, a third-year student at Prva gimnazija, the First Gymnasium, at the onset of the siege. As a student in the American Studies seminar I taught as a visiting scholar at the University of Sarajevo, Amira wrote an essay entitled, "My Experiences in the War," where she expressed her thoughts on life as an adolescent under siege and the significance of war schools to the students:

> During that time we were so desperate, especially young people. We couldn't understand how the whole world could just sit aside and do nothing to save us. I thought they wanted us to die. When we understood that nobody would do anything for us unless we did it ourselves, our fear gradually turned into a revolt. We didn't want to lose courage completely. It wasn't just the fight on the battlefield. It was also intellectual, spiritual. We started to go to school, because we felt we had the right to, the so-called "war schools." . . . We felt then and still do that we had the right to this city and to life, and no one could take it away. That's why we didn't give up. (1996)

Thus, to reiterate Mujo Musagić, "the most important value of schools during the war . . . can be measured by *the value of the significance of life*. . . . That's how we come to 'war schools'" (1998).

In the words of Anna Pawełczyńska, "The understanding of ultimate situations allows one to look life or death in the eye with courage" (1979:5). In this regard, I would offer a personal note to suggest that an understanding of the war schools of Sarajevo is critical in order to acknowledge and validate the courage and tenacity of the Sarajevo teacher, to whom Professor Jahić refers as "the warrior and pedagogical patriot of our land" (1996:27). I would argue that this recognition in the eyes of the outside world is no small matter since the failure of educators and scholars to recognize their efforts suggests not simply a critical gap in the history of the Bosnian war. Viewed in more critical terms, this failure obfuscates the work and perseverance of dedicated teachers who fought "the battle of the mind" during the siege of Sarajevo. "We did this on our own," said Professors Jahić and Sultanović. "We did this because we wanted to. It was a form of patriotism" (1998). In the words of Professor Jahić then, "the intention of the aggressor to destroy and burn school buildings, killing children and their teachers and wiping out our educational system, has not been achieved" (1996:11).

An Ethnically Diverse High School

Fast forward to 30 July 1999 in the aftermath of another Balkan war and the *Washington Post* article one day later entitled, "West to Bolster Balkans," with a subheading that read, "At Summit, Clinton Encourages Milosevic." Back in Sarajevo, at what the *Post* termed "a special summit conference . . . to work for stability and prosperity in the Balkans," some three years after the siege, Bill Clinton, the president of the United States, along with leaders of forty other nations, endorsed the Stability Pact for Southeastern Europe to mark the distribution of two billion dollars for Kosovar Albanian refugees (Babington, 1999:A15). At the same time, the pointed references to the removal of Slobodan Milošević as president of what is today the Federal Republic of Yugoslavia, who was left off the list of invited leaders, left no doubt as to another of the primary aims of the summit.

Tucked away on pages fifteen and sixteen of the first section of the paper, the article was hardly the primary news of the day. And hidden away in the course of the article was a short reference to a Clinton speech at what was simply termed, "an ethnically diverse high school in Sarajevo [where] the president reminded residents of Serbia . . . that they can expect no postwar help" until Milošević was removed from power. "'I hope that before long, Serbia, too, will participate in this economic reconstruction,' Clinton told several hundred people who received him warmly at the school," but no reconstruction aid would be forthcoming to Serbia "'as long as it rejects democracy'" (Babington, 1999:A15). With this brief reference to the audience, the ethnically diverse high school remained nameless to the reader, and there was no discussion in the article of the reasons for Clinton's visit to the school other than as a backdrop to his pointed message.

Yet a press release by the United States Information Service (USIS), dated 2 July 1999, almost a month prior to the summit, noted that the United States "has decided to provide more than two million KM [con-

vertible marks] to rehabilitate Sarajevo's Third Gymnasium School."
Although United States Agency for International Development (USAID)
monies to rehabilitate the school were approved in early 1998, the funds
were withheld because of the failure of the Bosnian government to fa-
cilitate the return of minorities in Sarajevo Canton as provided for in the
Sarajevo Declaration. While Clinton's remarks in the *Post* were restricted primarily to the future of the region, along with numerous references to Milošević, he also made specific reference to the reconstruction
of the school itself. With the release of the funding, Clinton offered the
audience assembled at Treća Gimnazija the following words:

> I'm very glad to be back in Sarajevo, and especially to come to this
> school to see the rebuilding that is going on. Not long ago the Third
> Gymnasium was at the center of the cruel war. Today, as we can all see,
> the building still bears the scars of the past. But thanks to you, it holds
> the promise of the future. . . .
>   I know that students sent letters to the Sarajevo canton asking that
> this school be repaired. One student wrote, please think of future gen-
> erations. This school is a monument to Sarajevo's proud tradition of
> teaching young people from all backgrounds. Saving this school will
> save that tradition and will help all young people to have the future they
> deserve. . . .
>   I want this school—this school rebuilt—to be the symbol of all of
> our tomorrows. And I will do my best to see that the United States is
> your partner and your friend. (USIA, 1999)

Unaware and no doubt unconcerned with the wider focus by the *Post* on
the Balkan region, the school community viewed the visit of the president of the United States as the historical highlight of the saga of the
school in the aftermath of the siege. To the teachers, the school does represent "the symbol of all of our tomorrows," if not the hope for the future of Bosnia and Herzegovina. Indeed, the reader of the *Post* reads
nothing of their story, while the reader of Clinton's speech knows nothing of "the scars of the past" that the school still bears. In fact, the release of USAID monies, combined with the ongoing assistance of the
city of Stockholm, Sweden, is designed for the reconstruction of the
school buildings that have remained empty since the onset of the siege of
Sarajevo during that horrific spring of 1992.

     In spite of a brief newspaper reference to a nameless high school, the
students, teachers, and administrators of the school have real names and
real stories to tell of their experiences of almost four years under siege.

This journalistic perspective is hardly unusual, however, for those who viewed the city under siege often adopted a cold and objective if not cowardly and inhuman attitude to rationalize their inaction. Perhaps the most striking feature of this perspective, at least in regard to education, is the abstract and dispassionate attitude towards those Bosnian educators caught up in "the battle of the mind" for the sanity of the youth of the country. In particular, the educational documents that record the status of schooling during the war offer only a superficial analysis of how schools functioned and suggest a minimal understanding of the experience of teachers, administrators, and students during this time.

At the highest level, we witness this attitude in the words of the UN secretary-general himself, Boutros Boutros-Ghali, who visited Sarajevo for part of the day, on 31 December 1992, nine months into the siege. After meetings in the Presidency and a motorcade around Baščaršija, the old quarter of the city, his last stop was a press conference at UN headquarters. There a reporter for a Sarajevo radio station, Vedrana Božinović, in a passionate outburst, offered comments to and asked questions of the secretary-general. In his book, *Love Thy Neighbor*, Peter Maas recalls the absurdity of the exchange:

> "You too are guilty for every single raped woman, for every single murdered man, woman and child. . . . You are guilty—"
> "Excuse me," interrupted Mik Magnusson, the U.N. spokesman. "What is your question?" . . .
> "We think that you are guilty for our suffering. What do you want before you will do something? How many more victims are needed before you act? Aren't 12,000 enough? Do you want 15,000 or 20,000? Will that be enough?" . . .
> [Ghali responded], "If I am guilty, then mea culpa. . . . You have a situation which is better than ten other places all over the world. I can give you a list of ten places where you have more problems than in Sarajevo." . . . "We are dying, Mr. Ghali, we are dying." (Maas, 1996:180–181)

The cold-blooded fashion in which the UN secretary-general himself dismissed the siege in favor of ten other places in worse condition than Sarajevo bordered on the insane. Peter Maas writes, "I remember thinking that the secretary general was mad. *Ten*? It seemed so absurd that neither I nor any other reporter in the room bothered to ask him to name the ten" (1996:181). In the movie, *Welcome to Sarajevo*, Woody Harrelson, playing the part of one of the reporters, asks the question. "Excuse me sir. Just out of curiosity, could you tell me what those other thirteen [ten] places are, and are we sliding up or down that scale?" (Winterbottom, 1998). Unfortunately, the attitude expressed in this episode by the secretary-general, captured so well in the sarcasm of the film, simply appears as the most blatant example of the dispassionate manner in which the United Nations perceived the Bosnian war. David Rieff, in his book, *Slaughterhouse: Bosnia and the Failure of the West*, offers commentary on the episode of December 1992, the views of the secretary-general, and the influence of these views within the UN hierarchy:

> Boutros-Ghali's impatience with the question of Bosnia only deepened during the years of UNPROFOR's deployment. Asked by an interviewer a few weeks before Srebrenica fell what the United Nations had learned from Bosnia, the Secretary General replied, "Bosnia has created a distortion in the work of the UN. We are paying less attention to what is going on in Burundi, in Georgia." His ambition, Boutros-Ghali said, was "to pay attention to the marginalized." That did not include Bosnia
> . . . .
> This was in 1995, three weeks before the greatest massacre to occur on the European continent since the Second World War. But Boutros-Ghali remained faithful to his initial view of the conflict, expressed in Sarajevo in December 1992. It was a rich man's war, not worthy of the attention it received. . . . He resented having had to deal with Bosnia, and he refused to confront its implications for the future of the UN. It was hardly surprising in an old-fashioned vertical hierarchy like the United Nations, that the Secretary General's views would permeate all the way to the most junior UNPROFOR clerk. (1996:244–245)

David Rieff's analysis of the mindset of UN officials towards the war in Bosnia, which emanated from the top down through the vertical hierarchy, suggests something of the insanity of the attempt to conduct schooling within this setting. Indeed, I witnessed the madness of it all firsthand upon my initial visit to Bosnia during February and March 1995 as an educational consultant to UNICEF with the University of Pittsburgh Bosnia Project. Who could even imagine that, during this time, the schools actually functioned, that students actually attended classes, that attendance was actually kept by teachers, that exams for the university were actually given?

This minimal understanding of schooling is clearly evident, for example, in a UNICEF document entitled, *Children and Women in Bosnia and Herzegovina: A Situation Analysis* (1994). Although the document provides an overview of schooling throughout Bosnia during the war to include the number of schools, students, classrooms, and teachers, the analysis provides minimal information to place these numbers into any meaningful context. Under a heading entitled "Specific Cases," the document provides educational statistics for Sarajevo city to include numbers of students, teachers, and schools, and thus suggests an understanding of the structural organization of schooling. "However," wrote Mujo Musagić, "my impression is, the most important value of the schools during the war can't be measured by numbers and statistics" (1998). In terms of the value of schools during the war and the actual operation of the educational system, not to mention something of the daily lives of teachers and students, the document is disturbingly lacking. Witness the following two paragraphs:

> In April of 1992 the assault on the city began, interrupting regular classes and eventually leading to the closure of the educational system for about a year. During this period, many dedicated teachers improvised ad hoc arrangements in which they met their students in basements and in their homes; any convenient place where they could feel relatively safe from the constant shelling. In many of these improvised schools, three or four grades would assemble in the living room of a home and the teacher would move in turn from group to group as time permitted.
> In March 1993, classes resumed for a partial 18-week school year .... A partial curriculum was re-established and the program was once again sanctioned, with diplomas given at the end of courses. However, as school buildings still could not be used due to the danger of shelling, classes continued to be held in the improvised locations with almost no teaching equipment. (1994:14–15)

The 1994 UNICEF document devotes but two brief paragraphs to the 1992–1993 school year in Sarajevo during which educators painstakingly reconstructed the framework of schooling throughout the besieged city. Indeed, the 1992–1993 school year did begin on 1 March 1993, but it began in drastically altered form as an adaptation to wartime conditions seen in the local community war schools during an eighteen-week session that ran until 16 July 1993. In fact, the truncated 1992–1993 school year served as the precursor of the 1993–1994 school year that began on time on 6 September 1993 and continued for thirty weeks out of a projected thirty-six week school year. There is no indication here that the 1993–1994 school year even began, or was functioning, yet the success of Sarajevo educators is seen most dramatically in the local community war schools that operated through the entire academic year. In short, the UNICEF report emphasizes the "ad hoc" nature of schooling in "improvised schools" in "improvised locations" at the expense of any thorough analysis of the organization and operation of the war schools of Sarajevo.

Three years later, in a follow-up UNICEF document entitled, *Bosnia and Herzegovina, Women & Children: Situation Analysis* (1997), the situation is updated with additional data but even less insight given the information and access available during the postwar era. The document repeats much of the discussion from the earlier analysis while providing another superficial overview of education during the war. A portion of the document that describes the situation for the educational sector is presented here as follows:

> On 6 April 1992 war broke out in Bosnia and Herzegovina. Within a short time the education system was in tatters, and schools were either destroyed, damaged, or occupied by military units or refugees. The country became a patchwork of ethnic pockets and fronts, severing all connection with the central authorities.

Following a discussion of the three entities within Bosnia and Herzegovina, the Serbian Republic, the Croatian Republic of Herceg–Bosna, and "the rump state of Bosnia and Herzegovina," the document moves into the following discussion of the effect of the war upon the schools:

> During the war enrollment in primary education dramatically decreased, as did the number of teachers (about 28,000 in 1993/94 down to 7000 in 1994/95). Figures are difficult to establish because of the process of destruction of schools, the movement of front lines, and the informal premises and the unlicensed (and sometimes technically 'unqualified') teachers who improvised an educational system during the war. Children were often targeted by snipers in schools and on their way to and from school.
>
> Education continued in the basement of buildings and in other shelters, often with two or three shifts per day to accommodate demand, and a decrease in the school workload of some 35–40 percent. The school term, such as it was during the first two years of war, lasted for about twenty weeks, but immediately increased to about thirty-five weeks after the cessation of fighting in 1995/96. (1997:15)

It is difficult to determine the context for the primary school figures cited given the preceding discussion of the collapse of central authority, that is, whether these figures are for the three entities or for the Bosnian republic itself. However, such figures are hardly difficult to establish given the meticulous documentation of schooling on all sides of the boundary lines. Again, the emphasis in the document is upon improvisation, here by "unlicensed" as well as "sometimes technically 'unqualified' teachers" with no sense of the efforts of those professional or "licensed" educators during the war. While it may be true that "everything was an improvisation," in the words of Professor Jahić (1998), at least at the beginning of the siege, the "organizing, coordinating, planning, and supervising of educational activities" required to reconstruct an educational system in systematic fashion to survive wartime conditions is given no mention (Jahić, 1996:12). Furthermore, the 1997 situation analysis repeats the errors of the 1994 document with references to the school term, "such as it was." In fact, the school term actually ran for thirty weeks of a projected thirty-six weeks during the 1993–1994 and 1994–1995 war school years, as opposed to "about twenty weeks," or in contrast to the 1995–1996 school year cited.

Indeed, the impression that is offered in such documents is that education in Bosnia in general and Sarajevo in particular was conducted in some sort of a haphazard fashion with no systematic effort to organize schooling across the city if not across the country. This is no small matter since the failure of UN educational officers and consultants to understand the nature of schooling during the siege is reflected in their failure to offer the critical assistance necessary to support the schools. Perhaps more importantly, this failure to recognize the capacity and the complexity of education during the war, viewed here in the organization of the war schools of Sarajevo, obfuscates the perseverance, dedication, and "pedagogical patriotism" of Bosnian educators in general and Sarajevo educators in particular. It is difficult, perhaps, for reporters to view a high school as something other than a presidential stopover on a day of summits in Sarajevo, or for UN consultants to perceive the work of Sarajevo educators as something other than "ad hoc arrangements." If only they had witnessed a masked ball organized by students in the shells of the buildings of Treća Gimnazija on a warm spring night along the old frontline, they would sense, perhaps, that there is something more here than a nameless school with nameless teachers and students.

The Second Battle Line

If the postmodern condition is "the contradiction between dreams and reality," in the words of Lawrence Grossberg, "the need to find meaning, and the impossibility of the task," this condition is seen in the world of this study whereby Bosnian educational institutions somehow continued to function and Bosnian educators somehow continued to teach (1989:108). In his article entitled, "No Pity for Sarajevo," Jean Baudrillard writes, "These people, who are absolutely disillusioned with reality, and who no longer even believe in the rule of political rationality that is very much a part of the European reality principle, have found an alternative source of courage, founded on surviving in a senseless situation" (1996:81). "OK. We have to survive," said Edina Dmitrović, an English teacher at Treća Gimnazija as of the second semester of the 1994–1995 school year, "Let's go and do it" (1996).

In his study of education and adaptation in postwar Japan, Nobuo K. Shimahara wrote that "adaptation is a continual process through which the organizations of society are modified to meet social and physical requirements; it is a dynamic strategy for solving problems of human existence" (1979:1). Although primarily concerned about the relationship between the Japanese cultural orientation and the structural conditions of Japanese society, Shimahara's explanation of structure and adaptation is relevant here:

> Structural conditions . . . consist of those institutional arrangements of human life that are constantly subjected to change; for example, economic, political, and social systems undergo transformation resulting from pressures for adaptive efficiency, such as modernization [or wartime conditions I would add here]. Institutional or organizational arrangements are amenable to modification, unlike cultural orientations, and such organizational amenability represents a societal competence to upgrade adaptability. (1979:2)

Here in this study, we are looking at adaptation and education as well, viewed through the structural conditions of education as an institutional arrangement of Sarajevo life that had to undergo significant transformation in order to survive the pressures for adaptive efficiency. We are concerned here not with cultural orientations but with "the culture of wartime" viewed, in educational terms, through the organization of the war schools of Sarajevo and the institutional adaptations of Sarajevo educators to wartime conditions during the siege.

The terminology used here concerning the adaptation of instruction to wartime conditions is taken directly from contemporary accounts of schooling during the war. In August and September 1992, for example, articles from Sarajevo daily newspapers recorded the official decisions of what, at that time, was the Ministry of Education, Science, Culture and Physical Culture of the Republic of Bosnia and Herzegovina (hereafter, Ministry of Education), to reorganize instruction. These articles indicate that, during those months between the onset of the siege and the conventional beginning of the 1992–1993 school year, the Ministry of Education made the decision to begin the school year with the country at war and the city under siege. A number of these articles appear among the regular entries in the *School Annual* of Treća Gimnazija and document the developing situation as it relates to education during this time. One of these articles from *Oslobođenje*, the major Sarajevo daily, dated 10 September 1992, to be cited in full in the following chapter, appears under the headline, "The Government of Bosnia–Herzegovina: Instruction to be Adapted to Wartime Conditions," and refers to the "Decision on the Registration of Students in Elementary and Secondary Schools and the Beginning of Instruction in the 1992/93 School Year":

> With this Decision, the Government of the Republic of Bosnia and Herzegovina ordered municipality and city community executive organs, that are responsible for the safety of students and teachers, to insure conditions for conducting normal instructional procedures in elementary and secondary schools.
>
> In harmony with this, municipalities, with regards to city communities, will decide about the beginning, the length, and the place for holding the registration of students in the first class of elementary and secondary schools, and the decision about the beginning and the place for holding instruction in the 1992/93 school year. (*Oslobođenje*, 1992:8)

In other words, with the country in a war for survival, and the capital of the country under siege, the Ministry of Education issued resolutions for school administrative units to begin the forthcoming school year in spite of these conditions. The article clearly indicates that the Ministry issued resolutions to school administrative units at the local level "to insure conditions" for the normal instructional process with specific reference to initiate the 1992–1993 school year, in other words, to adapt instruction to wartime conditions.

The same terminology referring to the adaptation of instruction to wartime conditions is also used by Abdulah Jabučar, the deputy minister of education of the Bosnian republic at the time, in an article entitled, "Organizing Schools in the War," when he writes:

> It is necessary to emphasize that the operation of schools followed the guidelines given by the Ministry, as well as guidelines made before the war, but which could not be applied in each situation. But, this guideline is applicable and it obliges each school to work, without regard to conditions—it is necessary *to adapt to conditions* and organize the work of schools. (1994:5, my emphasis)

These "Guidelines on Educational Activities of Preschool Institutions, Primary and Secondary Schools During the State of War" issued by the Ministry of Education for the operation of schools encompassed five areas: (1) measures of protection and safety; (2) organization of curriculum and instruction during the war; (3) the role of teachers during wartime conditions; (4) textbooks; and what is termed (5) evidence and documentation (Jabučar, 1997:293–295; 1994:4–5). While these five areas are interrelated, they represented specific concerns that, in practice, had to be addressed as they related to the reorganization of schooling during the state of war.

Each school was obliged to provide official documentation of student attendance and classroom performance, for example, to ensure that the section book of the class (*odjeljenska knjiga*) or the class book, also referred to as the class journal, was kept in accordance with legal statutes. The school was further responsible to secure and protect school documents, that is, "to hide the school documentation in a safe place." For the safety of students, the school was given the responsibility to survey the school premises and to "fix and adapt premises that can be used for teaching" (1994:5). If war threatened the premises, the school was to organize teaching in shelters or in safe places inside the building. The school was responsible to all students for regular instruction and for periodically assembling students for class examinations. "The municipality or the district, depending on a concrete situation, can interrupt instruction for a definite time, in other words, to determine a new deadline for the beginning of the school year as well as the beginning of the winter and summer holiday, but taking into account the total number of working weeks which have to be realized" (1994:5). The teacher assumed greater responsibility for any number of tasks that were much more complicated than during peacetime. These responsibilities included not simply classroom instruction but the protection and safety of students, including their evacuation when necessary, organizing first aid, and coordinating activities (the cancellation of classes, for example) with parents and the local communities to a far greater degree. In short, to reiterate Abdulah Jabučar, "provinces, municipalities, and particularly schools, as well as teachers, have to be maximally engaged and try to find all possible ways of successfully educating the children" (1994:5).

In an addendum to these "Guidelines" in his *Collection of Regulations from the Field of Education* (1997), Jabučar wrote in very explicit terms concerning the adaptation of instruction in Bosnian schools. "These guidelines were passed in December 1993," he stated, "and committed every school to work, regardless of conditions—*to adapt to the actual situation*" [my emphasis] (1997:295). Viewed in the image of educators such as Abdulah Jabučar, this study suggests that the story of the siege told in educational terms is the adaptation of instruction for wartime conditions by those educators who implemented the administrative decisions of the Bosnian Ministry of Education and the Sarajevo City Secretariat for Education in the war schools of the city.

It is clear then that the Ministry of Education of the Bosnian republic allocated responsibility to school administrators at the local level to implement Ministry directives. In particular, local school administrative units were responsible for implementing the decision to register students for the 1992–1993 school year and to determine the dates for the beginning of the school year depending on the circumstances. In the besieged city of Sarajevo, these instructions meant that what was then the City Secretariat for Education, Science, Culture and Physical Culture (hereafter, City Secretariat for Education), was responsible "to insure conditions" for beginning the normal instructional process and for "the decision about the beginning and the place for holding instruction in the 1992/93 school year" for Sarajevo schools. In fact, the 1992–1993 school year in Sarajevo did not commence until 1 March 1993 when it ran for a truncated, eighteen-week session through 16 July 1993.

Although it took approximately eleven months to reorganize schooling in Sarajevo since the onset of the siege in April 1992, these months were critical as Sarajevo educators struggled with the problems of initiating the new school year. As early as 3 May 1992, for example, educators gathered at the Pedagogical Institute in Sarajevo to confront the implications of the siege in educational terms. With the uncertainty over the continuance of the 1991–1992 school year, these educators looked to the future and the reorganization of schooling for the impending siege of the city. At this time, two educators from the Pedagogical Institute, Professor Hajrija-Šahza Jahić and Professor Melita Sultanović, took upon this task by conducting situation analyses of elementary and secondary education to determine the specific needs of the schools. As they told me in their own words, "Everything was an improvisation . . . the idea was to normalize the situation for the children, to start first with programs in one location and then implement these programs throughout other parts of the city" (1998). Thus wrote Mujo Musagić, "The psychology of people in the besieged cities . . . was trying to establish a 'normal' life" (1998).

> In July 1992, the Pedagogical Institute of Sarajevo took on the task of organizing, coordinating, planning and supervising the educational and recreational activities to be offered to refugee, resettled and local children in Sarajevo. Work was immediately started on developing a concept for working with children caught up in a war situation. . . .
>
> The aim of the teaching plan was to present, develop, revise and practise all the topics which had to be abandoned at the end of the first wartime school year, because the war had put a stop to them. The teaching plan began to take shape in the first so-called *war schools*, and the external and internal organization of these schools was taken on in "the normal" school year 1992/93. (Jahić, 1996:12)

From the beginning of the so-called war schools with the Bjelave School on 2 September 1992, to the so-called stairway schools of Dobrinja, the formation of groups of teachers and students at the local community level became the *punkts* or *punktovi,* the points, to be connected in systematic fashion in order to reconstruct schooling throughout the city. "The idea was to connect the small points, the micro-environments, which, at the beginning, operated independently," said Professor Jahić, "to develop a scheme, to develop a kind of organized system of war schools" (1998).

Just as teachers from the local schools have provided information critical to understand schooling at the microlevel of the local community war school, educators at the Pedagogical Institute have provided information critical to understand schooling at the organizational level or the macrolevel of analysis. The methodological approach was to first construct the story of Treća Gimnazija and, based upon the case study of one Sarajevo school, the research design was to adopt the inductive approach and construct a picture of schooling from the ground level upwards. Viewed from the ground level perspective, the design was to connect the story of Treća Gimnazija to the story of schooling throughout the city, which required an understanding of the pattern of war school organization at the *mjesna zajednica* (local community) level. This approach required movement back and forth between the micro- and macrolevels of analysis in order to form a holistic perspective of the organization and operation of the war schools of Sarajevo. In turn, this wider perspective of war schools is necessary in order to understand the organization and operation of one individual war school and the local community war schools under its administration.

Hence, the development of "a kind of organized system of war schools" was based upon connecting the punkts to each other within and across the boundaries of the local communities of Sarajevo. Thus the *School Annual* of Treća Gimnazija for 1–8 December 1992 records the following entry, "Our school received the obligation to come forward and organize the instructional lectures for the territory of local community Kovači, Sumbuluša, and Bistrik. That means registering students, finding premises where the lectures are to be conducted, and professors who need to conduct the instructional lectures." The local community school concept was finalized in February 1993 when, according to Melita Sultanović, 470 Sarajevo teachers attended a seminar conducted by the Pedagogical Institute on the organization of war schools throughout the city (1998). Documents from the Pedagogical Institute indicate that twenty-seven secondary schools or education centers were assigned the responsibility of organizing instruction for 5,635 students in at least seventy-two local communities in the four municipalities of "free Sarajevo" to belatedly begin the 1992–1993 school year on 1 March 1993 (Pedagoški zavod, April 1993).

Viewed within this perspective, the initial September entry for the 1993–1994 school year in the *School Annual* of Treća Gimnazija reflects the adaptations of the school within the framework of the local community school concept:

> The obligation of Treća Gimnazija is for the operation of war schools within the local communities, Avdo Hodžić, Danilo Đokić, Kumrovec, and Bistrik (gimnazija section) in which general educational lectures are being realized and two punkts: (1) the Agricultural and Veterinarian and Food School Center; (2) Ivan Krndelj Hrasno for the theory and practicum lectures of the chemical–technological profession and of civil defense for the students of Treća Gimnazija. (*Školski ljetopis*)

Viewed from another perspective, while "the obligation of Treća Gimnazija [was] for the operation of war schools" in four local communities
for the 1993–1994 school year, Treća Gimnazija students attended not
only these four local community schools but another fifty-five local
community schools organized and administered by other secondary
schools while still maintaining their enrollment at Treća Gimnazija.
Viewed from the microlevel of the local community war schools of
Treća Gimnazija, the picture clearly illustrates the macrolevel complexity of the organization of war schools across the city. Beginning with
those "small points, the microenvironments," formed during the early
months of the siege, such "a kind of organized system of war schools"
was critical in the daily life of Sarajevo, noted Professor Jahić, since
"school was the only institutional structure which could offer continuity
from pre-war life to the current life of refugees and war" (1996:11).

Korak po Korak

Before I even crossed the Sarajevo city limits during my first trip to the
former Yugoslavia, I traveled through checkpoints and across confrontation lines into the central part of the country in the late winter of 1995.
In educational terms, the images that remain with me are those of dedicated teachers who kept the schools in operation under the most difficult
of conditions. While the war in Bosnia imparted indelible images of the
human condition, the educational story was simply not revealed by my
initial visits to Bosnian schools. This story was constructed in methodological fashion, step by step, *korak po korak* a Bosnian would say, as
I struggled to understand the survival of schooling during the siege of
Sarajevo. The story of a war school in Sarajevo that I tell here dates
from the images of this first visit to Bosnia during wartime, but the story
was pieced together during subsequent visits in the aftermath of the war.

On this first trip to the country, I flew into Sarajevo under siege in a
UN aircraft where UNPROFOR soldiers at the airport hustled us off the
plane to sandbagged bunkers along the airport runway. Before I even
entered "free Sarajevo," I was travelling by UNICEF Land Rover
through checkpoints and across confrontation lines into Middle Bosnia.
Here I first visited a number of schools in Zenica and Novi Travnik as
well as schools in the surrounding countryside. In Zenica proper, I visited three vocational–technical schools operating in shifts while attempting to conduct classes in the one building of the Comprehensive

Metal Secondary School. The buildings of the other two vocational schools were taken over by the Bosnian army into which all male graduates of the three schools entered upon their graduation.

Travelling into the mountains outside of Zenica, I visited primary schools in the villages of Babino and Arnauti where the students were refugees from the Bosanska Krajina, from places like Sanski Most, Prijedor, Šipovo, and Kotor Varoš, as well as from the enclave of Žepa located in eastern Bosnia. The Hamza Hamo Elementary School, with locations in the upper village of Arnauti and the lower village of Babino, was formerly named Omer Maslić Elementary School after a *partizan* from World War II. The name change had come recently because a stairway in one of the buildings had a picture of the partizans with the 1945 date. According to the assistant principal, Avdo Avdić, the schools had no resources whatsoever, no means to maintain operations, no sanitation supplies, no electricity for heating. The 1,125 students not only had no school supplies but lacked basic winter clothing, especially footwear, and were eating bread made from husks of wheat. At the beginning of 1995, however, the students received new textbooks and school supplies from the Ministry of Education. As an assistant principal, Avdo Avdić had recently received the equivalent of fourteen German marks in Bosnian dinars from Sarajevo that would buy him "three packages of very cheap cigarettes." The teachers received the equivalent of seven German marks. All the schools in Zenica municipality were in similar straits, he said. The worst time, however, was the 1993–1994 school year when fighting between Croats and Muslims ravaged Middle Bosnia (1995). The visitor only had to travel through burned-out villages down the road, through villages such as Ahmići, where Croats massacred Muslims, or Križenćevo selo, where the favor was returned in kind.

I passed through these two villages near Vitez as we travelled across the confrontation line to visit a school in the "Hrvatska Republika Herceg–Bosna," the Croatian Republic of Herceg–Bosna, carved out of Middle Bosnia and surrounded by territory controlled by the Bosnian government. Here schools were supported both by the Croatian government in Zagreb as well as by the Ministry of Education, Science, Culture and Sport (Ministarstvo prosvjete, znanosti, kulture i sporta) of the self-styled Herceg–Bosna Republic from its capital of west Mostar in Herzegovina to the south. These monies came from taxes levied by "customs agents" at the borders on commercial traffic and on Bosnian Muslims entering Croat-controlled territory. Here was a whole separate school system comprised of some twelve municipalities in a whole separate republic that paralleled the "Republika Bosna i Herzegovina," the Bosnian Republic, with its capital of Sarajevo. Here I again observed the operation of three separate schools on a single school visit, Travnik Secondary School, Novi Travnik Secondary School, and Novi Travnik Elementary School, with some 2,300 Bosnian Croat students, attending school in shifts in what was once the elementary school building.

By the time I entered Sarajevo on the Blue Route over Mount Igman, the complexity of the situation, not to mention the sorrow and the tragedy, was overwhelming. Indeed, one day I was in the besieged city and the next day, with the UNICEF program officer in Pale, I travelled across confrontation lines through Bosnian Army, Bosnian Serb, and UNPROFOR checkpoints located around the airport. On the other side of the airport runway, we entered the "Republika Srpska," the Serbian Republic, the third separate "entity" that I visited within Bosnia and Herzegovina in a several week period. In the poignant words of Mirzeta Memišević, a student at Treća Gimnazija:

> I don't know what happened to my friend
> Because my friend divided himself in three.
> (*Almanah Treće Gimnazije*, 1998:43)

In Pale, schools were organized under the Ministry of Education, Science and Culture (Ministarstvo obrazovanja, nauke i kulture) of the Republika Srpska. Here in Pale, we met with Ljubomir Zuković, the minister of education, to gain some sense of schooling on the other side, an attempt by UNICEF to ensure nonpartisanship. Minister Zuković told us, "You help us the best if you help our children. It's happening all over the world and it's happening here. They're completely innocent" (1995).

The view from Mount Trebević overlooking Sarajevo on an early spring day was breathtaking in its clarity, and the Holiday Inn with its garish yellow paint now somewhat faded was the most prominent location dead on what was known as "Sniper Alley." To the accompaniment of small-arms fire in the background, we reentered the besieged city across the airport runway passing through checkpoints, sniper screens, and sandbagged bunkers. We then raced down Sniper Alley passing directly in front of the Holiday Inn, and I looked back up towards Trebevića in the attempt to view the lookout from where we had gazed down upon the city just hours before. From the guesthouse in Baščaršija, my journal records small-arms fire beginning that evening in the hills above the old quarter of the city.

The next morning, 11 March, I walked from the UNICEF offices just off Maršala Tita Street down towards the Faculty of Philosophy of the University of Sarajevo. Upon rounding a corner, I was to recognize at the last minute the Holiday Inn now dead ahead of me just across Sniper Alley from the Faculty buildings, and I was to learn the street was closed down later that day. According to the UNICEF program officer in Pale, two Serb children were killed by sniper fire in Grbavica located in Bosnian Serb territory. On Monday, 13 March, the newspaper account in *Oslobođenje* read, "Bloody Weekend in Sarajevo: Snipers Again Sow Death" (1995:11). The body count, according to the article, was three dead and one badly wounded, to mark "the aggressor's Saturday and Sunday activities in Sarajevo." The Blue Route over Mount Igman was now closed, and the airport was closed down as well because of small-arms fire and shelling. The headline of the feature article on the front page of *Oslobođenje* read, "Sarajevo Shelled," and cited five killed and two wounded from the shelling by 82- and 120-millimeter mortars and four now killed by snipers (1995:1). In the *School Annual* of Treća Gimnazija, the entry for Sunday, 12 March 1995, read as follows:

So the armistice is still on in Sarajevo. The snipers still fire and have killed more people. Near the school one child was shot to death, and on Darovalaca krvi Street the mother of our student Naida Podić II/1 [second class, first class section] was shot to death. At the very end of the session of the Teachers' Council a state of general danger was declared in Sarajevo. (*Školski ljetopis*)

The entry for Monday, 13 March 1995, read in similar fashion:

In agreement with the civil defense, the local communities, and the Army, regular classes were stopped until Thursday, 16 March 1995, due to the difficult situation in the city and on Heroes' Square where the school is situated. (*Školski ljetopis*)

As mortar rounds tore into Sarajevo and the crack of rifles echoed in the streets, sirens wailed, spotter planes dropped flares, and NATO jets buzzed the hillsides but did nothing. The ticker-tape message over the television, which was working that day, read, *Opasno/Opasnost u Sarajevu* (Danger/Dangerous in Sarajevo). It was just another day in Sarajevo, said one *Sarajlija* to me, in just another attempt at normality.

At the request of one young Bosnian refugee then in Pittsburgh, I visited the Fatima Gunić Elementary School located in Alipašino Polje in the western end of the city. We walked to and from the school behind sniper screens of tarps and trailers piled high on top of each other only to observe that the school had nothing. Mine awareness posters covered the walls, and UNHCR plastic foil covered the window openings in place of the glass. The image of elementary school students going to school in the besieged city remains with me to this day. Upon my return to the United States, I wrote an essay for teachers entitled, "In the City of Lost Souls" (1995), after a poem by a young orphan boy named Sanjin who wrote, "I live in the city of human shadows in the city of lost souls" (Videopress, 1993). The essay was my attempt to reconcile the academic perspective with the human condition in Sarajevo during the siege. If Ljubomir Zuković, the minister of education of the Republika Srpska, could speak of the innocence of the children, then I could write the following:

> The methodological slaughter of the children is perhaps the most horri-fying aspect of the Third Balkan War as the country once known as Yugoslavia disintegrates into its various entities. For those of you who teach the social studies, these are the hard facts on the children of the besieged city of Sarajevo and their struggle to survive during the last decade of the twentieth century. These hard facts suggest that it is the children of the former Yugoslavia who have suffered the war in such terms that they have become the developmental equivalent of combat veterans many years their senior. As the Third Balkan War grinds into its fourth year, the suffering of the children continues. (1995:200)

The suffering of the children who were "completely innocent" remains to somehow be rationalized by politicians and academics such as myself. Yet the hopes of these children were kept alive by the schools, and the story of the siege of Sarajevo told in educational terms is how dedicated teachers kept the schools open under conditions that most American educators simply cannot imagine.

The unforgiving impressions of life under siege conditions (not to mention that someone such as myself could get out) and of life in schools in particular, offered, in academic terms, the opportunity to learn more of the work of these dedicated educators during the war. I returned to Sarajevo during the summer of 1996 as a visiting scholar in the De-partment of English Language and Literature at the Faculty of Philoso-phy where, under the auspices of Professor Zvonimir Radeljković, I taught an American Studies seminar to undergraduate students. These undergraduates were high school students during the siege, however, and I learned much about schooling and war schools from my discussions with them. To practice their English, they wrote essays to tell me something about their common experiences as adolescents and the importance of schooling during wartime. Written in the immediate aftermath of the siege, I have included their words at various points in this essay for their stories provide the perspective of students attending schools other than Treća Gimnazija itself.

In addition to teaching on the Faculty of Philosophy, I also wanted to talk with teachers about their experiences in the war school classrooms. Left alone in the offices of the City Secretariat for Education, I told Safija Rašidović, the *saradnik za obrazovanje* (associate for education), that I wanted to visit a war school to talk with the teachers. Safija took me under her wing and introduced me to the teachers of Treća Gimnazija, then located on Trg Heroja, or Heroes' Square, in Hrasno, not far from the Malta Bridge, just down Sniper Alley from the Holiday Inn. The devastation of the apartment complexes of Hrasno that rise above the square revealed an urban combat zone within clear sight of the frontline just to the east of Hrasno Elementary School where Treća Gimnazija found refuge during the 1994–1995 war school year, and where it was still located at that time.

At Treća Gimnazija, Safija introduced me to Emina Avdagić, the school director, Avdo Hajdo, the assistant school director, and Edina Dmitrović, then the English teacher, who first introduced me to the life of a teacher in a war school located on the frontline. As a former high school teacher myself, I simply wanted to talk with the teachers of Treća Gimnazija about their experiences, to get some sense of life and teaching under siege conditions, to develop a picture of how educators kept the schools open during the war, to hear their stories. "Everybody has a story to tell," said Gordana Roljić, one of those educators, during an interview some two years later. Yet the memories of the killing and the trauma and the desperate struggle to survive are not easily forgotten, and the stories of the survivors are not casually revealed. The memories and the exhaustion often cloud the details of the stories as well. "Sometimes we forget even the year as well as the day," Professor Roljić said to me in response to my questions about her teaching schedule in the war schools, unintentionally revealing something of the heroic character of her own personal story as well (1998).

Several years ago, in the aftermath of another civil war that became a geopolitical struggle, I remembered similar stories of the killing and the trauma and the desperate struggle for survival not easily forgotten and the stories of Vietnamese survivors that are not casually revealed. I had returned to Viet Nam as a visiting scholar at the University of Ho Chi Minh City where, in addition to my teaching, I talked with Vietnamese about their experiences during what they term the American War in their country. "Every family has a story to tell," said Hoang Thi Mai Huong, who then proceeded to tell me some of those stories of Vietnamese who survived the American War (1992). Amidst the landscape of rice fields that extend to the horizon were the stories of a Vietnamese enemy that I once had the chance to tell, only to pass on the opportunity, with profound regrets. In the aftermath of the Bosnian war, the words of Gordana Roljić echoed the words of Hoang Thi Mai Huong, that "everybody has a story to tell." The story of the students and teachers of Treća Gimnazija as a Sarajevo community caught up in the siege is but one of those stories. "This is a story about war," wrote Belma Huskić, one of those students, "the truth and reality to me," a story seldom found in the history books that reveals something of the lives of ordinary people during the siege of Sarajevo (1995).

"It is a war story," wrote Chuck Sudetic, in a letter to my students in the Pennsylvania Governor's School for International Studies, about the choice of his book, *Blood and Vengeance: One Family's Story of the War in Bosnia* (1998), for our primary reading. Such "stories . . . envelop us."

> They allow us to identify with characters. And most importantly, they allow us to empathize—to put ourselves in someone else's shoes. . . . So when you sit down and begin reading the book, imagine what it would be like to be the people you're reading about. . . . What were their aspirations? . . . What were their choices? . . . How would you have behaved differently? Would you have survived? (1999)

I have tried to write this book about the Treća Gimnazija community in humanistic as well as academic terms, to allow us to identify with the teachers and students, to put ourselves in their shoes, to imagine what it might be like. How might we have behaved in their situation? Would we have behaved differently? Would we have survived? "The answers to such questions are generally feared," wrote Anna Pawłeczyńska, of life in the concentration camps. "People today do not desire a knowledge of life which compels the asking of such questions" (1979:4).

In the aftermath of my journey to Bosnia, I wrote a short article entitled, "The Heroes of Treća Gimnazija: A War School in Sarajevo" (1997). Perhaps the essence of the article may be summarized in the following words that serve as a forerunner to my acknowledgments:

Indeed, the story of Treća Gimnazija is perhaps the story of all schools, of all teachers, of all students, of all those who waged "the battle for the mind" during the siege of Sarajevo. . . . This is the story of "the heroes of Treća Gimnazija," the students who asserted their right to their education, and the teachers who answered their call. (1997:9)

Those discussions with teachers at Treća Gimnazija became the basis for my third visit to Sarajevo during the spring of 1998, again as a visiting scholar at the Faculty of Philosophy. On this occasion, I spent my time in the Department of Pedagogy through the assistance of Professor Miljenko Brkić, the department chair, and Mirjana Mavrak, the higher assistant in the department. I had returned to Sarajevo with a research agenda to explore a macrolevel focus on the organization of war schools in the local communities across Sarajevo city and a microlevel focus on Treća Gimnazija as a case study of a "war school" during the siege.

On this occasion, I was invited to attend the Treća Gimnazija *maskenbal*, the masked ball, held now as an annual event by the students of the school in the original school buildings on what is now Wilson Promenade along the banks of the Miljacka River. To this day, the damage to the school is visible to even the most casual observer. However, this damage takes on the surrealistic character of the siege itself during the masked ball held in the shells of those buildings along the old frontline. There is probably no more surrealistic sight than the "the picture of speckles, colors, and masks" of students dressed in the outrageous costumes of a masked ball dancing to rock music in the empty skeletons of school buildings pock-marked by shell craters and bullet holes.

"And the masked ball happened," reads the Treća Gimnazija *Almanac* (1998:41). The school held "the first postwar masked ball" in the spring of 1996 organized by the students of the third class whose first three years of high school were marked by the last three years of the siege of the city. "These are our five minutes," reads the newspaper headline. "A crazy night in the backyard of the destroyed school—the best masks chosen," reads the subtitle. Some of the story of the masked ball reads as follows:

Every year, the students of Treća Gimnazija organize the masked ball, with the motto, "Take us back to our school." Actually, the buildings of Treća Gimnazija have been completely destroyed, and therefore, the students of this school use Hrasno Elementary School while theirs is being rebuilt. . . . Every year the students of the third class have the responsibility to organize the masked ball. These are our five minutes, in order to forget about all the sleepless nights. (*Dnevni avaz*, 1998:12)

Indeed, the surrealism of the siege is matched only by the surrealism of the masked ball that has now become a rite of spring in the aftermath of the war. Yet the masked balls continue as a sign of resistance and of hope for the future, and the surrealistic images of the dancing offer a ghostly mirror that reflects the surrealistic images of the siege. On 6 April 1996, on the fiftieth anniversary of the founding of the school, the letter to celebrate the occasion is signed by "the students and teachers from Sniper Alley" (n.d.). Those students of the fourth class, the graduating seniors of Treća Gimnazija, who had attended all four years of high school during the siege, were known as the *ratna generacija* (war generation). Just down the Miljacka River from the original school location on Wilson Promenade, and just down the street from the temporary school location in Hrasno, the reality of the nightmare was expressed in the epitaph on the wall of a building near Malta Bridge just off Sniper Alley, which read, in English, "Welcome to hell!"

To an American educator who came late to experience the siege, the process of "doing research on the war schools of Sarajevo" is no small matter. Indeed, my initial impressions of schooling during the siege came from UN documents that focused upon "ad hoc arrangements," "a partial curriculum," and no reference to the local community war schools. It took several visits to understand, to reiterate the words of Hajrija-Šahza Jahić, that "the idea was to . . . develop a scheme, to develop a kind of organized system of war schools" (1998). The story of Treća Gimnazija is simply incomplete without recognition of the place of the school within the scheme, within the organized system of war schools that connected the basement classrooms and stairway schools together in order to survive under siege. Korak po korak, a Bosnian friend told me as I sought to put together the picture of the war schools of Sarajevo, "step by step," or, to rephrase the message in the more figurative terms of a Bosnian proverb:

Zrno po zrno pogača
Kamen po kamen palača!

Grain by grain bread
Stone by stone a palace!

Chapter Two

Schooling in Wartime Conditions, April 1992–September 1992

I thought that my little river had only currents of happiness. I never understood that I would come back to its source with longing. And I am coming back. I am coming back, because my pain and tears flow into it. My generation is crying, my generation is being killed. They too had their sources, their rivers, and their love. All that broke into the riverbed of my river. Its current is quiet and silent; will it hold on? It will have to. Its current will go wild, its waves will wash all the blood and tears. It will help that all rivers find their sources. And that we all quietly go to our sources. Full of pride, happy but still longing.

> —Azra Halimić,
> student of Treća Gimnazija

First Drop of Blood on the Asphalt

Dan Oslobođenja Sarajeva, or Sarajevo Liberation Day, dates from 6 April 1945 and the liberation of Sarajevo from the Nazi occupation of World War II. The *School Annual* of Treća Gimnazija records the significance of Monday, 6 April 1992, however, in somewhat cryptic terms:

> *6 APRIL:* School Day and the Day of Liberation of Sarajevo in *1945*. It is planned that this date be celebrated with a lunch for all employed workers of the schools as it is every year,
> but instead of that,
> *6 APRIL 1992.* (*Školski ljetopis*)

In addition to the record of school events, the *School Annual* contains excerpts from Sarajevo daily newspapers that record the trauma of those early days at the onset of the siege. Dated Monday, 6 April 1992, the headlines read, "A Night and a Day of Terror over Sarajevo," "The Battle for Sarajevo," "Shelling the Heart of Sarajevo," and "Shelling Killed Nine People." A second" entry for 6 April follows the newspaper clippings and reads simply:

> Classes interrupted for students. There is a state of emergency because of the danger of war. Employees are to show up for work. (*Školski ljetopis*)

Treća Gimnazija was one of seventeen secondary schools totally incapacitated during the siege of Sarajevo, one of ninety school buildings physically damaged, shelled into ruins at the onset of the siege, forty-four years to the day of her founding (Jabučar, 1994). Located at what was then 16 Omladinsko šetalište, or 16 Youth Promenade, today Vilosonovo šetalište, or (Woodrow) Wilson Promenade (after the American president), directly across the Miljacka River from the Grbavica settlement occupied by Bosnian Serb forces during the siege, the eviscerated shells of her buildings continued to stand. However, Treća Gimnazija, an academic secondary school whose purpose was to prepare students for the university, ceased to exist in traditional terms.

The weekend of 4–5 April 1992 marked the onset of the siege of Sarajevo, or "the third Bosnian war," to repeat the words of Misha Glenny, a siege that "pitted Serb irregulars . . . together with JNA and its awesome arsenal of heavy artillery against the sophisticated, urban dwellers of Sarajevo" (1994:171). The events of the weekend proved deadly for the citizens of Sarajevo most of whom in their naivete could hardly believe that another of the wars of Yugoslav secession was now on their doorstep. In the words of Lejla Polimac, one of my students at the University of Sarajevo, and one of those citizens:

> It is Sunday, 5 April 1992. I am sixteen years old, in the second year of secondary school. Something has changed but we cannot believe it. We don't want to believe. We don't want to accept the fact that war is here. My parents are confused. I never saw them looking like that. They don't know what to say, how to react, how to behave. The only thing they are saying is, "Everything will be just fine in a couple of days," and they kept saying that for four years. I know now that these words helped us to stay alive—mentally. (1996)

On the weekend of 4–5 April, the area teemed with thousands of people who had gathered on the plaza in front of the Parliament where the protest leaders declared a "National Salvation Committee" in a call for new elections. "The idea was to cross the bridge to Grbavica to show that the city still belonged to the people—all the people," recalled Samir Korić, of the events on that Sunday, 5 April. The Vrbanja Bridge, which crossed the Miljacka River and connected the Marijin Dvor and Grbavica areas of the city, was located just behind the Faculty of Philosophy and the Bosnian parliament buildings and the Holiday Inn across the street that became known as "Sniper Alley." Crossing the bridge to the barricades that day, Suada Dilberović, a twenty-one-year-old medical student at the University, was shot through the chest by a sniper in march to the barricades erected in Grbavica. "I remember Suada standing there that morning with her blonde hair and sparkling blue eyes, laughing. . . . Strange to say, war still didn't seem inevitable. It was only a few days later that there seemed no turning back, that we began to speak of Suada as the first person killed in the Bosnian war" (Silber and Little, 1996:227–228). Today a memorial plaque to Suada Dilberović on the Vrbanja Bridge, where *Sarajlije* often place offerings of flowers, reads in sobering terms for all to see:

Kap moje krvi	A drop of my blood
poteće	flowed
i Bosna	and Bosnia
ne presuši	does not run dry

Four years later, as a graduating senior, Jasna Hadžić, a first-year student of *Treća Gimnazija* at the time, wrote the following account of those early days at the onset of the siege:

> The first blossom in the trees. The first shot, the first drops of blood on the asphalt, the first tears. The colors and the smell of spring. Bosnia, Sarajevo, April 1992. That is how the war started in my country. It is still going on for more than three years now. The first death became the second, the third. . . . Today it is a regular occurrence. (1995)

Those in the protest march to the barricades in Grbavica were moving directly into the assault on the city by Bosnian Serb forces. Laura Silber and Allen Little describe those events on the morning of Sunday, 5 April, at the onset of the siege:

34 Chapter Two

> Serb paramilitaries laid siege to, and then attacked, the Sarajevo police
> academy on the southern edge of the city. The compound sat high
> above the city and enjoyed a commanding strategic position. It also
> housed a large stockpile of arms and ammunition. The military priority
> of the Serb forces was to move down from their positions on Vraca hill
> and enter the city from the south, where they would cross the [Mil-
> jacka] river near the parliament building and cut Sarajevo in half at its
> narrowest point. (1996:226)

As Bosnian Serb paramilitary forces were moving down from Vraca hill
into the Grbavica area, thousands of Sarajevo citizens were walking from
the parliament buildings across the Miljacka River into Grbavica directly
into their assault. Later that night, elements of the JNA seized control of
the airport on the outskirts of the city and cut it off from the rest of Sarajevo. On Monday, 6 April, from the upper floors of the Holiday Inn
where Radovan Karadžić and the SDS (Serbian Democratic Party) had
their offices, Bosnian Serb gunners opened fire on the demonstrators,
who were still in front of the Bosnian Parliament, killing at least six people and wounding others. In the words of the *School Annual* of Treća
Gimnazija: "Classes interrupted for students. There is a state of emergency because of the danger of war."

The events of the weekend are also recalled by Belma Huskić, another first-year student of Treća Gimnazija at the time who, in her innocence, echoes the words of other students and offers a premonition of the
next four years:

> The television is turned on. There is electricity of course. Friends from
> the city are calling and saying not to leave our apartment. We are
> hearing from everyone that barricades have been put up on the streets.
> Father is nervously walking up and down in the apartment. He is sens-
> ing something that I cannot even feel a premonition of. I am pleased
> because I will not have a math exam. Everybody is saying that most
> probably war is going to "happen." In elementary school I learned
> about war. A couple of people defend the country, the enemy from
> abroad attacks, but of course honor wins in the end. Maybe this could
> be the picture in a world of illusions, in a world of justice. But to us, it
> is the best version of a terrifying war. (1995)

The state of emergency that began the terrifying war extended to
schooling throughout Sarajevo, but for Treća Gimnazija, the implications
were particularly severe because of its location approximately a thousand
meters down the Miljacka River from the Vrbanja Bridge, perhaps a fif-
teen-minute walk on an early spring day. The Sarajevo Police Academy

that was the target of the Bosnian Serb assault on Vraca hill was located directly above Grbavica and provided "a commanding strategic position" with a clear view of both banks of the Miljacka River below. From Vraca hill, the Bosnian Serb forces moved down into Grbavica and, within several weeks, occupied the entire area. The Grbavica area was located directly across the Miljacka River from Treća Gimnazija to the south where the high-rise apartment buildings along the riverbank provided vantage points for Bosnian Serb snipers. In other words, where students once strolled on pathways under the linden trees along the river, they could no longer even come to the school that was now situated directly on the frontline in the battle to prevent the city from being cut in two.

From a distance, the most visible forms of evidence of the location of the school on the "first battle line" are the shell craters through the south and west walls of the main classroom building. Closer inspection notes the buildings are pockmarked from small-arms fire especially across the south walls that faced the enemy directly across the river. There are no windows in the entire building, and shattered glass lies across the school grounds. Many of the windows were shot out over the weekend of 4–5 April from across the river in Grbavica as a prelude to the assault. The shattered windows greeted the teachers when they arrived at school on 6 April, but they were replaced that day "because we didn't know that the war had started. We never believed there was going to be a war," said Mirko Marinović, the school director at that time, to me. "Otherwise, why would we have replaced the windows?" (1998). The linden trees in front of the school were not spared either. In fact, they were among the few trees left standing in Sarajevo as the inhabitants of the city, with no electricity during the winter, cut down the trees to build fires for warmth. The frontline along the Miljacka, however, was simply too dangerous a place to cut down trees.

In a report to the Fund for Secondary Education to request monies for building repairs, the *School Annual* notes the condition of the school buildings in August 1992, four months into the siege, just prior to the anticipated beginning of the 1992–1993 school year:

> The school consists of two buildings, the new and the old, which are connected to make one entity.
>
> The object is located on the first front (fighting) line at 16 Youth Promenade and is constantly exposed to shelling and machine gun fire.
>
> The new building of the school is badly damaged. The roof construction made of "Salonit" boards is pierced in many places. This caused the greatest damage on the second floor, where there are labs for chemistry and physics.

All the glass surfaces on the building are broken.

Gutters on both buildings are badly damaged.

Most of the carpentry work is either damaged or destroyed, including inside and outside walls and part of the furniture.

The roof on the physical education hall is damaged to a very great extent, and therefore the parklet got wet and raised and lost its form. It was noticed that the residents of the surrounding buildings come and collect pieces of parklet, take it home and burn it. . . .

The beginning of the 1992/93 school year is uncertain. (*Školski ljetopis*)

With the physical destruction of her buildings at the onset of the siege, Treća Gimnazija became a *ratna škola* (war school), a school that continued to survive in both an administrative and functional sense without a physical structure or single permanent location. Dated April 1–15, 1992, the *School Annual* provides the first references to the "war schools" of Treća Gimnazija and notes the attempt to continue with schooling in some sort of normal fashion:

The aggression against the Republic of Bosnia and Herzegovina is still continuing. Life and work in the surrounded city is exceptionally difficult, including instruction in the war schools that were organized in the district offices. However, with an exceptional effort of the teachers and the students, regular instruction is going on in satisfying scope in the war schools in the districts of Kovači and Sumbuluša for which Treća Gimnazija is responsible. The Teachers' Boards were formed and overall instruction is professionally offered, with the exception that one part of the instruction is given by TA's in the districts of Kovači and Sumbuluša. The instruction is given in many objectively hard circumstances which are not possible to control by the school like, for example, the lack of textbooks and materials. . . . The students' attendance is, for the most part, regular. The instruction in the general courses will end on 2 July after eighteen weeks, and afterward, additional instruction in some subjects will be organized if it is necessary. (*Školski ljetopis*)

Under these conditions, the administrators of the school attempted to organize instructional programs, the teachers attempted to coordinate classes, and the students attempted to attend classes in various locations, complete assignments, and study towards the university examinations. The intent was to somehow continue classes in order to complete the 1991–1992 school year, but the entry of 20 April notes the impossibility of these efforts as the situation continued to deteriorate:

The sixth meeting of the Teacher's Board was held this school year. By recommendation of the appropriate city committees, the city Parliament, the inspection services, and the Pedagogical Institute, even with the interrupted school instruction, the grades of students are concluded for the third nine weeks based on the grades students made from the beginning of the school year to the present. The plan and program of instruction was not followed because of the teachers' strike and because of the circumstances in Sarajevo. (*Školski ljetopis*)

The strike reference refers to the teachers' strike organized by the independent union of secondary school teachers in Bosnia during March. The loss of class time during the strike combined with the interruption of classes during the assault rendered the continuation of schooling during this third term a virtual impossibility. The objective and reasoned entry of 20 April in the *School Annual* belies the fact that Sarajevo was in chaos as the fighting intensified. Just two short weeks later, the entry of 2 May 1992, suggests just how much the situation had deteriorated within less than a month after the initial assault on the city:

Life and work in the city are made extremely difficult after all city transportation stopped working, after a large number of telephone lines were cut down, and the rest of communications as well. Every day a great number of citizens are killed and wounded. Going out on the street is extremely dangerous due to shelling of the city and also because of snipers. In such conditions [students] have stopped coming to the school—and it is also being shelled daily. . . . In that period a school crisis headquarters was formed and a work obligation was instituted for certain workers. (*Školski ljetopis*)

The Decision on Establishing a Work Obligation actually was published in the *Official Gazette* on 9 April 1992 making work compulsory for employees in selected professions and critical industries (*Službeni list RBiH*, 1992). In the schools of the city, crisis headquarters were formed to direct school operations and selected teachers were obligated to continue with work at their respective schools. At Treća Gimnazija, five employees were assigned to the crisis headquarters: Mirko Marinović, the school director, Jasminka Tomić, the deputy director, Jure Dimopulo, the president of the school council, Azemina Osmanagić, the secretary, and Julka Vukmirović, the bookkeeper. The names of another nine teachers and one maintenance man appeared under the work obligation list in the 2 May 1992 entry in the *School Annual*. The adaptation of the work obligation to the educational profession, entitled the "Law on Determining Conditions of Temporary Internal Organization and Systematization and

Assigning of Workers in the Institutions Working in the Field of Education, Science, Culture and Physical Culture during the War or in the Case
of Immediate War Danger," was published in the *Official Gazette* on 9
July 1992 and noted the working obligation of teachers (Jabučar, 1997).

Although teachers and administrators attempted to continue with the
school routine, classes at the school itself were simply impossible because of the location of the school directly on the frontline. The 2 May
entry indicates that if the 1991–1992 school year did not effectively end
on 6 April, it is quite clear that it ended in mid-May since students "have
stopped coming to school" within a month after the initial assault on the
city. Abdulah Jabučar, the deputy minister of education for the Republic
during the war, and for the Federation today, explained the end of the
1991–1992 school year on 15 May in the following terms:

> The Ministry of Education, Science, Culture and Physical Culture had
> been following the development of events and reacted on time. When
> the chetnik's euphoria gained the upper hand, we had to stop the pro-
> cess of teaching lest children would be killed, so the Ministry sug-
> gested, and the Presidency of Bosnia and Herzegovina issued a regula-
> tion with legal force concerning the end of the school year—the fif-
> teenth of May 1992. (1994:4)

Deputy Minister Jabučar was referring to the "Law on the Completion of
Teaching in the 1991/92 School Year in Primary, Secondary and Higher
Schools; Faculties and Art Academies in the Republic of Bosnia and
Herzegovina," which appeared in the *Official Gazette* dated 5 May 1992,
and provided the legal documentation for closing the schools on 15 May
1992 before the end of the 1991–1992 school year (Jabučar, 1997). Selected articles of the law read as follows:

> Taking into consideration the continuation of the aggression and ter-
> rorism against the Republic of Bosnia and Herzegovina, instruction is
> discontinued and completed for the 1991/92 school year in all elemen-
> tary and secondary schools in the Republic of Bosnia and Herzegovina
> as of 15 May 1992.
>
> The students of elementary and secondary schools in the Republic
> of Bosnia and Herzegovina who attended school in the 1991/92 school
> year and completed a class, year, or education which shall be recog-
> nized and all that in accordance with the achieved performance up to
> the moment when instruction was discontinued. . . .
>
> Enrollment of students in elementary and secondary schools and
> students in higher education institutions in the next school year, organi-
> zation of the entry exam to gimnazija, that is, the qualifying exam for

entry to higher education institutions, shall be done when conditions for its organization are made. . . .

Due to the end of this school year before its time, the next 1992/93 school year shall begin when conditions are made for normal instruction and work of all elementary, secondary, and higher schools, faculties and art academies in the Republic of Bosnia and Herzegovina. (Jabučar, 1997:175–176)

Schools were effectively closed to students as of 15 May 1992 with the "aggression and terrorism" against the new Bosnian Republic, while the enrollment and registration of students for the next school year was held in abeyance until conditions improved. With conditions throughout the city deteriorating, the state of the situation was described by Misha Glenny who wrote, upon entering the city during early May, "It is an unfathomably surreal experience." Racing down Sniper Alley at eighty-five miles an hour, Glenny wrote, "Never have I witnessed such an eerie scene. Broad daylight in a capital city and there is not a soul on the streets. Newspaper skips in the wind. This is not Sarajevo—this is the Twilight Zone, and it is real" (1994:175).

The Geography of Murder

The 2 May entry in the *School Annual* of Treća Gimnazija summarizes the events from the four previous weeks of school that began with the 6 April entry and recorded the onset of the siege. Either the 2 May entry was a premonition of the day's events, or an attempt to record the magnitude of the assault on Sarajevo as captured in the 3 May 1992 headline in *Oslobođenje* that read, in Cyrillic, "Brutal Attack on Sarajevo." In their book, *Yugoslavia: Death of a Nation* (1996), Laura Silber and Allen Little offer perhaps the most thorough description of the events of the day as they unfolded. I will offer their description here in some detail because these events served to entrench the siege lines around the city for the duration of the war and, in this regard, have particular relevance for Treća Gimnazija. The description also provides an indication of the mindset of the Bosnian Serb political leaders towards the inhabitants of the city and the implications for both the conduct of the war and the adaptation of schooling to wartime conditions. Silber and Little write:

The second of May had seen a serious escalation of the war not only in Sarajevo but elsewhere in Bosnia. . . . It was also the day that [Radovan] Karadžić's forces tried to implement, by military might, his plan to divide the city into separate Muslim and Serb quarters.

Karadžić always made plain his ambition to partition Sarajevo. He had a vision of a city divided into Serb, Croat and Muslim sectors that was sharply at odds with Sarajevo's centuries-long tradition of peaceful coexistence and ethnic intermingling. Without shame, he would advocate to journalists and diplomats alike the need to build a wall through the heart of the city. He wanted a Berlin Wall through a city in which every district, every neighborhood, every street, every apartment block was ethnically mixed. In his mountain headquarters at Pale, Karadžić would happily spread out his maps of the city and show anyone who was interested the route that his proposed wall would take. The extreme east of the city, the narrow winding streets of the Turkish old town, together with the broad boulevards of the neighboring nineteenth-century Hapsburg quarters, were for the Muslims and Croats. Everything to the west of Marijindvor—including most of the city's twentieth-century industrial and commercial infrastructure, and most of its residential capacity—was to be inhabited exclusively by Serbs. This was decided on the preposterous grounds that the farmland and villages on which the modern city had been built was originally populated mostly by rural Serb communities. Karadžić made no apologies for devising a plan which would cram the vast majority of the city's people into the smallest most crowded sector of the town. "It is the habit of the Muslims to live in this way," his deputy, Biljana Plavšić, once memorably declared. "They like to live on top of one another. It's their culture. We Serbs need space."

On May 2, as Izetbegović was returning from Lisbon, Karadžić's forces tried to cut the city in half. For weeks they had occupied the high ground, encircling the city from all sides. Now they moved into the town itself. From the south, they moved down from the Vraca and Trebević mountains into the city-center district of Grbavica. One column of armored vehicles crossed the narrow bridge at Skenderija and came within a hundred yards of the Presidency building. Its progress was covered by artillery and mortar fire from the surrounding heights. Artillery- and tank-rounds slammed into the red-brick facade of the city municipal headquarters [which contained the offices of the City Secretariat for Education]. . . .

In Croatia, Serb and JNA forces had proved themselves almost incapable of capturing urban territory without first reducing it to rubble. They enjoyed overwhelming firepower superiority; but they did not have the infantry to follow up artillery attacks. The pattern now repeated itself in Sarajevo. Both armored columns were halted by a relatively small number of Patriotic League, the recently-formed armed wing of the SDA [Party for Democratic Action] and Bosnian territorial defense members equipped with nothing more than shoulder-launched antitank missiles. At Skenderija, they immobilized the lead vehicle in a street so narrow that it blocked the passage of the rest of the column, which was then forced to retreat. . . .

It was a half-hearted effort, but it was not wholly unsuccessful. For the first time it brought the Serb front line into the heart of the city. It gave Karadžić's forces control of Grbavica and part of the neighboring district of Hrasno. . . . The inner-city front lines established by the Serbs' bungled invasion of May 2 held firm for the rest of the war, and formed the basis for a *de facto* partition of Sarajevo; thus Grbavica and Nedžarići would, from now on, find themselves part of the self-declared "Serbian Republic of Bosnia–Herzegovina," separated from Bosnian Government controlled districts by a Beirut-style green line, across which rival armies (and former neighbors) faced each other in a constant, and often deadly, stand-off. It was a line that divided naturally cohesive inner-city communities, and separated parents from their children, a wholly artificial and arbitrary military barrier which, overnight, became, in effect, a new frontier between enemy states. (1996:232– 234)

From the heights of Mount Trebević down to the ridge line of hills that paralleled the Miljacka River, Bosnian Serb forces controlled Vraca hill above Grbavica, Hrasno hill above Hrasno, and, further down, Mojmilo hill above Otoka and Alipašino Polje. In addition, the occupation of Mojmilo hill and the Nedžarići area to the west isolated the suburb of Dobrinja, located alongside the airport, from the main part of the city. The "Beirut-style green line" ran southeast down the slopes of Mount Trebević through the old Jewish cemetery to the Vrbanja Bridge. From the southwest, the line ran along the slopes of Mojmilo hill over to Hrasno hill and then down around Grbavica Stadium, the home of the Željezničar Football Club. From the stadium, the line ran straight along what was then Milutina Đuraškovića Street to the Miljacka River, approximately one kilometer downstream from the Vrbanja Bridge.

The landscape that saw Bosnian Serb forces hold the high ground above the city and the Grbavica salient is characterized by Kemal Kurspahić, who lived in the adjacent Hrasno neighborhood, as the "geography of murder" (1997:173). The Bosnian Serb forces that first occupied the police academy on Vraca hill on 5 April, and ventured down to terrorize the inhabitants below over the next several weeks, had taken virtual control of Grbavica by the weekend of 2–3 May. During this time, they began the process of cleansing Grbavica of undesirable inhabitants and imposing their rule upon those who remained. "The Serbian Territorial Defence force called a tenants' meeting," wrote Elma Softić of telephone conversations with relatives trapped in Grbavica, "at which they

42   Chapter Two

informed them that they now belong to the Serbian Republic of Bosnia–
Herzegovina. . . . Grbavica. So near, and yet infinitely far. So familiar,
and so appalling. A different country. And a hostile one" (1996:28,148).

The frontline that partitioned this area of Sarajevo was the Miljacka
River itself separating occupied Grbavica, referred to simply as "the
other side," from the territory known as "free Sarajevo." In other words,
the school buildings of Treća Gimnazija were a stone's throw directly
across the river from the enemy. The inhabitants of the school were no
longer secondary school students in the throes of adolescence but Territorial Defense forces who became the forerunner of the Bosnian Army.
And directly across from Treća Gimnazija on the Grbavica side of the
river, the inhabitants of the Borisa Kovačević Elementary School were
no longer elementary school students but the paramilitary forces of the
Serbian Republic of Bosnia and Herzegovina, the Republika Srpska. In
the words of Emin Čustović, one of the elementary school teachers:

> The "Borisa Kovačević" Elementary School found itself playing a role
> in this horror that was taking place in the city. This school was located
> in Grbavica where the winds of war were destroying everything in their
> path. . . . The school bell was last heard on 3 April when it was re-
> placed by gunfire from the barricades that were placed at the Pofalići
> crossroad.
>
> Illusions had to be burned, forced to face reality and flee from the
> left bank of the Miljacka to the right or across the water to freedom.
> The tradition of the school in its thirty-fourth year was brutally ended
> by the ruthless war, and it destroyed any hopes of the faculty and their
> students in a quick return to their school.
>
> The school was "captured" by Serbian chetniks, "white eagles,"
> and "hawks," and they created a lair from which their snipers, artillery,
> mortars, shells, grenade launchers, machine guns and grenade launchers
> fired upon the citizens of the right bank of the Miljacka River. All of
> these innocent civilians would spend their nights hiding in cellars and
> shelters, not sleeping and thinking of what tomorrow will bring. Until
> the month of June, Wilson Promenade and the area of the "Brotherhood
> and Unity" Bridge was covered with dead people. Their bodies served
> as meals for the numerous scavengers and the stench of them decom-
> posing was unbearable.
>
> In mid-June of 1993, "Borisa Kovačević" was destroyed by fire
> . . . . Most of the faculty members and students are displaced all over
> the country and until this day their fate is unknown. (1994)

The surrealism of schools occupied by armies became but one of the ironies of the Bosnian war. With the siege lines now entrenched for virtu-

ally the entire length of the siege, we know that the faculty and students of Borisa Kovačević Elementary School were displaced and that the elementary school became a "war school" like many others. As for the students and teachers of Treća Gimnazija, their story unfolds in the pages of the *School Annual* and in the words of those who remained behind in the besieged city. A final April entry reflects something of the barriers erected between communities and neighborhoods, and, in this case, between teachers as colleagues:

> From the sixth to the thirtieth of April, the following workers never came to school: Mirjana Popović, Biljana Helesa, Čedo Miletić, Savka Krčmar, Gordana Mimić, Slobodan Potpara, Vlado Baškarada, Ratko Hršum, Danica Vujović, Ljiljana Preković, Julija Anzić, Sadeta Joldić, Dragica Trubelja, Zdravko Plavšić, Radivoje Puhalo. (*Skolski ljetopis*)

In other words, on Monday, 6 April, amidst the state of emergency that was declared throughout the city, a number of teachers and staff never showed up for classes at the school nor did they ever show up at the school during the month of April. In fact, they never showed up at all. They simply disappeared. The 30 April entry also notes the disappearance of the school treasurer:

> Mirjana Knežević, the school treasurer, took needed money from Novo Sarajevo municipality for employee salaries for the month of April. She gave half the employees their part and the other half of the employees never saw the money since she never showed up at work. (*Školski ljetopis*)

In the August entries that conclude the truncated 1991–1992 school year, the *School Annual* records that sixteen teachers simply disappeared while the treasurer and a coordinator made for a total count of eighteen workers "who stopped work." As of 31 May 1992, these workers were fired from their jobs for their failure to come to work after a waiting period of twenty days. Article 6 of the "Law on Determining Conditions of Temporary Internal Organization and Systematization and Assigning of Workers in Institutions Working in the Field of Education, Science, Culture and Physical Culture during the War or in the Case of Immediate War Danger," that appeared in the *Official Gazette* dated 9 July 1992, reads as follows:

> To the employees whose employment stopped in accordance with the law, or those who were absent without an excuse from work for more

than twenty days or who went over to the aggressor's side and against
the Republic of Bosnia and Herzegovina after the Decision on Establishing a Work Obligation . . . entered into force, the director is obliged
to bring a decision on terminating employment. (Jabučar, 1997:129)

These eighteen employees were all Serbs who went to "the other side,"
as their colleagues would say, to the other side of the Beirut-style green
line, to the other side of the river, to Grbavica, to the enemy state on the
other side, to the Republika Srpska. However, not all Serb teachers went
to "the other side," and those who remained behind performed truly heroic service under the most difficult of conditions. In this regard, Abdulah Jabučar, referring to the 9 July 1992 law, wrote the following:

In the beginning of the war, a large number of teachers of Serb nation-
ality joined the aggressor's side, a certain number of them ran away before the aggressor's assault, and a certain number of teachers were engaged to do other things, so schools were, in large part, without their
staff. In order to overcome this situation, a Regulation with legal force
has brought about the temporary inner organization and systematization
of workers in institutions in the areas of education, science, culture and
physical education in the war period or in the case of the state of war.
This Regulation foresees that in a war situation the teacher can be engaged to teach 35 hours a week. (1994:4)

In another of the ironies of war, the coordinator responsible for vocational education programs "who stopped work" and failed to return to the
school was Zdravko Plavšić, the brother of Biljana Plavšić, the deputy to
Radovan Karadžić, the political leader of the Republika Srpska.

In the final count of 1991–1992 employees, a total of thirty-six
teachers and administrators remained under contract while six teachers
remained on a "waiting list" because of questions about their status.
Seven teachers appear on the list of part-time workers to include Misim
Gegić whose whereabouts in April was unknown. Six teachers who
taught at other schools were now temporarily assigned to Treća Gimnazija because of the proximity of their residence. One Treća Gimnazija
teacher was now assigned to the Comprehensive Agricultural, Veterinarian and Food Secondary School located in another area of the city. A
total of sixty-one teachers and administrators (who also taught) were ac-
counted for on the roster of Treća Gimnazija employees under one category or another in the concluding August entries of the *School Annual* by
the end of the 1991–1992 school year.

Razvlačenje pameti
(Stretching the Brain)

If the onset of the siege in April 1992 was traumatic, the month of May was a prelude to somewhere beyond the "awful nightmare" of Lejla Polimac as the siege of the city intensified. While May began with the attempt by Bosnian Serb forces to cut Sarajevo in two and carve out their own slice of the city, Sarajevo was also in the process of being pounded into ruin. The pattern of urban warfare seen at Vukovar, for example, repeated itself here in the attempt to reduce the city to rubble with superior firepower in order to then seize it. The imagery of the destruction of Sarajevo gave rise to the term "Urbicide" at an October 1993 Sarajevo exhibition entitled, "Warchitecture," to suggest the killing of the urban identity, not to mention the people. "What does it mean to 'murder a city'?" asked Bogdan Bogdanović, the former mayor of Belgrade, in an essay called, "The City and Death." "It means to snuff out its strength, stifle its metaphysical eros, its will to live, its sense of self, its means of scattering its memory to the winds, annihilating its past along with its present" (1995:72–73). The physical and psychological annihilation of Sarajevo intensified with the relentless shelling of May 1992. The middle of May was especially deadly. The headlines in the 14 May 1992 issue of *Oslobođenje*, read, for example, "Sarajevo Defended Itself from Attack." The subheading read:

> Criminal bombarding of the city from early morning and attempts of the chetnik-terrorists to penetrate settlements one by one was broken by a defense wall. . . . Karadžić requested air attack from Milošević. (1992:1)

In fact, the entire city was under attack, from the western settlements of Stup, Nedžarići, Alipašino Polje, Otoka, and Hrasno, to the Vrbanja Bridge in the center of the city, and on to Stari Grad, the Old City, on the eastern end. A 14 May story read: "Pictures of Horror in Hrasno" which cited "New Victims of the Bombardment of Sarajevo" (1992:3). The intensity of the early battles for Sarajevo is captured by Elma Softić who recorded the events of 12–16 May in her diary of life under siege. In the process, she reveals the increasing hardships as the basic essentials of life, water, bread, and electricity, became a day-to-day proposition:

12 May 1992: Today, all day, the pounding of bombs. . . . It's a horrifying sound, the whistling that trails after a mortar shell as it flies overhead, but at least you know it's flying over you. They say it's the one you don't hear that kills you.

14 May 1992: A bloody fourteenth of May. The bombardment is horrific. All over the city. . . . The dead and wounded wait for hours until someone comes for them. Firefighters are being fired upon. Doctors are being fired upon. [Grave-diggers] are being fired upon. . . .

15 May 1992: I waited for hours for bread. A mob of people had been standing since early morning by the Eternal Flame waiting for the bread truck. I was suffocating with fear as I stood there waiting for the damn truck, and waiting for a bomb to fall. . . . I didn't get any bread—it didn't arrive at all.

16 May 1992: There is no running water. They've bombarded the installations of the pumping station that provides water to the districts of New City, New Sarajevo, and the city centre. Almost the whole city is without water and the greater part of the city is without electricity. (1996:29–30)

In the *School Annual* of Treća Gimnazija, the only May entry, other than the 2 May description of the siege, is dated 20 May and reads: "State of war declared and general mobilization of the entire Republic of Bosnia and Herzegovina." In a review of significant battles, the Bosnian army newspaper, *Prva linija* (First Line), notes the critical importance of these early battles for Sarajevo during the spring of 1992. In the process, the article updates the description by Silber and Little of the events of 2–3 May when Bosnian Serb forces attempted to cut the city in two, which established the siege lines for the duration of the war:

> The first decisive armed battle won by the defenders of Sarajevo was the battle in Pofalići on 16 May 1992. The intention of the chetniks to try splitting Sarajevo in two in order to win it completely was discovered two days earlier. The main intention was to connect chetniks from Orlića and Hum hill, as well as those from Grbavica and Vraca, over the Vrbanja Bridge with the Marshal Tito barracks in the center of this linkage. The determining moment was the forceful charge by the defenders of Sarajevo who were positioned only 50 meters from the chetniks. The battle for Pofalići has opened tactical space for the liberation of Orlića on 8 June 1992 as well as the further liberation of Zuč hill. (Gagula, 1994:6)

The last week of May witnessed the most intense shelling of the city since the onset of the siege. On 27 May, at least three mortar shells tore into a line of people waiting for bread on what was then Vase Miskina

Street leading to Baščaršija falling precisely between buildings on either side of the narrow walkway, killing 17 and wounding at least 156 (Smajkić, 1992). "The bloody bread of Sarajevo," wrote Elma Softić (1996:40). Known as the Breadline Massacre, today a memorial plaque commemorates the slaughter:

NA OVUM SU MJESTU	AT THIS PLACE
SRPSKI ZLOČINCI	SERBIAN CRIMINALS
27-5-1992 UBILI 17	ON 27 MAY 1992 KILLED 17
GRAĐANA SARAJEVA	SARAJEVO CITIZENS

In her personal diary, Jelena Andrić, then a first-year student at Prva gimnazija, recounted the Breadline Massacre on the following day. Her entry confronts us with the trauma of siege in human terms:

Thursday, 28 May 1996 (11:30) Sarajevo: Yesterday was the bloodiest day in the history of Sarajevo. Yesterday morning a terrible massacre happened in front of Trznica in a breadline. People were waiting for bread to come to the Klas store when three shells exploded in the middle of the crowd of 200 to 300 people. . . . Fourteen people died and one of them is Lala's sister Gordana. When it happened the TV was there and we saw everything. Blood was everywhere, and people were lying on top of each other. I was scared. . . . At that moment I knew that my mom was working and her hospital is right beside Trznica. . . . Mom came home shaking and crying. Dad was hugging her trying to calm her down. She told us later that as soon as she put her uniform on, she heard the explosions followed by the terrible screams and all of them ran out in the hope that they could help someone but there was nothing left to help. They could not put pieces of bodies back together. . . . There is this terrible feeling in me that reminds me all people lost someone yesterday and recognized some of their friends or family members laying on that pile of death. But it looks like that was not enough for the beasts that are so tempted to destroy our town, so they continued the shelling at night. Our building was hit last night when a shell flew right into somebody's apartment in building #7, we live in #11, and the girl was killed. I did not know her but I am very sorry for her. . . . Oh God that was close. I am so sick of watching all this happen. I do not want to see blood anymore. I am not a mean person but I wish all the worst for the people that are destroying my and everyone else's lives while bombing our town. . . . WHY ALL THIS????. (n.d.)

Yet the shelling continued into June. On 4 June, Jelena Andrić wrote in her diary that "the war is still going on and Sarajevo is slowly dying. There are more weak and hungry people. . . . They shelled the town again and just during the night they destroyed more than in all fifty days of the war" (n.d.). Four days later, on 8 June, John Burns wrote an article in the *New York Times* entitled, "The Death of a City: Elegy for Sarajevo." The elegy provides a poignant overview of the dying city of Sarajevo:

> Two months into a civil war that turns more murderous by the day, Sarajevo, the capital of Bosnia and Herzegovina, is a skeleton of the thriving, accomplished city it was. It is a wasteland of blasted mosques, churches and museums; of fire-gutted office towers, hotels and sports stadiums, and of hospitals, music schools and libraries punctured by rockets, mortars and artillery shells.
>
> Parks have been pressed into service as emergency cemeteries, and the pathetic lines of graves march ever farther up the hillsides toward the gun emplacements.
>
> What is happening here, in a European city that escaped two World Wars with only minor damage, is hard to grasp for many of those enduring it.
>
> It is a disaster of such magnitude, and of such seeming disconnectedness from any achievable military or political goals, that those who take shelter for days in basement bunkers, emerging briefly into daylight for fresh supplies of bread and water, exhaust themselves trying to make sense of it. (1992:1)

One day later, on 9 June, Burns cites a recording of radio communications between Bosnian Serb officers in the hills above the city. In the conversation, General Ratko Mladić, the military commander, is speaking to two of his officers, through the Bosnian Serb practice of using Muslim code names, on 27 May, the day of the Breadline Massacre. Burns relates portions of the recording:

> *General Mladic:* Open fire a little to the right. You know where.
> *Mustafa:* O.K.
> *General Mladic:* Bombard Velesice [*sic*], burn it all.
> *Zijo:* It is better to bombard Pofalici.
> *General Mladic:* Why Pofalici?
> *Zijo:* Because there are not many Serbs there.
> *General Mladic:* O.K., you bombard both of them, Velesice [*sic*] and Pofalici. Leave the 82-millimeters and the 120-millimeters, and use the heaviest. (1992:10)

In my view, Burns misses not simply the extent but the key elements of the transmissions. In fact, there were several conversations recorded between Bosnian Serb Army officers during the shelling. These recordings reveal that General Mladić did not know the proper name of the area of Sarajevo known as Velešići, written here as Velesice, but which he pronounced as "Velušići," but he knew enough to command that three primary streets in the center of the city be shelled: Humska, Dobrovoljačka (today Hamdije Kreševljakovića), and Đure Đakovića (Alipašina). The more extended version of the conversation cited by Burns above is presented here as follows:

General Mladić: Vukašinović?

Colonel Vukašinović: Yes, sir.

General Mladić: What are those from Hresa firing on?

Colonel Vukašinović: They are firing on the presidency and the congress buildings and before that they shelled Velešići and Pofalići.

General Mladić: Fire on Velešići and Baščaršija from both sides and on the presidency.

ColonelVukašinović: Yes, sir.

General Mladić: Fire with three batteries on all sides.

Colonel Vukašinović: Yes, sir.

General Mladić: Is it best for you to fire from Hresa?

Colonel Vukašinović: Yes, it is.

General Mladić: What are your suggestions for next targets?

Colonel Vukašinović: Well, I ordered the three batteries . . .

General Mladić: I know you ordered the three batteries but what group of targets do you suggest that we fire on next?

Colonel Vukašinović: I would stop firing on our old targets and I would fire on Pofalići.

General Mladić: Don't do that, why Pofalići?

Colonel Vukašinović: Because, so far we have fired only one platoon on that area.

General Mladić: Fire on Velušići.

Colonel Vukašinović: You mean Velešići.

General Mladić: Yes, Velešići and fire on Pofalići because there aren't many Serbian inhabitants living down there. Shell the following streets: Humska, Dobrovoljačka and Đure Đakovića. Is it clear?

Colonel Vukašinović: Understood.

General Mladić: Watch from your post as you are shelling so they won't be able to sleep and this way we will stretch their brains.

Colonel Vukašinović: Yes, sir.

(Videoteka "Vankee," n.d.)

What Burns left out of the conversation was the direct order by General Mladić to shell the city so the inhabitants "won't be able to sleep and this

way we will stretch their brains." "Now, I have finally begun to understand what Mladic meant when he said to his commanders: "Stretch their
brains!" recalled Zoran Bečić. "There is nothing here any more, no
memories, nothing to remember, and nothing to hope for (Dizdarević,
1994:65–66). "Right now, I am not afraid but if the shellings start again,
I would go out of my mind," offered Alma Duran over the Internet during a lull in the bombardment three years into the siege. "Those things
are the worst experiences in my whole life—besides seeing my best
friend's brain blown away" (Castra, 1995). "*Razvucite im pamet!*"
Mladić said. "Stretch their brains!"

The War Continues, the Work Continues

An appreciation of the intensity of the siege provides something of the
background to better understand the adaptation of schooling to siege
conditions. The question of schooling under such conditions is not simply a difference of context that provides a rational academic framework
for understanding the reconstruction of schools and the instruction provided at various classroom locations. Something of the fear and the
trauma if not the degradation of the human condition must be acknowl-
edged in order to understand the truly heroic character of schooling under siege. Viewed against this backdrop, Hajrija-Šahza Jahić locates
schooling within this context during those early months of the chaos:

> April 1992, May 1992, a tale of destruction, fires, cellars, screams, si-
> rens, the wounded and the dead, day and night fused into a gigantic
> hell, and in parallel, our inner compulsion to organize a school, as
> quickly as possible and whatever the cost, to normalize the lives of
> children living in totally impossible circumstances. (Jahić, 1996:11)

After the shelling and destruction of April and May 1992, the first entry
for June in the *School Annual* of Treća Gimnazija records the situation of
the school two months after the initial assault on the city:

> *5 June:* Mirko Marinović, school director, was the first one who en-
> tered the school building since 30 April to see the building situation,
> the equipment, and the necessary applications for the accounting of
> salaries. The soldiers of the Territorial Defense are using the school.
> Great damage to the building and missing equipment were registered.
> (*Školski ljetopis*)

Director Marinović told me that he not only had to receive special permission from the Army to come to the school to retrieve school records, but that he "had to crawl to the school" in order to get there. Accompanied by a soldier with a machine gun, he found "great damage" to the buildings that included the destruction of the computer laboratory by the computer teacher himself who had gone over to "the other side" (1998).

With the entry of 10–20 June in the *School Annual*, the teachers began to return to the school "with great risk and danger" in order to retrieve school documents and student registers. Around this time, Director Marinović managed to secure two rooms at the Mješovita srednja poljoprivrodno-veterinarska i prehrambena škola, the Comprehensive Agricultural, Veterinarian, and Food Secondary School, located on what was then Dobrovoljačka Street in Stari Grad, the Old City, "which was a really dangerous place." Here in the eastern end of the city just up the Miljacka River from the original school buildings is "where all the register books, complete student documentation, all class books, all documentation for the employees, curricula, and other important pedagogical documentation and registers are found" (*Školski ljetopis*).

There is a single entry in the *School Annual* for the entire month of July. Dated 1–31 July, this entry suggests that the chaos of the siege was not going to totally disrupt the educational process and eliminate the intentions to continue with the regular process of schooling. Against this backdrop, the entry by Director Marinović reflects the policies of the new government and reads, in no uncertain terms, that the work of school would continue:

> When a general mobilization was declared, and working obligations because of the state of war, the employees do not have a right to annual leave. Duty rosters for everyday were defined and work is being done on the conclusion of the school year, current jobs, and jobs on planning the start of the new school year. Life and work in a city under blockade is extremely difficult. No water, no food, no electricity, and no communication, besides constant danger to life.
>
> Some of our employees are in the *BiH Army*, among them: *Mustafa Halilović* in Dobrinja under siege, *Osman Tabaković* on Kobilj Glava, *Muris Klipo* on Zlatište, etc. Another group of our workers are engaged in *civil defense* like Šemsudin Hrapović, Gordana Roljić, Azemina Osmanagić, Igbala Šačiković, . . . many are engaged in local communities [and in] humanitarian organizations. . . . And Slobodan Đurasović, professor, football player, poet . . . fights in his own way with a pen. (*Školski ljetopis*)

The August entries conclude the 1991–1992 academic year in the *School Annual*, yet they also provide critical insight into the school years that follow. The month of August preceding the regular beginning of the new school year in September appears to be a particularly crucial time for the future of education in the new Republic of Bosnia and Herzegovina. Based upon the roster of school employees and the class rosters of students, it is clear that Director Marinović made a conscientious effort to account for the teachers and students of Treća Gimnazija who were scattered across the city and to normalize the situation as much as was humanly possible. However, the initial August entry in the *School Annual*, much like the entries of the previous months, again reflects the uncertainty of the situation:

THE WAR CONTINUES

Life and survival in the city is getting more and more difficult. The majority of the employees are having their own tragedies. The daughter of Vildana Abdurahmanović was killed. The brother of Alma Karahasanović was killed as well. The destiny of Misim Gegić who lived in Hadžići is unknown. Many of the employees in the school do not know anything about their loved ones: parents, children, spouses, cousins. . . . All communications are practically down. Some of the workers are blockaded in certain parts of the city: Grbavica, Dobrinja. Many had to leave their apartments and now live with their relatives or with friends as refugees. To some, their apartments have been destroyed or burned down. . . . Some of the workers are probably on the side of the aggressor, even though we do not have liable proof. We had to submit a claim to higher court against one worker, Mirjana Knežević, who was the school cashier and who had been one of the most conscientious workers, because she took but did not distribute the salaries for the month of April to one group of employees.

Every arrival to the rooms where classes are being held presents danger due to the constant shelling of the city, snipers, and war activities in general. The start of the following school year is uncertain and with that the financial assistance to employees. But in spite of it all—

THE WORK CONTINUES

At the same time that schools such as Treća Gimnazija were struggling with simply keeping count of school employees, the grim nature of wartime conditions is revealed in the headlines and narratives of the Sarajevo daily newspapers. In bold capital letters accompanied by stark pictures of the casualties, the headlines of *Oslobođenje* portray an ever more frightening reality for the people trapped inside the siege lines. The headline for 1 August 1992 reads, for example, "Unbreakable Sarajevo" noting "new brutal attacks by the aggressor on the capital of Bosnia and Herzegovina." The 5 August headline screams, "Sarajevo Blackmailed with Water!" noting the "city runs out of ninety percent of water which it now has at its disposal." On 17 August, the headline reads, "Darkness by Aggressor's Plans," which records the "critical electroenergy situation in Bosnia and Herzegovina" accompanied by another article that states "Supplying water is still critical." The 18 August headline states, "Baščaršija [the Old Quarter] in Flames," with pictures of the Ferhadija mosque burning, and wounded in an emergency room. By 24 August, the headline reads, "New Wounds on the Soul of Sarajevo," with pictures of the "everyday destruction" of buildings, a dead child accompanied by the question, "What is the guilt of this child?" and women with "pain on the face of every expression."

The casualties continued to mount during the month that saw its climax on 30 August when a single 120-millimeter mortar round tore into a marketplace on Solidarity Square in the Alipašino Polje apartment complex of western Sarajevo where people were waiting for bread. At least fifteen people were killed and over one hundred were wounded, many of whom were not expected to survive. According to *Oslobođenje*, the shelling came from the direction of Lukavica near the airport under control of "bloodthirsty Serb–Montenegrin criminals." The headline read, "Massacre at Alipašino Polje," and the article was particularly bitter in its condemnation of the enemy:

> The sight at the scene was horrifying: tens of people in blood, massacred bodies, limbs dismembered. . . . The massacre on Solidarity Square is one more warning to world civilization of a final time to curb Serb–Montenegrin bloodlust, which kills, destroys and burns with incomprehensibly sickening impulse. Until everything that happens, *Sarajlije* must understand that every exit on the street becomes a game of Russian roulette. All the weight of blood tribute of a Serb-chetnik shell on a market in Alipašino Polje is being demonstrated by the reports of three main emergency points in Sarajevo. (1992:1)

The marketplace massacre in Alipašino Polje added to the casualty figures recorded by the Republican Institute for Public Health (Republički zavod za zdravstvenu zaštitu) and the Republican Crisis Committee for Health and Social Security (Republički krizni štab za zdravstvenu i socijalnu bezbjednost). In fact, "The Bulletin" of the Institute/Crisis Committee recorded casualty figures throughout the years of the war on a daily and weekly basis. By 6 September 1992, "The Bulletin" had recorded 2,037 killed, 6,630 missing or "liquidated," and 26,963 severely or lightly wounded in Sarajevo after five full months of the siege (Smajkić, 1992). The numbers of displaced persons throughout the country and the number of registered cases of various illnesses were recorded as well. With casualties mounting and health deteriorating, "The Bulletin" makes a dramatic appeal for outside assistance:

> Hello, Hello. . . . Is that the Security Council of the UN?
> Hello, Europe, Is that the European Community? Sarajevo and Bosnia and Herzegovina are calling! Do you hear us? . . . Will you help us? Let us say to you once more: in this country of war, terror, famine, epidemics, genocide, poisoning and mass dying, there are still living creatures whom you can help if you want! (Smajkić, 1992)

Somehow in a country at war and in a city where Russian roulette was played on the streets, where "everyone of us has a mortar round that awaits him/her," as Sven Alkalaj wrote in his foreword to the book, students and teachers alike were beginning preparation for the 1992–1993 school year, whenever it was going to get underway.

Against the background of the siege of the city, the work of the schools continued for Sarajevo educators to include the teachers of Treća Gimnazija as seen in the August and September entries of the *School Annual*. Alongside the regular entries, contemporary newspaper accounts record the official decisions and guidelines of the Ministry of Education of the new government of the Republic of Bosnia and Herzegovina concerning the future of education throughout the country. These accounts also record the official decisions and guidelines of the City Secretariat for Education of Sarajevo concerning the future of education in those portions of the four city municipalities that remained under Bosnian government control. This documentation provides clear evidence that a government being forged during a state of war was attempting to cope with the exigencies of schooling to begin the 1992–1993 school year.

Dated 8 September 1992, for example, an article appears in *Oslobođenje* entitled, "War Determines the Term: Maximum care will insure that children and their parents are not exposed to danger." This is but one of several articles that concluded the entries of the 1991–1992 school year and set the stage for the 1992–1993 school year to follow. The article is cited in some detail here for the background it provides about "some kind of 'slippery' beginning" of the 1992–1993 school year:

The preparation of plans for registration in the secondary schools in the Republic is in progress. The authorized ministry states that the date of the beginning of the school year will be given later because it highly depends on war operations and the situation at the front.

Therefore, it can be spoken about some kind of "slippery" beginning of the school year. Municipalities will individually decide about the beginning of the school year depending on the circumstances. In the Ministry of Education, Science, Culture and Physical Culture, four different school program proposals are prepared which will determine the length and duration of classes. Because of the war, however, they are likely to be changed.

According to the Decision on Conditions and Temporary Criteria for Registration of Students in the First Class of Secondary School, the secondary school registration requirements will be announced through the media, and will be based on the grades of the last four years of elementary school. . . .

The registration plan is based upon the estimates of last year's statistics and the actual number of students. Considering the war in the region, ethnic cleansing and the large migration, the actual number and classes of students today is disastrous, even though there is a certain optimism in the Ministry that, in spite of everything, instruction will be given as planned.

In the Ministry they want to deny rumors about the possibility of creating ethnic schools or classes. The unified plan and program of schooling does not mention that possibility nor consider it a good solution.

When it comes to elementary schools, the conditions are similar to secondary schools. Maximum care will be taken that children and their parents do not expose themselves to any kind of danger when they go to schools or while they are in schools, which will be taken care of by the municipalities in which the schools are located. . . .

In the end, there is still a question of how instruction will be implemented in practice. Many schools have been demolished, some serve as shelters, and parents fear letting their children go farther than the yard of the house. Possibly this will be yet another problem that will be attract the interest of officials. (1992:4)

On the following day, 9 September 1992, the "Decision on the Registration of Students in Elementary and Secondary Schools and the Beginning of Instruction in the 1992/1993 School Year" appeared in the *Official Gazette* of the Republic of Bosnia and Herzegovina. "On the recommendation" of the Ministry of Education of the new government, the Decision reads as follows:

I

The executive organ of the municipality and/or city community, in co-operation with the jurisdictional, district secretariat for social work, is responsible, taking into account the safety of students and teachers and securing the conditions for normal instructional procedures in elementary and secondary schools, to bring about:

1. A Decision on the beginning, duration, and place where the registration of students for the first class of elementary school and the first class of secondary school;

2. A Decision on the beginning and place where instruction is to be conducted for the 1992/93 school year in elementary and secondary schools.

II

The registration of students for the first class of elementary school shall be done for those students who will by 1 September of this year be seven years of age.

In exceptions, in elementary schools that have the space and the teaching staff, it is permitted to register children who will, by 1 September of this year be six years of age.

The registration of children, as described above, will proceed according to the lists of children in the school-age group, of the municipality administrative organ responsible for education, or on the basis of applications submitted by the parents of the children from the territory of the municipality, as well as on the basis of applications submitted by the parents or legal guardians of the refugee children or displaced persons residing in the respective municipality.

III

The registration of students in secondary schools will proceed on the basis of open competition for student admission into the first class of secondary school for the 1992/93 school year, a decision on equal criteria and evaluation for admission of students into secondary institutions, and the Plan for registration of students in the first class of secondary school in the Republic of Bosnia and Herzegovina in the 1992/93 school year, which will be decided upon by the Republican Public Fund for Secondary Education and Upbringing, in agreement with the Minister of Education, Science, Culture and Physical Culture. (*Službeni list RBiH*, 1992)

It is clear that the Ministry of Education allocated responsibility to school administrators at the municipal and local community levels to implement the decision to initiate the 1992–1993 school year. Given wartime conditions in the immediate area of their respective schools, these administrators were, in the words of *Oslobođenje*, to "individually decide about the beginning of the school year depending on the circumstances." In Sarajevo, the responsibility for these decisions rested with the City Secretariat for Education, the school administrators in the four municipalities of "free Sarajevo" that remained under the control of the Bosnian government, and the local communities of each of these four municipalities. The beginning of the new school year in Sarajevo would be decided whenever "the question of how instruction will be implemented in practice" would be resolved.

On the next day, 10 September 1992, another article entitled, "Instruction to be Adapted to Wartime Conditions," cited in the previous chapter, appeared in the pages of *Oslobođenje* reviewing the Decision enacted the previous day. The article reiterates the Decision on the registration of elementary and secondary school students for the new school year and clarifies the curricular organization for the instructional process. The article is cited in full here as follows:

> The Government of the Republic of Bosnia and Herzegovina yesterday adopted a Decision on the Registration of Students in Elementary and Secondary Schools and the Beginning of Instruction in the 1992/93 School Year.
>
> With this Decision, the Government of the Republic of Bosnia and Herzegovina ordered municipality and city community executive organs, that are responsible for the safety of students and teachers, to insure conditions for conducting normal instructional procedures in elementary and secondary schools.
>
> In harmony with this, municipalities, with regards to city communities, will decide about the beginning, the length, and the place for holding the registration of students in the first class of elementary and secondary school, and the decision about the beginning and the place for holding instruction in the 1992/93 school year. . . .
>
> Instruction in elementary schools and secondary schools will be carried out according to the program that was designed by Educational–Pedagogical Institute of the Republic of Bosnia and Herzegovina, and the organization and supervision of instruction in harmony with the Decision of the Government of the Republic of Bosnia and Herzegovina will be executed by the appropriate secretariat that works in wartime conditions—it was said in the report from yesterday's meeting of Government of the Republic of Bosnia and Herzegovina. (1992:8)

In other words, with the country in a war for survival, and the capital of the country under siege, the new government of the Republic of Bosnia and Herzegovina, "on the recommendation" of the Ministry of Education, issued a Decision for school administrative units to initiate the start of the forthcoming school year in spite of wartime conditions. These school administrative units were to decide not only upon the registration of new students at the elementary and secondary levels, but upon the appropriate places for instruction and the duration of the new school year as well. "Taking into account the safety of students and teachers," these school administrators were to create the conditions for the regular instructional process," in other words, to adapt instruction in the schools to wartime conditions. In the besieged capital of Sarajevo, these instructions meant that the City Secretariat for Education, the school administrators of the four remaining municipalities of Sarajevo city, and the representatives of the local communities, were responsible for the beginning of the new school year.

On 8 September 1992, the very same day that *Oslobođenje* made reference to a kind of "slippery" beginning of school, and one day prior to the Decision for local school administrative units "to secure conditions for normal instructional procedures," Jelena Andrić, now a second-year student at Prva gimnazija, wrote the following entry in her diary:

> I really do not understand what the hell is happening with all the people around me. Suddenly, everyone is depressed. All right, I understand, we have no water, no electricity, no life, but that is not the reason for me to bang my head against the wall the whole day. . . . It is true that Bosnia is becoming hell and that people are suffering. Sarajevo's spirit is dead and people are desperate. Through the town you can see the speeding ambulances or the cars with dead bodies in the back. Blood is everywhere and the everyday question arises: "Am I going to be so lucky to see sunshine tomorrow or is my life going to disappear in the coldness of Sarajevo's night?" The people are in lines everywhere. What are they waiting for? They do not know. They are just waiting. Waiting for bread, and bread is not coming. Waiting for water, and water is not even in the town, listening about the possibility of getting electricity, and all of this is just a big lie. . . . I am studying English every day, and I am trying to keep my brain in shape. I do not feel like letting my brain die just because of the war." (n.d.)

"Razvucite im pamet!" said General Mladić. "Stretch their brains!"

Chapter Three

The War Schools of Sarajevo, September 1992–March 1993

During that time we were so desperate, especially young people. . . . We couldn't understand how the whole world could just sit aside and do nothing to save us. I thought they wanted us to die. When we understood that nobody would do anything for us unless we did it ourselves, our fear gradually became a revolt. We didn't want to lose courage completely. It wasn't just the fight on the battlefield. It was also intellectual, spiritual. We started to go to school, because we felt we had the right to. The so-called "war schools" were organized and everyone went to the nearest one. Each neighborhood had a few war schools and I had to go to Prva gimnazija [the First Gymnasium] to take exams—I had to risk it, because it was far away from my home. I don't know how many times I heard sirens while going to school, so I had to run into the nearest building and stay there until the shelling stopped. It was terrible. But we felt then and still do that we had the right to this city and to life and no one could take it away. That's why we didn't give up, that's why we are here now.

—Amira Prcić,
student of the Department of English Language
and Literature,
Faculty of Philosophy,
University of Sarajevo

The Schools of Bjelave and Dobrinja
as Forerunner to the Local Community War Schools

With the beginning of the 1992–1993 school year on 1 March 1993, Treća Gimnazija had become a *ratna skola* (war school), a school that continued to survive in a functional sense, as an administrative entity, without a physical structure or single permanent location. Under these conditions, the administrators of the school continued to organize school programs and direct the teachers, the teachers continued to coordinate classes and teach the students, and the students continued to attend classes, complete assignments, and study towards their university examinations. For the students, teachers, and administrators of Treća Gimnazija, the work of school continued along with the siege.

Although it took approximately eleven months to reorganize schooling in Sarajevo, these months were critical as Sarajevo educators struggled with the questions of the adaptation of instruction to the siege. In the fall of 1992, for example, educators from the Pedagogical Institute of Sarajevo recorded "that over two hundred individual contacts of educational advisors and workers took place" (Bešlija et al., 1995:22). As early as 3 May 1992, however, a small group of educators gathered at the Pedagogical Institute to confront the siege in educational terms. With the uncertainty over the continuation of the 1991–1992 school year, these educators looked towards the future and recognized the need for a collaborative approach to educational reorganization. Although their immediate aim was to reopen the schools for the 1992–1993 school year, the underlying goal was to reorganize schooling for students as a long-term adaptation to the siege. During May 1992, two educators from the Pedagogical Institute, Hajrija-Šahza Jahić and Melita Sultanović, took this task upon themselves by conducting the first situation analyses to determine specific school needs throughout the city.

In their own words, Professors Jahić and Sultanović told me that, at the outset, "everything was an improvisation. . . . The idea was to normalize the situation for the children, to start first with programs in one location and then implement these programs throughout other parts of the city . . . but we were the cell of the organization" (1998). During the war, "the cell of the organization" was officially termed the Inter-Municipal Pedagogical Institute Sarajevo (Medjuopštinski pedagoški zavod Sarajevo), hereafter, simply the Pedagogical Institute (Pedagoški zavod) of Sarajevo. Professor Jahić wrote about the responsibilities undertaken by the faculty of the Institute for the reorganization of schooling across the four municipalities that remained under Bosnian government control:

In July 1992, the Pedagogical Institute of Sarajevo took on the task of organizing, coordinating, planning and supervising the educational and recreational activities to be offered to refugee, resettled and local children in Sarajevo. Work was immediately started on developing a concept for working with children caught up in a war situation. The plan covered children between the ages of 5 and 15 years.

The aim of the teaching plan was to present, develop, revise and practise all the topics which had to be abandoned at the end of the first wartime school year, because the war had put a stop to them. The teaching plan began to take shape in the first so-called *war schools*, and the external and internal organization of these schools was taken on in the "normal" school year 1992/93. (Jahić, 1996:12)

Based upon the situation analyses conducted during May, several fundamental principles to organize curriculum and instruction for the war schools of Sarajevo were developed and are summarized here as follows:

1. Formation of pupil groups based on residence with due regard for safety.
2. Involvement of teachers from the local community in which the war schools were organized with due regard to the teachers' safety.
3. Expanded teaching content to go beyond socializing and academic elements to include the recreational.
4. Voluntary participation.
5. Maximum lessons of thirty minutes.
6. Maximum school day of three or four lessons with a weekly total of up to eighteen lessons.
7. Curriculum basis to include the following subjects: the mother tongue, foreign language, mathematics, biology, art, music, and free activities. (Sultanović, 1996:8–9)

The initial educational program began in the Bjelave School, named after the Bjelave area of the city, which had begun operation in February 1992 three months prior to the siege for 160 refugee children from eastern Bosnia (Bešlija et al.,1995). The Institute created a small "Bjelave team" of elementary and secondary educators, conducted seminars for the teachers, organized the refugee students into age groupings, and developed curricular programs for the age-level groups. The idea was for teachers to take programs developed by Institute educators to the refugee students of the Bjelave School. In the words of Professor Jahić, "Children didn't go to school, school came to them" (1996:15). While the beginning of the 1992–1993 school year was held in abeyance for schools in Sarajevo, the Bjelave School commenced operations as one of the first war schools in the city on 2 September 1992 with a reorganized curriculum and a reorganized elementary grouping to include: (1) preschool children combined with grades one and two; (2) grades three and four; and (3) grades five through eight similar to the American middle school organization (Sultanović, 1996; Jahić, 1996). Professor Sultanović wrote about the rationale for the reorganization of schooling in this manner:

> To implement this type of work, a special Teaching Plan was drawn up to guide the socialization, study and leisure activities of refugee children from these areas (children from five to eleven). It was based on the normal curriculum but adapted to children who had experienced the horrors of war.
>
> The teaching plan strongly emphasized recreational activities. This plan was the basis of a new attitude/method of working with children who had already experienced war trauma, and was used by all the teachers as the basis of their own lesson plans (1996:8).

At approximately the same time as the Institute programs were being introduced at the Bjelave School, small groups of students and teachers, especially at the elementary level where there was greater need for the supervision of children, began to form in other areas of the city. These groupings were the *haustorska škola*, often referred to as "stairway schools," although perhaps a more accurate translation might be "corridor schools," a term taken from the Dobrinja settlement adjacent to the Butmir airport, an area of apartment complexes with virtually no protection from the frontlines. "Dobrinja was a special place," said Behija Jakić, a sociology and philosophy teacher at Treća Gimnazija, who was trapped in her Dobrinja neighborhood during the early stages of the siege. "Are you crazy?" her friends asked her when she refused the opportunity to leave Dobrinja. "You have gone from a siege to a siege within a siege" (1998). Completely cut off from the main part of Sarajevo during the first several months of the war, Dobrinja was Sarajevo at its most severe, "a siege within a siege" (*opsada po opsadom* or *opsada u opsadi*), which created in the residents who were trapped there a determined resolve to survive. Even after Bosnian Army forces relieved some of the pressure, the only connection between Sarajevo proper and Dobrinja, other than UN vehicles, was the trench line that ran around the bottom of Mojmilo hill. The severity of conditions forced those educators who, as residents of Dobrinja, remained inside the settlement, to organize schooling much earlier than in most areas of the city if for no other reason than to ensure the day-to-day safety of the children.

In a paper prepared for the *Schooling in War Conditions* Symposium in Sarajevo on 18 April 1994, entitled, "The Stairway School: A Model of Educational Work in Dobrinja," Seniha Bulja, of the Pedagogical Institute, explains the situation in Dobrinja that led to the creation of the first stairway school located on what was then Salvador Allende (today Esada Pašalića) Street "in a building that was on the frontline. You will have to admit," she wrote, "that took courage and guts":

> The children of Dobrinja can't go to school. They don't have any. These schools are dead and destroyed monuments. It is war. Constant shelling prevents children from gathering in one place.
> The children can't play in the streets, they can't be in the apartments. Basements and only basements. Because they spend most of their time in basements, that is where school initially began. Soon, all over the settlement of Dobrinja, shelters, stairways and other secure spaces received a new designation—they were transformed into little classrooms. They were the birthplace of the first stairway schools. (1994)

Although the force of the siege was perhaps at its most severe in Dobrinja, Professor Bulja's description of wartime conditions is applicable throughout the entire city. In other words, many of the schools were deliberately targeted as cultural monuments, and many others were unsafe simply because of their location. The streets were unsafe to walk much less play, and even the home residences, whether a house or an apartment, were often unsafe as well. These conditions led to the situation in Dobrinja where the siege proved a worse-case scenario, that for schooling to survive, a dramatic reorganization of the traditional pattern of schooling must be accomplished. Professor Bulja describes the first stairway school on Salvador Allende Street as a model for schooling:

> Professors and students who worked under such conditions expressed their way of resisting the aggressor at the same time.
> The first parent-teacher meeting took place on 17 June 1992 because until then movement on the streets of Dobrinja was impossible . . . . With the help of the Command Headquarters and the Dobrinja Brigade and the local communities of Dobrinja, 28 facilities were established for the purposes of schooling. These facilities were equipped with the necessary materials that were recovered from "Simon Bolivar" Elementary School which was totally destroyed. . . .
> All students of Dobrinja were placed in available school facilities depending upon which municipality they reside in. The safety of students was the main priority and that is why those students attended

classes in their own apartment complex. Most of the subjects were divided among the faculty members which created essential conditions
for school operations. (1994)

These local schools became the *punkts* or *punktovi*, the points or checkpoints, after the German, to be connected in the attempt to reconstruct
schooling throughout the Dobrinja settlement and eventually throughout
the entire city. "The idea was to connect the small points, the micro-
environments, which, at the beginning, operated independently," said
Professor Jahić, "to develop a scheme, to develop a kind of organized
system of war schools . . . to be more safe" (1998). To connect the points
or *punkts* to each other, educators from the Pedagogical Institute went to
the *mjesna zajednica* (local community) of the *opčina* (municipality), the
local unit of government in the city, perhaps most analogous to the
American political ward. "A local community is a main autonomous
community based on a territorial principal," wrote Miodrag Višnjić, in
his analysis of the role of local communities within the political system
of the former Yugoslavia:

> In a large number of local communities there are very intensive social
> and humanitarian, educational, cultural, artistic, recreational, sport, fire-
> fighting and other activities, depending on the needs and interests of the
> working people and citizens. . . . By joining activities and resources of
> working people and citizens, organizations of joint activities and com-
> munities of self-governing interests in many local communities, many
> communal buildings have been constructed . . . buildings for cultural
> and educational, health and other needs. A broad range of activities are
> developed by almost all local communities especially in the field of na-
> tional defense and social self-protection. . . . The role and influence of a
> local community, in large extent, needs to develop within a municipal-
> ity, because that is . . . the only way for affirmation of a local commu-
> nity in the entire social and political system. At the same time there is
> no self-governing municipality without self-governing relations devel-
> oped in local communities. (1979:5, 18–19, 42)

The local community had a wide range of functions within the political
framework of the municipality. Until the siege of the city, however, these
local community offices were minimally staffed and primarily responsible for such matters as local grievances, social functions, and civil defense activities in a peacetime setting. Each local community had com-
munal buildings, so educators from the Pedagogical Institute, along with
their teacher counterparts, requested rooms from local authorities to create the local community school classrooms. Professor Bulja notes, for

example, that "with the help of Command Headquarters and the Dobrinja Brigade and the local communities of Dobrinja," twenty-eight facilities were located within the settlement for the purposes of elementary schooling. With the help of the local civil defense authorities, chairs, tables, stoves, and plastic for the windows were provided to create the semblance of classrooms. Although Institute educators even created models for the "organization of teaching space" and for the "organization of teaching in different spaces," the reality of these classrooms was described by Professor Bulja for the first stairway school in Dobrinja:

> At the parent-teacher meeting we decided that the best place for the school would be in the facilities of stairway number 9. These facilities were prepared as best as possible.
> These nine little children sat bravely at their desks which were not standard, not for schoolboys . . . but as long as they could sit, the desks and chairs were okay. The student classroom is small, nine of them could barely fit together. Next to two of these student desks are two even small teacher desks. The classroom has three walls. The fourth is a hallway and leads outside of the stairway into the street in front of the building. . . .
> On the left side of the classroom, leaning next to the wall, is a board for table tennis. Sometimes that board is used for art shows and other times for complicated mathematics assignments, laws of physics, and chemistry formulas.
> The source of light for the classroom is a student-made candlelight. The way it is made is by filling a glass half with oil and half with water. Then two thin cotton threads are taken through a cork of a wine bottle and placed in the glass. When those cotton lines are soaked in oil, they are lit, and they stay lit as long as there is oil.
> Above the names of the students written on the wall, it says:
> *First Stairway School "Dobrinja 2B."* (1994)

In the words of Professor Jahić, "Lack of equipment, teaching aids, textbooks, basic paper, pencils, heat, light, bread and water presented no obstacle to the work of the *war schools*" (1996:15).

In one sense, the suburb of Dobrinja was further along in the efforts to reorganize schooling than the rest of Sarajevo city. Forced by its isolation to confront the educational realities, Dobrinja educators forged "a model of educational work" not just for Dobrinja but what became, in many respects, a model of educational work for the rest of the city as well. "The elementary education unit [of the Dobrinja War School Center] is the birthplace of the 'stairway school' which later on became the basic model for the organization of educational activities in Dobrinja," wrote Vesnić Smail, the Center director. "The model of the 'stairway school' born in Dobrinja, enriched with faculty experience and a high level of the concrete adaptation of work conditions, remained as the basic groundwork for the organization of educational activities throughout the territory of the city during the period of the war" (1994:18–19). In a September 1992 Pedagogical Institute document entitled, "Operational Plan in Wartime Conditions for 1992," Dobrinja is discussed in these very terms to clarify the role of the Institute in the reorganization of schooling throughout Sarajevo:

> The advisors of the Institute will take an active part in compilation of instructional programs under war conditions for elementary and secondary education which means compilation of operational plans for individual subjects, compilation of technical guidelines for the operational plans, and makeup programs and processing the missed instruction for the previous year.
>
> To this end, the experience gained in the operation of the Dobrinja Educational Center, which links all segments of education, culture and information and represents a novelty in our educational system, should be used in view of the efficient and successful organization of all activities. . . .
>
> The new situation requires, on the part of school institutions, a swift and efficient restructuring and different organization at internal and external levels. The experience gained in the operation of the Dobrinja Educational Center should be used here. (Pedagoški zavod, 1992)

The experience gained from the organization of the Bjelave School and the stairway schools in Dobrinja was transformed into the organization of war schools throughout Sarajevo. The individual classroom locations or punkts, such as the Dobrinja 2B Stairway School, located within the boundaries of a *mjesna zajednica* (local community), were connected and integrated into the *ratna škola mjesne zajednice* (local community war school) under the administration of the nearest regular school in the area. Thus, for example, the individual punkts located within the boundaries of the Bistrik local community, located in Stari Grad municipality, were integrated into a single local community war school known as the *Ratna škola mjesne zajednice Bistrik* (War School of the Bistrik Local Community). At the next level, these local community war schools were then integrated within the administrative framework of the school which had responsibility for schooling in that particular area, the *matična škola*, the home school or the "school of register." Thus, in the words of the *School Annual* of Treća Gimnazija, dated 1–8 December 1992:

Our school received the obligation to come forward and organize the instructional lectures for the territory of local community Kovači, Sumbuluša, and Bistrik. That means registering students, finding premises where the lectures are to be conducted, and professors who need to conduct the instructional lectures. (*Školski ljetopis*)

1992–1993 School Year
(War)

"In the end, there is still a question of how instruction will be implemented in practice," stated the 8 September 1992 article in *Oslobođenje* entitled, "War Determines the Term," at what would have been the normal start of the 1992–1993 academic year. Based upon the experience of those educators who began with the Bjelave School and gradually developed a network of local community schools, Professor Sultanović wrote of the importance of this experience for the future of schooling in wartime conditions. "Taking into account that this manner of work in these spaces and conditions has demonstrated the only possible solution . . . one can openly consider that this work has created good preconditions for the beginning of the ensuing school year 1992/93, and that schools in the same spaces and in the same manner have started with the implementation of the shortened curriculum and work in extraordinary conditions" (1993:4). Although the beginning of the 1992–1993 school year was uncertain, there is clear evidence that the adaptation of schooling to wartime conditions had moved beyond the stage of discussion and into the realm of the local communities of the city.

The new school year was introduced in the pages of the *School Annual* of Treća Gimnazija with the cryptic headline above, introducing this section. Although the Ministry of Education had issued resolutions concerning the start of the new school year, the initial entry for September 1992 suggests the uncertainty of the situation for the opening of schools and something of the uncertainty of the situation in a city under siege:

The school year didn't begin at its usual time and it is uncertain when it will. The city blockade and the aggression continue with an even stronger intensity. Due to that, minimal conditions for school to start work don't exist. The school buildings are mainly damaged and destroyed. The city is not provided with electricity. The number of children in the city is unknown. (*Školski ljetopis*)

The new "war school year" that was to begin in September was inaugurated by intensive shelling of the city that continued into October and November. The blockade of the city, the lack of electricity, the impending winter, and the shortage of food and water, all contributed to a difficult fall season. Ed Vuilliamy poignantly captures the desperation of the situation eight months into the siege:

> By October 1992 Sarajevo was not just under siege—the Serbs could have taken it if they had really wanted to—it was on the rack. The capital had become a torture chamber and the daily dealing out of death, inquiry and mourning had become an endurance test beyond physical loss and suffering. The shelling was cynical and calculated to terrify as well as to kill. . . . The looks on the faces that peered round the hollowed-out doorways of the flats in between those two shells that evening showed nothing that could be described as 'getting used' to the sound of those grey metal cases landing, exploding and splintering into flying shrapnel. People looked out as though the air itself was menacing them and could tear their bodies to shreds, their faces vitrified in the frozen effort of concentration and fear." (1994:186–187)

The intensity of the description stands in stark contrast to the matter-of-fact tone that marks the entries in the *School Annual*. In this regard, it is sometimes difficult to comprehend the desperation of siege conditions if we were to rely solely upon these entries. Nevertheless, the regular entries in the *School Annual* reflect the attempts by school administrators to continue with the regular, day-to-day business of schooling.

In addition to the reference to the blockade in the initial September entry, the *School Annual* also noted the employment situation given the uncertainty over the new school year. The war "leads to a situation where 10–15 percent of the school workers will be employed, while the rest of the workers will be put on a waiting list, receiving minimum salaries." In fact, eight workers at Treća Gimnazija remained on the employment rolls under "work obligation." These employees included Fahrudin Isaković, the new school director, Mirko Marinović, the previous director who now served as deputy director and chemistry teacher, the secretary, the bookkeeper, one pedagogue or counselor, and three of seven members of the Management Board of the school, one of whom was a teacher.

The initial entry in the *School Annual* for October continues to reflect the uncertainty of the situation for the beginning of the school year and for the course of action that schools might follow:

1–10 October: We are already in the second month of this school year. The real beginning of it is uncertain. From time to time, someone from the City Parliament gives a statement with various versions on the possibilities of organizing school lectures. It is assumed that unless the war danger ceases, instructional lectures will be organized for students in appropriate classrooms. In the last couple of days, the Ministry of Education initiated an action with an aim to determine by way of a poll what number of students from our school stayed in Sarajevo. (*Školski ljetopis*)

The entry reveals that the school year has yet to begin and the difficulty of implementing plans for the instructional process at the classroom level. The following October entry relates to the initial September entry and the difficulties of those school employees who were placed on the waiting list at the beginning of the school year:

10–11 October: The teachers who are on the waiting list for work sometimes come to our new offices [in the Comprehensive Agricultural, Veterinarian, and Food Secondary School on Dobrovoljačka Street]. Most of them have changed and have lost a lot of weight. They have all been found in very bad financial situation with minimum salaries of a guaranteed amount of 2,700 dinars. For the sake of orientation, just a note that one loaf of bread costs 150 dinars. (*Školski ljetopis*)

An 11–20 October entry notes that although there were no regular classes yet, there was much work for the eight employees on work obligation. This work included a detailed review of school documents to include what is referred to as the *dnevnik rada* (school or work journal) or *odjeljenska knjiga* (class section book). Concerns were expressed for the location of the class section books "that are in the apartments of the classmasters because of the shelling." Particular concern was expressed that "the IV/4 class section book [fourth class, fourth class section] is with the class-master, Olga Đerković, who is a 'prisoner' in Dobrinja." As Abdulah Jabučar, the deputy minister of education noted, one of the five "Guidelines on Educational Activities" that clarified the responsibilities of schools was to protect school documents during wartime. The critical importance of providing official records of school attendance and classroom performance meant ensuring that school documentation and specifically, each work journal or class book, was kept in accordance with legal statutes (1994:5). The 1–9 November entry again refers to the IV/4 class section book and indicates the extent to which school administrators would go to retrieve school documents:

With the assistance of the Territorial Defense HQ, we managed to get the IV/4 class section book that was with the class-master, Olga Đerković, in Dobrinja for a full seven months. In that way, we avoided the great responsibility of reconstructing the documentation for 34 students. Besides that, the students of this class got the opportunity to enroll in a Faculty [of the University] valid as of 5 November 1992.

Unfortunately, we had to reconstruct the data for students from the I/1, I/2, and IV/6 class sections that were in the work journals in those parts of the city that suffered damage in the winds of war. (*Školski ljetopis*)

In other words, the documents of school attendance and academic progress were considered of such importance that school administrators would request the services of the Bosnian Army forces defending Dobrinja to secure the grade book for a single class. These records remained critical documents for students at schools such as Treća Gimnazija, an academic preparatory school designed to prepare students for a university education. Without the opportunity for students to enroll in one of the Faculties (or Colleges) of the University of Sarajevo, a school such as Treća Gimnazija simply had no purpose, even during wartime. The loss of such documentation meant that the teachers had to reconstruct the academic programs of the students in order to provide them with the required documentation for graduation and for admission to the university.

Entries in the *School Annual* through October and November of 1992 continue to record the difficulties of the times. The entry for 20–30 November, for example, reads that "the eventual start of the school year is yet uncertain." This entry records the organization of what is termed "instructional lectures" for the students at localized classroom locations:

Meetings were held on the possibilities of conducting instructional lectures for some subjects, as has been done in some elementary schools. Everything is still in the stage of discussion. However, teachers in separated parts of the city with their own arrangements, organized self-initiated instructional lectures for students who pay in a foreign currency. The attention of the authorized school organs should be turned at that as an inadmissible appearance and that in a time when such a form of lectures can be legally mentioned, and the teaching staff gets fully paid for their work. . . .

On Wednesday, 18 November, a meeting of secondary school principals was held, at which a string of guidelines was given on what is to be undertaken for the instructional lectures to start in the local communities in mid-December. (*Školski ljetopis*)

By the week of 1–8 December 1992, there is clear evidence that the reorganization of schooling had moved beyond the stage of ideas and discussion. At this point, the entry in the *School Annual* indicates that Treća Gimnazija has been assigned specific organizational responsibilities designed to initiate schooling in specific areas of the city:

> Our school received the obligation to come forward and organize the instructional lectures for the territory of local community Kovači, Sumbuluša, and Bistrik. That means registering students, finding premises where the lectures are to be conducted, and professors who need to conduct the instructional lectures. (*Školski ljetopis*)

With the administrative offices of Treća Gimnazija now located on Dobrovoljačka Street in Stari Grad (Old City) municipality in the eastern part of the city, the school "received the obligation" to organize classes in that area of the city as well. At its original location on Youth Promenade in Novo Sarajevo (New Sarajevo) municipality, Treća Gimnazija was the only gimnazija in the western or newer part of the city, and many of its students came from that area. Now forced to find another location for the school, it could only secure two rooms in the Comprehensive Agricultural, Veterinarian, and Food Secondary School up the Miljacka River in Stari Grad. Consequently, Treća Gimnazija was now assigned the responsibilities for education in four local communities, Bistrik, Kovači, Sumbuluša I and II, all located in Stari Grad, to begin the 1992–1993 school year. The first December entry also records another casualty of the Treća Gimnazija community:

> On the seventh of this month, as a soldier of the Territorial Defense, Bakir Hrapović, the son of our Professor Šemsudin Hrapović, was killed. Bakir was a student of our school. (*Školski ljetopis*)

Bakir Hrapović, a former student of Treća Gimnazija, was killed in the battle for Mount Trebević, another of those early and critical battles, in what the Bosnian army newspaper, *Prva linija*, called "the heroic defense" of Sarajevo (Gagula, 1994:6). Dated 10 December 1992, the obituary read, "Bakir (Šemsudina) Hrapović was killed as a martyr in defense of his people, 7 December, at 22 years of age" (*Oslobođenje*, 1992:7). Bakir's sister, Ehlimana, a Treća Gimnazija student who would attend the Bistrik Local Community War School during the belated 1992–1993 school year, no doubt wrote about the loss of her brother in an essay that she called, "The Wounded Youth of My Town":

72   *Chapter Three*

The departure of some dear and close people from this world left an incurable wound in the heart and soul. The wound is the symbol of the
town, of the generation. A single look back is enough to the pain from
that wound. (1994)

Dated 25 January 1993, a joint memo from the Ministry of Education
of the Republic of Bosnia and Herzegovina and the Sarajevo City Secretariat for Education directed to all secondary schools in Sarajevo, concerns the "organization and operation of the secondary school in local
communities." Based upon a joint meeting with secondary school directors on 21 January 1993, directives for the upcoming school year, dated
25 January 1993, included the following listing of school responsibilities:

> All secondary schools in the area of Sarajevo city, in line with previous
> agreements, should organize teaching by local communities and realize
> the abbreviated instructional plan and program for general educational
> subjects. Instruction in secondary schools will begin on 8 February
> 1993.
> The essential form of teaching in the realization of the instructional
> program should be the direct work of teachers with students. In the im-
> plementation of this form of work, the teachers should realize the in-
> structional materials, gather information and assess students, and all re-
> cords should be kept in suitable class books. For the time being, work
> with students must be organized in a five-day week. A lesson cannot be
> shorter than 35 minutes. . . .
> School directors are obligated to the individual local community
> for the organization of operations and the realization of instructional
> programs by local communities (the list of obligations of directors for
> individual local communities is enclosed). (Ministarstvo obrazovanje
> and Sekretariat za obrazovanje, 1993)

In accordance with this joint directive, the 25 January–5 February entry
in the *School Annual* notes that, in accordance with school responsibilities, the local communities accomplished the enrollment of students for
the first year of secondary school, and the 6 February entry records the
enrollment of students for all four years of secondary school. The entry
for 7 February notes the decision to begin the 1992–1993 school year on
10 February, while on 8 February 1993, *Oslobođenje* ran an article entitled, "'School Bells' for Secondary Schools" in which the opening of
schools was anticipated on that very day. The subheading read that "the
school year will last for 18 weeks, but the instructional plan and program
is reduced by 50 percent." A portion of the article reads:

Today in Sarajevo instruction begins for students of secondary education. Instead of in normal school premises, "school bells" will ring in
suitable premises at local communities, apartments, business premises,
in fact at premises which will provide minimal work conditions and
maximum safety for students and the teaching staff. (1993:4)

The article also notes the following basic information about the projected
school year:

The 1992/93 school year will last for 18 weeks plus one more week in
reserve and the instructional plan and program have been reduced by 50
percent by width and length. . . . In the city, during the last school year,
in ten city municipalities, 26,000 students attended classes at 25 secondary schools. This year, given the high spirits of the citizens, but elimi-
nating the occupied municipalities, instruction should be attended by
about 10,000 students. (1993:4)

In other words, the projected student numbers from the end of the 1991–
1992 school year were down by perhaps as many as 16,000 students or
approximately 61.5 percent. The article then cited Abdulah Jabučar, the
deputy minister of education, who again makes specific reference to
schooling by local communities:

Schools of register must have an absolute survey of students by local
communities, but then their duty is making contact with the students
and organizing definitive hours for the professional–theoretical group
of subjects and also organizing practicum instruction if it is possible.
(1993:4)

Again, schooling did not begin on 8 February, but throughout the month,
the preparation of schools for the delayed opening of the new school year
was underway with discussion of organized lectures in classrooms as
well as "instructional lectures" for students who could not attend the
regularly scheduled classes. The framework for the local community
school concept was finalized in February 1993 at a Pedagogical Institute
seminar attended by 470 teachers on the organization of war schools in
preparation for the beginning of new school year (Sultanović, 1998).
    The entry for 8–28 February in the *School Annual*, however, notes
that "the lectures have not been fully organized yet in the local communities." As late as 16 February 1993, a brief item appeared on the last
page of *Oslobođenje* that read, "Secondary Schools: Term of Enrollment
Extended," which pushed back the final day for enrollment of first-year
students in secondary schools from 17 to 24 February. The article also

noted that about one thousand students had been enrolled but that each school had additional space for students except for Prva gimnazija. Finally, the article noted that "the criteria for enrollment hasn't changed, and all interested candidates can bring an application to the local community which will forward the requests and declarations to the responsible institutions" (1993:8).

Although delayed for six full months, the 1992–1993 school year finally began on 1 March 1993 and ran for eighteen instructional weeks until 9 July, "plus one more week in reserve." As noted in the *School Annual*, 16 July 1993 marked the formal end of the 1992–1993 school year. While a truncated version of the regular academic year, the eighteen-week session served to establish the framework for schooling for the 1993–1994 school year to follow. From the beginning of the siege on 6 April 1992 until the beginning of the new school year on 1 March 1993, it had taken approximately eleven months to reorganize schooling in the besieged city of Sarajevo.

In a June 1993 article in *Prosvjetni list,* Mehmed Hromadžić reflects upon the beginning of the school year three months previously. Hromadžić made reference to critical comments that the delayed opening for secondary school students in March 1993 meant, for all practical purposes, the loss of the entire school year. His response to such comments is reflected in the title of his article, "The School Year is not Lost":

> To organize and perform instruction for secondary school students in occupied, destroyed, constantly shelled and sniper-exposed Sarajevo— is equal, without exaggeration, to real heroism. In conditions when bombs were falling for days, hours, months, and weeks—a full 15 months, one shift after another, when snipers, anti-aircraft guns, and other deadly iron from hill-billy people from the surrounding hills did not allow us "to open an eye"—we had to gather students and teachers together and not allow the school year to be lost. Besides all war conditions, in spite of those people from the hills and one hundred reasons "against," it was decided to start with "war schools"—in one real, safe, and applicable way of organizing instruction. (1993:3)

In spite of one hundred reasons not to begin the school year, this statement in an official government newsletter makes it quite clear that the truncated 1992–1993 school year served a larger purpose than simply the instructional process in the classroom. The idea here was not to "lose" the school year to an uncivilized enemy who besieged the citizens of Sarajevo from the hills above the city. Even in spite of wartime conditions, the message was clear, that schooling would continue as an essential fabric of the normal life pattern albeit in altered form. Although a truncated version of the regular academic year, the 1992–1993 school year established the organizational framework for schooling in the local communities of Sarajevo for the 1993–1994 school year to follow. In this regard, the article concludes with the following statement:

> We are already taking into consideration the new school year. That organization as well as the progress will depend on war conditions and for now we foresee that the school year should be divided into three sessions. As soon as this wildness of cannons and other artillery from the hills stops, everything will be much easier. . . . We are planning to start with the 1993/94 school year in the beginning of September. . . . Experience from this school year will be useful for us in the new school year, so all of us who have been involved in the implementation of those tasks are expecting that this school year will be more successful. (Hromadžić, 1993:3)

Noose around Sarajevo

Dated 2 March 1993, a memo from Fehim Spaho, the secretary of the Sarajevo City Secretariat for Education, was issued to all secondary schools and to all local communities. The subject of the memo, "The Organization and Operation of Secondary Schools in Local Communities," reflects the concern of school officials with the safety of schooling, just one day after the beginning of the new school year on 1 March 1993. The memo is particularly notable for the tone that it takes, which suggests that previous directives were not followed and that schooling was operating in a haphazard fashion in certain locations across the city. A portion of the memo, "warning secondary school directors and local community secretaries," reads:

> The harsh conditions of life that we are facing and the need to constantly take care of the lives and success of the younger generation impose the need to discover safe and efficient forms of work in secondary education. That is how it happened that in the short period of time of our work we have noted some shortcomings of educational instruction among which are the following:
>
> • Teaching is taking place under persistent threats of shelling of the city;
> • Educational instruction leads to the mass gathering of students in some localities;

- The concern by parents due to broader moves is present;
- The dispersion of students started since they are coming from various local communities to one locality;
- Students from hilly parts of the city are neglected;
- Educational instruction is not unified even in its minimum requirements (privatization, illegal opening of schools, teaching by non-qualified persons);
- It is difficult to monitor and control teaching.

Taking all these circumstances into account as well as the numerous suggestions which we keep receiving, we are warning secondary school directors and secretaries of the local communities in Sarajevo, about the following changes in the further functioning of educational instruction. . . .

1. The form of classroom teaching that was explained in the first part of the former letter is abolished. Teaching at places of mass gatherings, where its verification was organized at the same time, is also abolished.
2. Until further notice, work with students of secondary schools will take place exclusively at the premises of the local communities or other available space of its area. Work under these conditions need not be unified. Contact with students. (Spaho, 1993)

The memo speaks to specific forms of the instructional process by emphasizing both the organization and operation of the local community schools. In this regard, the memo cites the importance of small groups of students, that students should be fully informed about the instructional schedule, that teachers are obliged to implement the abbreviated war school curriculum, and that the instructional lessons should extend for a thirty-minute period. Viewed against the backdrop of the siege, and written only one day after the opening of the school year, Fehim Spaho was addressing the memo to community and school administrators to ensure the systematic organization of schooling consistent with the principles that underlay the development of local community schools in the first place. In other words, the organizational framework designed to ensure the systematic operation of local community schools would be clearly established at the outset.

Secretary Fehim Spaho's memo was no small matter viewed against the nature and number of enemy forces that besieged the city at the start of the new school year. In the second issue of *Prva linija*, dated 1 February 1993, a feature article entitled, "Noose around Sarajevo," explained the nature of the siege complete with a map showing the location and type of enemy forces that surrounded the city. "The disposition of the aggressor's artillery on the hills shows that that the siege of the capital of BiH was prepared in detail and for a long time," read the subheading. The weapons employed by Bosnian Serb forces included 82- and 120-millimeter mortars, 76- and 100-millimeter cannons, 105- and 155-millimeter howitzers, 128-millimeter Multiple Barrel Rocket Launchers (MBRL), and T-55 and T-35 tanks deployed in battalion level strength. The analysis, which notes that it does not include information about the 280 antiaircraft weapons used to fire upon the city, reads:

> The siege of Sarajevo was diligently prepared at a high military level of the former JNA. . . . More that 2,100 barrels on the 60-kilometer frontline ARE POINTING ON SARAJEVO AT THIS MOMENT. The aggressor has disposed 35 fieldpieces per 1 kilometer of frontline, and in the history of war, the greatest concentration of artillery was registered around Berlin, 25 pieces, on one side. . . . Sarajevo was otherwise attacked with 5,600 artillery pieces, 110 tanks and 180 armored personnel carriers. About one-half these weapons were destroyed. (1993:2–3)

The quantitative nature of the military analysis belies the effect of the siege upon the life and death of the citizens of Sarajevo caught inside the noose, not to mention on the organization and operation of schools. In more specific terms, a contemporary situation report from the Pedagogical Institute, dated April 1993, indicates the effect of the siege on Sarajevo secondary schools. Entitled, "Information on the Beginning of Instruction in Secondary Schools, 1992–1993," the report provides information concerning the contemporary status of secondary education while another portion of the document, to be discussed in the following section, reveals the extent of the local community–secondary school network. The Institute document was an attempt to provide quantitative data concerning secondary level education in Sarajevo by citing numbers of students, teachers, and classes on 1 March 1993 at the beginning of the 1992–1993 school year. These figures were then compared to figures from the 1991–1992 school year, as of 1 April 1992, just several days prior to its effective ending on 6 April 1992.

The figures cited in table 3.1 clearly indicate that the numbers of students and faculty are down significantly from the abbreviated end of the 1991–1992 school year in April 1992. The student population at the beginning of the 1992–1993 school year is down by 18,166 students to approximately one-fourth of the student population at the end of the previous year or 25.6 percent. The number of faculty is down by 719 or approximately 49 percent of the prewar figure.

Table 3.1. Sarajevo Secondary Schools: Number of Students and Faculty

	1 April 1992	March 1993
Number of Registered Students	24,406	6,240
Number of Faculty	1,412	693

Source: Pedagoški zavod (1993).

Table 3.2. Six Sarajevo Secondary Schools: Number of Students

Schools	1 April 1992	1 March 1993
Treća Gimnazija ——(Third Gymnasium)	1,297	318
Prva gimnazija ——(First Gymnasium)	1,042	578
Druga gimnazija ——(Second Gymnasium)	1,153	424
Srednja ekonomska škola ——(Economics Secondary School)	1,547	450
Mješovita srednja škola —za elektroenergetiku ——(Comprehensive Electroenergy ——Secondary School)	1,362	780
Mješovita srednja —drvno–šumarska škola ——(Comprehensive Wood-Forestry ——Secondary School)	819	80
Šumarski školski centar ——(Forestry School Center)	385	11
Drvna tehnička škola ——(Wood Technical School)	434	79

Source: Pedaogoški zavod (1993).

Table 3.3. Treća Gimnazija: Number of Students and Faculty

	1 April 1992	1 March 1993
Number of Registered Students	1,297	318
Number of Faculty	67	36

Source: Pedagoški zavod (1993).

In the particular case of Treća Gimnazija, the numbers might be viewed relative to several other secondary schools to better understand the comparisons, as seen in table 3.2. If we first look at Treća Gimnazija relative to the two other gimnazija, Prva and Druga gimnazija, the academic preparatory schools, it is clear that the Treća Gimnazija numbers are down further than the other two schools. Prva gimnazija retained somewhat over one-half of its students, 55.5 percent, some 270 more than Treća Gimnazija, while Druga gimnazija retained 106 more students than Treća Gimnazija or 36.8 percent of its students. In fact, Treća Gimnazija lost 979 students from the previous year or 75.5 percent of its student body, a figure made even more dramatic when compared to the losses of the other two gimnazija. No doubt the primary consideration here is that neither Prva or Druga gimnazija lost their buildings and were able to continue with classes at their respective locations in the heart of the city.

Prva gimnazija, located on what was then Zmaj Jove Jovanovića (today Gimnazijska) Street, was directly on the boundary line between Centar and Stari Grad municipalities, a narrow street that affords, in relative terms, some protection. Druga gimnazija is located in an open parklet area off Sutjeska Street in Centar municipality, but the school, if for nothing more than administrative purposes, had a permanent location in its original buildings. Treća Gimnazija, of course, not only had no buildings or permanent physical location, but its administrative offices were two rooms in the Comprehensive Agricultural, Food, and Veterinarian High School, located on what was then Dobrovoljačka Street on the boundary line between Centar and Stari Grad municipalities. To further complicate the difficulties for the continuing enrollment of students, Treća Gimnazija was now located right across the Miljacka River from Prva gimnazija, the most prominent gimnazija in the city, which had retained its buildings and remained at its original location.

If we look at the figures for Treća Gimnazija relative to the three other schools near the original location along the Miljacka River in Novo Sarajevo, the numbers offer interesting comparisons as well. In fact, there were four schools located adjacent to each other just off the banks of the Miljacka, between "Sniper Alley," or what was then Vojvode Radomira Putnika Street, and Youth Promenade. Each of these schools was shelled and at least partially destroyed, each of these schools was located too near the frontline to even consider their reconstruction at the time, and each of these schools, in administrative terms, was moved to another location. In fact, Mješovita srednja škola za elektroenergetiku, the Comprehensive Secondary School for Electroenergy, moved in with Prva gimnazija, while Srednja economska škola, the Economics Secondary School, moved in with Druga gimnazija. Of the four schools, only the Electroenergy Secondary School retained a majority of its student body, 57.3 percent, perhaps partially due to its move to a somewhat more advantageous location. The Economics Secondary School, located right next to Treća Gimnazija, lost 1,097 students out of 1,547 or 70.9 percent of its student body. The buildings that housed the Mješovita srednja drvno-šumarska škola, the Comprehensive Wood–Forestry Secondary School, were the original buildings of the Drvna tehnička škola, the Wood Technical School. The Šumarsksi školski centar, the Forestry School Center, previously located in Ilidža, was occupied by the enemy early in the spring of 1992, and the forestry and wood schools were now housed together in their new location on what was then Blagoja Parovića (today Paromlinska) Street in Novo Sarajevo municipality. The Wood Technical School, located near Treća Gimnazija directly on the Miljacka River, lost 355 of its 479 students, while the Forestry School Center suffered the loss of almost its entire student body, 97.1 percent, or 374 of its 385 students. All of these schools or centers were vocational–technical schools except for Treća Gimnazija, which was the only academic preparatory school at this location, but the numbers suggest something of the impact of the dislocation upon the continuing enrollment of students as well as the implications for the future.

When we look at student and faculty losses for Treća Gimnazija, the numbers cited in table 3.3 indicate that the situation for Treća Gimnazija on 1 March 1993, at the beginning of the 1992–1993 school year, was critical. The school had lost 75.5 percent of its student body or a total of 979 students, 31 of its faculty or 46.3 percent of its prewar total, and both of its buildings, as well as its physical location on the banks of the Miljacka River. The difficulties of the systematic operation of schooling for Treća Gimnazija at the onset of the new school year are reflected in the *School Annual,* dated 1–15 April 1993, which reads as follows:

> The aggression on the Republic of Bosnia and Herzegovina continues. Life and work in a city under siege is extremely difficult, as well as teaching in war schools that have been formed within the local communities. However, with the effort of the teachers as well as the students, regular instruction in the war schools within the local communities of Bistrik, Kovači, and Sumbuluša, for which Treća Gimnazija is obligated, are being realized in good extent and within the frame of possibilities that a war situation permits. (*Školski ljetopis*)

Life and work in a city under siege are reflected in the casualties and tragedies of the Treća Gimnazija community as well. In the following entry, dated 16–30 April, we see the siege hit the Treća Gimnazija community once again. A portion of the entry reads:

> Unfortunately, our employees are still going through their personal tragedies. Mustafa Halilović, philosophy professor, was killed by sniper fire in Dobrinja. He was a member of the armed forces. A brother of Zora Mandić, chemistry professor, was killed. The destiny of chemistry professor, Misima Gegić, is still unknown. The only professors or other employees who sometimes send word about themselves are Dragica Richtmann, Kulina Stanko, Danica Vujović, Klara Hadžihodivić, who are all in occupied territory or in refugee camps. Dragica Trubelja works on the education of refugee children in Split. (*Školski ljetopis*)

Amidst the chaos of the siege and the dislocation of schools, faculty, and students, education in the war schools of a city with a noose around its neck was finally underway with the start of the 1992–1993 school year. The resources for Treća Gimnazija included the remaining 318 registered students, 36 of the faculty, and two rooms in another school building at the other end of town. Treća Gimnazija also had the local communities of Bistrik, Kovači, and Sumbuluša I and II for which it now assumed administrative and instructional responsibility over a truncated eighteen-week version of the regular academic year.

The Local Community War School

The April 1993 document of the Pedagogical Institute entitled, "Information on the Beginning of Instruction in Secondary Schools, 1992–1993," referred to in the previous section, provides important data on the organization of the local community war school. This document clearly indicates that the organizational structure for schooling was in place at the beginning of the school year as seen in the relationship between secondary schools and local communities. The data provided by the Pedagogical Institute also indicates the extent and complexity of the relationship between the twenty-seven secondary schools or school centers and the seventy-two local communities across the four Sarajevo municipalities. The Institute document suggests that an understanding of the local community war schools under the administration of a particular secondary school such as Treća Gimnazija, viewed at the microlevel of analysis, must encompass an understanding of the war schools of Sarajevo at the macrolevel of analysis as well. A more focused look at the Institute document will illustrate this observation.

It is clear from the previous entries for the 1992–1993 school year in the *School Annual* of Treća Gimnazija that a working relationship between the school and the local communities was in the process of being developed. A 20–30 November 1992 entry refers to the administrative decision of the City Secretariat to initiate schooling in the local communities. The entry reads, "On Wednesday, 18 November, a meeting of high school directors was held, at which a string of guidelines was given on what is to be undertaken for the instructional lectures to start in the local community in mid-December." Of course, the start of the school year was delayed but, to reiterate once again the 1–8 December 1992 entry, Treća Gimnazija "received the obligation" to organize the instructional lectures for the local communities of Bistrik, Kovači, and Sumbuluša I and II. That obligation meant that the school was responsible for the registration of students to the local community war schools under its administration, finding classrooms in these local communities, not to mention finding teachers to teach those classes. In fact, all secondary schools in Sarajevo "received the obligation to come forward and organize the instructional lectures" in the local communities to which they had been assigned.

The Pedagogical Institute document states that, "in general, every secondary school received the obligation to organize instruction on a territory ranging from three to five local communities. The City Secretariat for Education and Culture, in cooperation with the Institute, gave those instructions in the month of January" (Pedagoški zavod, 1993:5), but the *School Annual* of Treća Gimnazija clearly indicates that they received those instructions at least as early as December. Furthermore, the paper presented by Treća Gimnazija faculty at the *Schooling in War Conditions* Symposium on 18 April 1994 referred to the December date for the organization of schooling by local communities as well:

> During the month of December after receiving instructions, preparations began on organizing lectures in the war schools within the local communities. . . . Based on the decision of the Ministry of Education, Science, Culture and Physical Culture of the Republic of BiH, dated 15 December 1992, instructional lectures were organized for secondary school students in Sarajevo. Initiation of the activities encouraged me, as an educator and as a citizen of Sarajevo, because for me they meant opposing the nightmare and absurdity of war. Instructional lectures were organized by local communities and the bearer of the activities

was the secondary school from the territory of the local community. (Sakal et al., 1994:1)

Nevertheless, the idea that each secondary school would be responsible for three to five local communities is consistent with the responsibilities of Treća Gimnazija for the three local communities located in Stari Grad municipality in the eastern end of the city. In geographic terms, this assignment was consistent with the relocation of the school to the Comprehensive Agricultural, Veterinarian, and Food High School in Stari Grad and the idea of local community war schools. In this regard, the Institute document indicates that safety concerns provided the underlying rationale for the development of the local community school concept:

> This period has been characterized by the need for securing safe grounds for the school areas (which even today is a major problem), providing faculty, and gathering students. Our main idea was for students to register themselves in their local communities where those local communities would provide safe areas so students would not be subjected to great risks. This rule applies to faculty members who would also register themselves in their local community. During this period schools will start at different times from each other and not entirely with all students expected because these student gatherings even though necessary are still voluntary based on students and their parents. (Pedagoški zavod, 1993:10–11)

It appears that some secondary schools actually began instruction earlier than the formal beginning of the school year on 1 March once their local community schools were organized. The document notes that the school year "officially began on 1 August 1992," although it is clear that only in certain situations such as Dobrinja, or in some of the elementary schools, were regular classes underway. One portion of the document notes that "most of the local communities (75 percent) started their school programs in January and February, while it is not known if 19.8 percent of the schools will start at all" (1993:9). Nevertheless, the Pedagogical Institute document reads in somewhat greater depth:

> The end of January brought a decision to start the 92/93 school year which would be mandatory for all students and faculty registered in their war schools by local communities. . . . Some schools were previously in intensive preparation at evening schools even from January. Most of the schools started in February, some in March, and the last one started on the first of April. It is necessary to emphasize that all

schools did not start because they are in areas under constant enemy
fire (Vratnik, Sedrenik, Gazin Han). (Pedagoški zavod, April 1993:12)

The document further notes the continuing concerns over safety in many
of the local communities once the school year actually had begun. At
least "one-half of the following local communities are subjected to constant danger caused by enemy aggression: Vratnik I and II, Gazin Han,
Sedrenik I and II, Toka, Đoka, Hrid, Jarčedoli, Babića Bašta, Bistrik,
Mahmutovac in Stari Grad municipality, and Hrasno Brdo, Trg Heroja,
Ivana Krndelja local communities in Novo Sarajevo municipality, and in
Centar municipality Podtekija and Skenderija" (1993:9). Of the seventy-
two local communities in Sarajevo that were cited where schooling was
underway, fully seventeen were considered extremely dangerous for
schooling within a month after the beginning of the new school year, not
to mention that all of them were within sight of the enemy in the hills
above. Schooling in the local communities of the Dobrinja settlement, for
example, is not even mentioned here. In fact, the very premise of the
school by local community arrangement was that students would be at a
lesser risk attending local community schools than if they attended their
school of register. In other words, normal school conditions are hardly
applicable when almost one-quarter of the schools are "subjected to constant danger" in a city that is under siege. The document goes on to indicate the nature of these conditions in the local community schools:

> The conditions under which schools are operating are far from normal,
> because students are not in regular classrooms but in other facilities
> such as ex-offices, bomb shelters, and even private apartments. From
> the entire number of classes [293], 37 of them operate in apartments, 45
> in bomb shelters, 102 in premises of different designation, and 49 in
> school, mainly, cellar premises. Taking into consideration such facili-
> ties, it is not surprising to hear that only seven of them had heat, 18
> schools said there was no heat at all, and 16 of them said that they had
> electricity, and only 13 of the spaces had sanitary premises. (Pedagoški
> zavod, April 1993:17)

Thus Dino Ćatović, a first-year student at Treća Gimnazija during the
belated 1992–1993 school year, attended classes at the punkt in the KUD
(Kulturno-umjetničko društvo/the Cultural-Artistic Society) Ivo Lola
Ribar located on what was then Blagoja Parovića Street. Dino offers the
student's perspective on attending classes under conditions that were far
from normal:

KUD Lola was pretty close to my home. It takes maybe five minutes to get there. It was at kind of a bad place because it was close to the second main post office in town and not protected by other buildings. . . . Classes were held in the basement of KUD Lola, so once you were inside, it was pretty safe. . . . Students from all schools were together in the same punkt in that school year. It was very dark in the classroom, because windows were at the ground level and very small and few, so sometimes it was too dark to write although we wrote. . . . Conditions were impossible, but it worked. They decided that something is better than nothing. (2000)

With the acknowledgment of these impossible conditions, and that something is better than nothing, the war school year began on 1 March 1993 in the local communities of the city. The complexity of these organizational arrangements between secondary schools or school centers and local communities across the city can hardly be underestimated. Although the actual operation of these arrangements will be discussed in more detail in the following chapter, the intent here is to indicate the complexity of the organizational framework that guided the operation of secondary schools during the early years of the war.

In this regard, table 3.4 indicates the assignments of schools by local communities, and I will list the school assignments in full here to indicate the extent of this relationship across the city. I have listed the schools by the specific names indicated in the document, at least their names at that time while, in parentheses, I have noted the contemporary school reference since the names of schools and school centers have changed a great deal even during the wartime period.

Several comments must be offered on the organization of this table. First, anyone attempting to compare contemporary schools or local communities with those listed above that date from the prewar era will observe several inconsistencies. Today, for example, there are, to the best of my knowledge, ninety-two local communities spread across the nine municipalities of Sarajevo Canton (Kanton Sarajeva) but, at the time of the siege, Sarajevo City (Grad Sarajeva) retained only portions of four municipalities (Stari Grad, Centar, Novo Sarajevo, and Novi Grad) and, to my knowledge, the seventy-two local communities noted previously. The inclusion of Gimnazija Dobrinja with responsibility for the Dobrinja Educational Center (Nastavni centar) accounts for seventy-three local communities, although today the Dobrinja settlement is comprised of four local communities. Second, the names of many of these local communities have been changed as have the names of all sorts of locations to include, most notably, street names, causing many of those who grew up

Table 3.4. School Obligation for the Organization of Instruction by Local Community, 1992–1993 School Year

School	Local Communities
1. Mješovita srednja poloprivredno– veterinarska i prehrambena škola	Podtekija Skenderija Mahmutovac Mjednica Širokača
2. Srednja muzička škola	Logavina I Logavina II
3. Mješovita srednja ugostiteljsko–turistička skola	Breka
4. Srednja stručna trgovinska škola	———
5. Školski centar "Pero Kosorić" (Mješovita srednja škola peta gimnazija i birotehnička škola)	Olimpijsko Selo Mojmilo Otoka Petar Dokić Kumrovec Avdo Hodžić 25 Novembar
6. Zubozdravstvena škola (Srednja zubotehnička škola)	Trg Oslobođenje II Koševo Džidžikovac
7. Srednja škola za medicinske sestre–techničare	Višnjik Park Podhrastovi
8. Srednja medicinska škola	Mejtaš I Mejtaš II Bjelave
9. Srednja škola primjenjenih umjetnosti	———
10. Prva gimnazija	Trg Oslobođenje I Centar Hrid Jarčedoli
11. Druga gimnazija	Ciglane
12. Mješovita srednja građevinsko–geodetska škola	Soukbunar Babića Bašta
13. Srednja mašinska tehnička škola	Koševo I
14. Mješovita srednja elektrotehnička škola	Adem Buć Marijin Dvor Marinko Obradović
15. Četvrta gimnazija	Koševsko Brdo Crni Vrh Gorica

Table 3.4—Continued

School of Education	Local Communities
16. Šumarski školski centar	Omer Maslić
(Mješovita srednja drvno–šumarska škola)	Blagoje Parović
17. Grafički školski centar	Medeseta
(Srednja grafička technička škola)	
18. Željeznički školski centar	Hrasno Brdo
	Trg Heroja
	Ivan Krndelja
19. Gimnazija Dobrinja	Nastavni Centar
20. Srednja ekonomska škola	Baščaršija I
	Baščaršija II
21. Saobraćajni školski centar	Velešići Donji
(Mješovita srednja saobraćajna škola)	Velešići Gornji
	Pofalići Donji
	Pofalići Gornji
22. Treća Gimnazija	Kovači
	Sumbuluša I
	Sumbuluša II
	Bistrik
23. Tekstilni školski centar	Vratnik I
(Mješovita srednja tekstilna škola)	Vratnik II
	Gazin Han
	Sedrenik I
	Sedrenik II
24. Drvna tehnička škola	Mladost
(Mješovita srednja drvno–šumarska škola)	Ivo Andrić
	Jedinstvo
	6 April
25. Srednjoškolski centar Velešići	Podhrastovi II
26. Mješovita srednja škola za elektroenergetiku	Bratstvo Jedinstvo
27. Srednja škola metalskih zanimanja	Ivo Lola Ribar
	Aneks
	Petar Dokić
28. Škola za mentalno retardirane učenike	Pavle Goranin
	Staro Hrasno

Source: Pedagoški zavod (1993:6–9).

in Sarajevo to say that they don't even know the streets in their own city anymore. "My native language is Serbo–Croatian, but now I'm told it's Bosnian," wrote Tatjana Kovačević, one of my students at the University of Sarajevo, in an essay entitled, "How Did I Survive the War?" "Every street has a new name now, so in Sarajevo where I was born, I don't know any streets" (1996). Thus Treća Gimnazija is located on the street that runs along the Miljacka River known during the Tito era as Youth Promenade and today as Wilson Promenade, which was the name of the street prior to World War II when it was (re)named after the American president, Woodrow Wilson. Caught up in a frenzied attempt to construct a country amidst the chaos of the siege, the renaming of locations, not to mention the language, became a means for the new republic to carve out an identity, and the renaming of local communities became part of this process.

Thus, for example, the names of all three local communities for which Treća Gimnazija assumed responsibility for the 1993–1994 school year were changed in the process of renaming the city. Mjesna zajednica (MZ) Avdo Hodžić, where the Avdo Hodžić Local Community War School was located, is now MZ Čengić Vila I; MZ Danilo Đokić, where the Danilo Đokić Local Community War School was located is now MZ Kvadrant; while MZ Kumrovec, where Kumrovec Local Community War School was located, is now MZ Čengić Vila II. In addition, new local communities have been carved out of local communities that previously existed adding to the total number and confusing anyone who attempts to simply equate old names with new names one for one. There are now at least five Alipašino Polje local communities, for example—Alipašino Polje A-1, A-II, B-I, B-II, and C-I—and, as noted above, there are at least four Dobrinja local communities as well—Dobrinja A, B, C, and D—at least in the Bosnian federation. Portions of Dobrinja that are now part of the Republika Srpska are another question.

Perhaps the most prominent example of renaming locations is the former Princip Bridge, renamed after World War I for the Serbian nationalist who assassinated the Archduke Franz Ferdinand, and today renamed the Latin Bridge, its original name before the war, during the siege. At the beginning of the 1992–1993 school year, however, the names of the local communities above were, to my knowledge, the correct names, although I have some concern about the reorganization of these local communities and their corresponding contemporary names. Certain Sarajevo agencies and municipalities are, at times, extremely reluctant to provide information on local community organization, so I will defer to another scholar any corrections that might be offered here.

Third, the adaptation of instruction to wartime conditions meant the reconfiguration of schools as well. These new configurations are seen, for example, in the division of the Comprehensive Wood–Forestry Secondary School (Mješovita srednja drvno–šumarska škola), noted in the previous section, which was originally located near Treća Gimnazija.

The school buildings were destroyed early during the war and, by the 1992–1993 school year, the school had retained only 11 of the 385 students from the previous year. Although the school in its entirety was eventually relocated, the school was divided into two school centers for the 1992–1993 school year, the Wood Technical School (Drvna tehnička škola), assigned four local communities, and the Forestry School Center (Šumarski školski centar), assigned two local communities. Another configuration involved a school such as Druga gimnazija, for example, which retained the services of its buildings in their original location. On the one hand, classes for the gimnazija students were conducted at the original school location for those who could attend classes there, but Druga gimnazija was assigned local community responsibilities as well. For the 1992–1993 school year, Druga gimnazija was assigned the responsibility for the local community of Ciglane, the massive apartment complex located on the hillside above the school, but by the following year, it was reassigned the local communities of Staro Hrasno and Pavle Goranin located in Novo Sarajevo.

The case of Druga gimnazija points to a fourth point of clarification, that school responsibilities for local communities changed as their responsibilities and locations changed during the war. These changes will be seen quite clearly in the next chapter with the discussion of the responsibilities of Treća Gimnazija. At this point, however, we might note the Economics Secondary School (Srednja ekonomska škola), also located next to Treća Gimnazija. With the destruction of its buildings, the Economics School moved from its original location in Novo Sarajevo into the buildings of Druga gimnazija located in Centar municipality, although students living nearby sometimes took exams in rooms of the original buildings that faced away from the frontline. However, given its new location, the school was given the responsibility to organize schooling in the local communities of Baščaršija I and II, just up the street from Druga gimnazija in Stari Grad municipality. Likewise, the Školski centar "Pero Kosorić," also referred to as Mješovita srednja škola peta gimnazija i birotehnička škola (Fifth Gymnasium and Comprehensive Office–Technical Secondary School), after the area then known as Pere Kosorića Square, today Heroes' Square, assumed responsibilities for seven local communities: Olimpijsko Selo, Mojmilo, Otoka, Petar Dokić, Kumrovec, Avdo Hodžić, and 25 Novembar, located across both Novo Sarajevo and Novi Grad municipalities. The School Center was created as a temporary administrative adaptation to meet the immediate needs of students in the area but, by the following school year, some of the responsibilities for these local communities had been assumed by the

Table 3.5. Sarajevo Secondary Schools: Number of Schools, Local Communities, Punkts, Classes, Students, and Faculty, 1992–1993 School Year

Schools	Local Communities	Punkts	Classes	Students	Faculty
27	74	77	293	5,692	532

Source: Pedagoški zavod (1993:13-16).

secondary schools themselves. With its move to Novo Sarajevo, Treća Gimnazija, for example, took on the responsibilities for the local communities of Avdo Hodžić, Kumrovec, and Danilo Đokić for the 1993–1994 school year.

Finally, we might also note the case of Dobrinja, which had no gimnazija prior to the war but where one was created given the numbers of secondary students trapped in the siege within a siege and unable to attend their schools of registration. The local community responsibilities for Gimnazija Dobrinja were simply assigned to the Dobrinja Educational Center (Nastavni centar Dobrinja), referred to also as the Dobrinja War School Center (Ratni nastavni centar Dobrinja), which had coordinated all instruction at both elementary and secondary levels throughout the besieged suburb. The story of the reconstruction of education in the besieged settlement of Dobrinja, not to mention the story of the siege of Dobrinja itself, remains as but another story to be told of the siege of Sarajevo.

The data on the number of secondary schools engaged in instruction in the local communities, to include the number of classes, the number of students actually attending classes, and the number of faculty teaching these classes, is presented in table 3.5. The figures presented in the Pedagogical Institute document were somewhat less than the anticipated number because figures for eight local communities assigned to three schools were unavailable, although there are now seventy-four local communities cited. Thus the data cited earlier in table 3.1 noted 6,240 registered students for the beginning of the 1992–1993 school year on 1 March 1993, which was approximately 25 percent of the total of those registered by the end of the 1991–1992 school year. The number of faculty is also less no doubt for the very same reasons.

One other important element on the figures presented, referred to in the previous chapter, concerns the number of punkts or punktovi, the number of points or specific classroom locations within each of the local communities. Although these figures are taken from a very early stage in the development of the local community schools, acknowledgment of the punkts within the local communities is important in understanding the actual operation of the local community schools. At the time of the survey, many local communities only had one location for classes, while several had none at all. However, the example of the Školski centar "Pero Kosorić" suffices here.

At the beginning of the school year, the School Center assumed responsibility for seven local communities in Novo Sarajevo and Novi grad municipalities. At this time, the figures indicate a total of eleven punkts, the actual physical location of the classrooms spread across the seven local communities. In other words, the direction was towards the creation of several points or classroom locations within each local community to minimize the risk for students. Students would attend classes at the nearest punkt while teachers would circulate between these punkts to teach their classes. As the local community schools developed, there were often five or six classroom locations within the boundaries of each local community. To reiterate the words of Professor Hajrija-Šahza Jahić, "The idea was to connect the small points, the micro-environments, which, at the beginning, operated independently, to develop a scheme, to develop a kind of organized system of war schools" (1998). Connecting these points within the local community resulted in the development of the local community war school. Thus the five or six punkts that represented the classroom locations within the local community of Avdo Hodžić were developed into the Ratna škola mjesne zajednice Avdo Hodžić, the War School of the Avdo Hodžić Local Community, one of the war schools under the administration of Treća Gimnazija. We will explore the organization and operation of the Treća Gimnazija war schools in greater depth in the next chapter.

In a memo to the secretaries of the local communities, dated 6 September 1993, Fahrudin Isaković, the secretary of the City Secretariat for Education at the beginning of the 1993–1994 school year, noted his concerns about the "conditions for organizing instruction in secondary schools." The memo indicates the importance of local communities to secondary school organization and expresses the hope that conditions in the local community schools will improve. The memo thus serves to summarize the operation of the local community schools during the truncated 1992–1993 school year and serves to address "the improvement of conditions for work with students in the forthcoming school year 1993/94." In this regard, I will cite the memo here in its entirety:

> We would like to express our appreciation for the unselfish collaboration by local community services with the directors of the secondary

schools of register and their coordinators during the past school year. At the same time we apologize for all mistakes which happened in the one form of work in which we did not have any experience in previous times.

In the interest of better collaboration which is of vital social importance, the City Secretariat for Education, Science, Culture, and Physical Culture, in agreement with the Ministry of Education, Science, Culture and Physical Culture, taking into account some mistakes on our part, is using this opportunity to point to the necessity for some measures which could bring about the improvement of conditions for work with students in the forthcoming 1993/94 school year:

- Wherever possible work with students should be organized in as decent as possible premises which can be achieved by better re-scheduling of space;
- Maximum attention should be paid to sanitary-hygienic conditions;
- Hygiene and appearance of premises where teaching is organized should be kept at a decent level which can be assisted by students' parents as well as civil defense services;
- Civil defense services should take care of order during teaching activities to stop mischief by hooligans and others who disturb order;
- Local community services together with directors and school coordinators, should constantly monitor the functioning of schools and should point out accompanying problems and propose optimal solutions;
- Where appropriate, provide lighting of premises where teaching is organized, and especially, although we know what kind of difficulties we are facing, any kind of heating of improvised classrooms.

We are appealing to the local community services that, within their realistic possibilities, fulfill some of these measures in the interest of those who are least held responsible for what is happening to us at this particular moment. Let us do it together with the aim to protect the physical health and sound spirit of our children for our better times. (Isaković, 1993)

Chapter Four

The War Schools of Treća Gimnazija, March 1993–July 1994

Life in Sarajevo is going on. We, the youth of this loving town, we are going on with sadness in our hearts and new experiences.

The first question we ask ourselves as young people is: What is waiting for us in the future? The thing that makes me happy on our way back to peace is that our desire for freedom is greater and stronger than the hatred of the enemy. It's there that we find support for everything else. Naturally, personal experience is hard and painful and it will remain forever as a kind of eternal shield for the future. We are badly wounded, but we shall look for strength within ourselves. . . .

So, we have to fight. The breakdown that I experienced, and so did most people of my age, can be felt even in these lines. Each sentence is a beginning. . . .

The departure of some dear and close people from this world left an incurable wound in the heart and soul. The wound is the symbol of the town, of the generation. A single look back is enough to feel the pain from that wound. . . .

The people who have been trying to bring us back to health, our parents and our teachers, they have been giving us the resolve. We must wake up with the spring, we must be friends and live new lives. New music, new society must cure the wounds.

With our experience as our shield, with our lives as the new beginning, we shall try to make the wounded youth of this town healthy again.

—Ehlimana Hrapović,
student of the Bistrik Local Community War School,
Treća Gimnazija

The Bistrik Local Community War School, 1992–1993 School Year

With the beginning of the 1992–1993 school year on 1 March 1993, the two March entries in the *School Annual* of Treća Gimnazija were nondescript stating only that the classes in the local community schools have been well organized. In these entries, the *School Annual* makes no reference to the number of teachers who remained with the school at the beginning of the abbreviated school year. However, the paper presented by Treća Gimnazija faculty at the *Schooling in War Conditions* Symposium on 18 April 1994 referred to thirty-three teachers with "a permanent working obligation together with thirteen external collaborators from other schools [who] realize the lectures" in the local community schools. Another seventeen faculty were on a waiting list, three were in the Armed Forces, "and for thirty-four workers employment was discontinued" because, in the words of one teacher, "they simply disappeared" (Sakal et al., 1994). The Pedagogical Institute document, dated April 1993, refers to thirty-six faculty, which is not inconsistent with the thirty-three permanent faculty plus the three faculty serving in the armed forces. Nevertheless, the number of faculty is down to approximately 53.7 percent of the prewar number while the number of students, cited in the tables of the previous chapter, is down approximately 24.5 percent compared to the student numbers at the end of the truncated 1991–1992 school year.

The April entries in the *School Annual* are more substantial and point to the difficulties of schooling under wartime conditions in the four local communities for which Treća Gimnazija was responsible: Bistrik, Kovači, and Sumbuluša I and II. In this regard, the 1–15 April entry describes the situation as follows:

> The aggression on the Republic of Bosnia and Herzegovina continues. Life and work in a city under siege is extremely difficult, as well as classes in war schools that have been formed within the local communities. However, with the effort of the teachers as well as the students, regular instruction in the war schools within the local communities of Bistrik, Kovači, and Sumbuluša, for which Treća Gimnazija is obligated, is being realized in good extent and within the frame of possibilities that a war situation permits. In the local communities of Bistrik and Kovači, instruction is being taught by graduate students. The instruction is followed by a string of difficulties that can not be solved by the school, for example, a lack of books. (*Školski Ljetopis*)

Amidst the dislocation of schools, faculty, and students, schooling in Sarajevo was finally underway albeit a shortened eighteen-week version of the regular academic year. The paper presented by Treća Gimnazija teachers for the *Schooling in War Conditions* Symposium noted above also refers to the difficulties of initiating classes in the local community war schools at the onset of the new school year:

> At the beginning the groups of students were very small. One of the reasons is that parents and students were not informed. The shelling of Sarajevo intensified especially at the beginning of January. This was another reason for students not to come to school. The persistence and enthusiasm of the teachers produced results and the groups increased daily. . . . Considering the experience gained so far in the instructional lectures, the war school gains in quality. Groups of 10–20 students are being organized, gimnazija students are being separated from the students of vocational training due to different instructional plans and programs. Work journals are being restored, the knowledge of students is being graded, and the cooperation between the teachers and the students is at a level of tolerance and understanding, considering war conditions. (Sakal et al., 1994:2)

The resources for Treća Gimnazija for the 1992–1993 school year included the remaining 318 registered students and 36 of the faculty with their persistence and dedication. The school also had two rooms in a school building at the other end of town to administer schooling in the four local communities for which it now assumed responsibility, groups of ten to twenty students in the classes, and "a level of tolerance and understanding, considering war conditions."

There are several entries in the *School Annual* for June and July that point to the regular schedule of classes and lectures in the war schools of Bistrik, Kovači, and Sumbuluša local communities in Stari Grad municipality. The regular classes that began on 1 March continued without interruption for eighteen instructional weeks ending on 9 July, according to the *Work Journal* (*Dnevnik Rada*) of the Bistrik Local Community War School, "plus one more week in reserve." As noted in the *School Annual*, 16 July 1993 marked the formal end of the 1992–1993 school year. Viewed in light of the general reference of the symposium paper to the local community war schools for which Treća Gimnazija was responsible, a closer examination of the work journals reveals the nature of the local community war school operation in greater detail. In the process, the paper provides a basis for understanding the organization and operation of these schools in the 1993–1994 school year to follow.

Mirko Marinović, the former school director of Treća Gimnazija, was the coordinator for the *Ratne škole na području mjesne zajednice Bistrik* (War Schools on the Territory of the Bistrik Local Community), hereafter, the Bistrik Local Community War School. According to Director Marinović, the primary responsibility of the coordinator was the safety of the students, so it was essential for him to find classroom locations or punkts in close proximity to the students' residences. Many of the local communities in Stari Grad, the Old City, dated from the Ottoman period, and were located on the hillsides above the area known as Baščaršija, the old market quarter of the city. Comprised of older houses and narrow walkways, these local communities in Stari Grad were generally smaller than those in Novo Sarajevo and Novi Grad, which formed the newer part of the city to the west. Within these older local communities, it was somewhat easier to locate punkts closer to the students than in the apartment complexes of western Sarajevo.

For the Bistrik Local Community War School, Professor Marinović located six punkts in shelters or basements below the ground and on the first floor of buildings close to the ground. As the war school coordinator, Professor Marinović was also responsible for the supervision of teachers and the organization of a regular schedule of classes that met over a five- or six-day school week, not to mention the cancellation of classes in the event of shelling or snipers. He was directly responsible for all administrative matters to include a regular attendance record for students, regular entries by the teachers that noted the content of classes, and regular evaluations of students for the purposes of grade reports. In his eyes, the most important responsibilities he assumed were the safety concerns for his students, including responsibilities to the parents of the students as well. Given the inherent danger of conducting schooling during this time, the coordinator was the one person whom parents could contact directly in regard to school concerns. In addition to his role as coordinator, Professor Marinović was also a chemistry teacher who taught classes in the different punkts of the Bistrik Local Community War School (Marinović, 1998).

In contrast to the usual accounting of teachers and students in the *School Annual*, there is no record, to my knowledge, of the number of students or class sections of Treća Gimnazija nor the number of students or class sections in the local community schools during the 1992–1993

Table 4.1. Bistrik Local Community War School: Class Sections and Students, 1992–1993 School Year

Class	Class Sections	Students
Class I	2	36
Class II	2	45
Class III	1	39
Class IV	1	32
Total	6	152

Source: Treća gimnazija, *Dnevnik rada, Ratne škole na području mjesne zajednice Bistrik* (1992–1993 School Year).

school year. Nevertheless, the work journals that are available allow us to construct a picture of the organization of these schools under the administration of Treća Gimnazija. In this regard, the work journals provide information on the students who attended classes, the teachers who taught those classes, and the lessons for each class section by subject area. Based on an examination of the work journals for the Bistrik Community War School, the numbers of students and class sections appear in table 4.1 above. Viewed against the numbers of the local community war schools for the 1993–1994 school year that follows, the 1992–1993 numbers appear consistent both in terms of the number of class sections and the number of students. The Bistrik work journals indicate that at least 152 students in all four secondary classes or grades attended six different class sections at the Bistrik Local Community War School under the administration of Treća Gimnazija.

Furthermore, examination of the work journals indicates that, with one exception, there were separate gimnazija and vocational class sections. It appears, for example, that there were at least two gimnazija sections created for at least fifty-six, first- and second-year students registered at gimnazija across the city. The records indicate that that twenty-six students attended classes for the first-year or class I gimnazija section where they received instruction in fifteen different subjects from sixteeen different instructors analogous to their regular gimnazija program. There was a separate gimnazija section for the second-year or class II students as well. The number of gimnazija students and their schools of register appear in table 4.2. While the majority of students who attended the gimnazija classes were indeed Treća Gimnazija students, it is clear that the Bistrik Local Community War School, under the administration of Treća Gimnazija, included both gimnazija and vocational students who were registered at schools other than Treća Gimnazija. Only one incon-

Table 4.2. Bistrik Local Community War School: Gimnazija Students and School of Register, 1992–1993 School Year

Class	School of Register	Students
Class I (gimnazija section)	Prva gimnazija	5
	Treća Gimnazija	18
	Peta gimnazija	3
Total		**26**
Class II (gimnazija section)	Prva gimnazija	1
	Druga gimnazija	2
	Treća Gimnazija	27
Total		**30**

Source: Treća gimnazija, *Dnevnik Rada, Ratne škole na području mjesne zajednice Bistrik* (1992–1993 School Year).

sistency marked these class rosters involving one gimnazija student who attended one of the vocational class sections. In other words, students were not haphazardly assigned to classes but, if possible, organized into class sections depending upon grade level, instructional program, and school of register. This form of adaptation of instruction is also seen in the records of the Avdo Hodžić Local Community School during the 1993–1994 school year to follow.

Those work journals available for the Kovači Local Community War School, however, suggest that the organization of war schools by instructional program was not uniform. In the case of Kovači, gimnazija and vocational students were mixed together in at least two of the class sections. The thirty students whose names were listed in a class I section included ten gimnazija students, ten vocational students, as well as ten student withdrawals. The seventeen students in a class II section included seven gimnazija students and ten vocational students, although a single class II and class IV section was composed of twelve vocational students; two gimnazija students, and three withdrawals were noted (Treća gimnazija, Ratne škole na području mjesne zajednice Kovači, 1992–1993 school year). From those teachers with whom I've talked, however, they consistently point to the organization of classes, and the punkts where these classes were held, by the instructional program if at all possible. In the case of Bistrik, as well as in the case of Avdo Hodžić, to be discussed in the following pages, this form of instructional adaptation was implemented in the majority of the individual class sections of the local community war schools.

Table 4.3. Bistrik Local Community War School: Vocational Students and School of Register, 1992–1993 School Year

Class	School of Register	Students
Class I (vocational section)	Mješovita srednja poloprivredno i veterinarska i prehrambena škola	1
	Srednja zubotehnička škola	3
	Mješovita srednja elektrotehnička škola	2
	Srednja medicinska škola	2
Total		**8**
Class II (vocational section)	Srednja medicinska škola	5
	Srednja ekonomska škola	1
	Mješovita pravno–birotehnička srednja škola	2
	Mješovita srednja saobraćajna škola	2
	Mješovita srednja škola za elektroenergetiku	4
	Mješovita srednja elektrotehnička škola	1
	Srednja škola za medicinski sestre–tehnicare	1
	Mješovita srednja građevinsko–geodetska škola	1
Total		**17**

Source: Treća gimnazija, *Dnevnik rada, Ratne škole na području mjesne zajednice Bistrik* (1992–1993 School Year).

The vocational class sections of the Bistrik Local Community War School are simply referred to as *srednja škola*, or secondary school class sections, and were also composed of students who were registered in schools from across the city. In the class I vocational section, eight students received instruction from eighteen different teachers in fifteen different general education subjects, and in the class II vocational section, seventeen students received instruction from sixteen teachers in fifteen general education subjects. The vocational students in the two class sections who attended the Bistrik Local Community War School are listed by their schools of register in table 4.3. As would be expected, none of the students in the vocational class sections are registered at Treca Gimnazija but at vocational–technical schools located across the city in all four Sarajevo municipalities. These students were taught a regular schedule of general subjects in the Bistrik Local Community War School, but for the specialized instruction required in their vocational–technical instructional program, they attended classes at various punkts in the city. Dated 10 May, the *School Annual* explains the process in the following manner:

The Pedagogical Institute and the Republican Fund for Secondary Schools organized working meetings to begin organizing vocational–theoretical instruction. Vocational–theoretical instruction for the chemical–technological profession is organized at three punkts and they are: in the Agricultural, Veterinarian, and Food School Center for the students from Stari Grad and Centar municipalities, in the Hrasno [Ivan Krndelj] local community for the students from Novo Sarajevo and Novi Grad municipalities, and a punkt [War School Center] in Dobrinja. (*Školski ljetopis*)

Thus the *Work Journal* for the punkt at Ivan Krndelj in Hrasno records eleven students enrolled in the chemistry–technology technician program who were taught fourteen different subjects in the field by eleven different instructors. These courses included everything from general chemistry technology to courses in practical apparatus and advanced courses in physical and analytical chemistry. It is clear, however, that the students in the chemistry–technology technician program needed specialized vocational instruction in the field. For this reason, they attended specialized classes held at the Ivan Krndelj punkt in Hrasno while attending general education classes in their local community schools, which were under the administration of Treća Gimnazija (Treća gimnazija, punkt: Ivan Krndelj, 1992–1993 School Year).

The entries in the *School Annual* refer to "general education lectures" or to "lectures of general subjects" of the kind held at the Bistrik Local Community War School, and to "vocational–theoretical instruction" or "professional education" at specific punkts. The entry for 1–10 June provides an example of this distinction:

General education instruction in the war schools within the local communities of Bistrik, Kovači, and Sumbuluša was conducted without great difficulty, as well as the instruction for professional education for the chemical–technological profession at three punkts. (*Školski ljetopis*)

This feature of the Bistrik school provides an indication of the rationale that underlay the local community war school concept. The intention was to organize students in relatively small class groupings located in their immediate neighborhoods and bring subject-area classes to the students to minimize the risk of school attendance. This required a major reorganization of schooling that involved not simply an adaptation by a single school such as Treća Gimnazija but an adaptation of instruction that involved every secondary school located in the city. This form of instructional adaptation allowed students who were enrolled at their school of register prior to the war, the *matična škola*, to maintain their enroll-ment and thus complete their instructional program during the war. Fur-ther adaptations were made for students of the gimnazija directed to-wards preparation for the university and for vocational–technical students as preparation for a career. The Bistrik Local Community War School allows us to see the beginnings of the local community school adaptation in the small group sessions that characterized the abbreviated 1992–1993 school year. The 1993–1994 school year that followed repre-sents the development of this form of adaptation in the local community war schools in even greater complexity.

One additional note marking the 1992–1993 school year concerns the appointment of the new school director that was to have a profound im-pact on the course of Treća Gimnazija through the years of the war. On 1 May 1993, the entry in the *School Annual* notes that Fahrudin Isaković, the school director, appointed less than nine months previously, on 15 August 1992, was appointed the new Secretary of the City Secretariat for Education in the Sarajevo city government. The 3 May entry notes that he was replaced as school director by Emina Avdagić, a mathematics teacher with thirteen years' experience at the Mješovita sredna elektro-tehnička škola, the Electrotechnical High School, and ten years' experi-ence at Prva gimnazija before. Director Avdagić was to set the course for Treća Gimnazija through the extremely difficult times that lay ahead and to see the school through its dislocation and relocation back to its origi-nal location in the western end of the city. Her efforts culminated in the reconstruction of the school buildings during the postwar era marked by the visit of President Clinton to the school on 30 July 1999 and, ulti-mately, the return of the teachers and students to the original school buildings in March 2000. Her efforts will be duly noted here in this chapter, as well as the next, for without her direction, Treća Gimnazija might not have survived the siege of Sarajevo as the third gimnazija in the city.

The Local Community War Schools of Treća Gimnazija, 1993–1994 School Year

With the beginning of the 1993–1994 school year on 6 September 1993, a working document from the Pedagogical Institute indicates that schooling was organized by twenty-eight secondary schools or school centers in seventy-two local communities, which is consistent with fig-ures previously cited by the Pedagogical Institute document of April

1993. However, even though the number of schools and local communities remained the same, the document revealed major shifts in school administrative responsibilities (Pedagoški zavod, 1993–1994 school year). For example, Prva gimnazija still had responsibility for Centar local community, but now shared responsibility for Trg Oslobođenja I with Srednja škola primjenjenih umjetnosti, the Applied Arts High School. Druga gimnazija, which had responsibility for Ciglane during the 1992–1993 school year, now assumed responsibility for the local communities of Pavle Goranin and Staro Hrasno. Mješovita srednja ugostiteljsko–turistička škola, the Comprehensive Hotel Management–Tourism Secondary School, assumed responsibilities for Hrid and Jarčedoli local communities. Responsibility for the local communities of Olimpijsko Selo, Mojmilo, Otoka, Petar Dokić, 25 Novembar, Kumrovec, and Avdo Hodžić, previously held by Školski centar "Pero Kosorić," was now divided between four secondary schools including Treća Gimnazija.

The administrative responsibilities of Treća Gimnazija had shifted significantly during this period. Originally responsible for the local communities of Bistrik, Kovači, and Sumbuluša I and II during the 1992–1993 school year, the responsibilities of the school for the 1993–1994 school year now shifted to the local communities of Avdo Hodžić, Danilo Đokić, and Kumrovec, although responsibility for Bistrik was still retained. This shift in responsibilities was no small matter and relates directly to the concerns for developing "an organized system of war schools" expressed by Hajrija-Šahza Jahic. The idea was not simply to connect the punkts to form the local community war schools but, in the larger sense, to develop the local community school network into an organized system of war schools across the city. We see the development of this war school network to its full extent in the organization of the local community war schools of Treća Gimnazija during the 1993–1994 school year.

With the shelling of its buildings on Youth Promenade in Novo Sarajevo municipality during the spring and summer of 1992, Treća Gimnazija had acquired several rooms in the Agricultural-Veterinary School on Dobrovoljačka Street just inside the boundary of Stari Grad municipality. Given the location of the school and the conditions of the siege, the locus of control for Treća Gimnazija had shifted from Novo Sarajevo on the western side of the city to the local communities of Stari Grad on the eastern side. Thus, to repeat the entry in the *School Annual*, dated 1–8 December 1992: "Our school received the obligation to come forward and organize the instructional lectures for the territory of local community Kovači, Sumbuluša, and Bistrik." These local communities for which Treća Gimnazija first assumed responsibility for the 1992–1993 school year were all located within immediate walking distance of the new administrative offices in Stari Grad municipality.

With the beginning of the 1993–1994 school year, however, the major responsibilities of Treća Gimnazija shifted back to Avdo Hodžić, Danilo Đokić, and Kumroveć local communities in Novo Sarajevo nearer to its original location. According to Emina Avdagić, the new school director, the tradition of Treća Gimnazija was here in Novo Sarajevo in the western end of the city (1998). With the move to Stari Grad, the relocated offices of Treća Gimnazija on Dobrovoljačka Street were just across the Miljacka River from Prva gimnazija, whose building remained intact, and which had a long tradition in the area. Furthermore, Druga gimnazija was located within walking distance just up the street in Centar municipality. With the destruction of its buildings, Treća Gimnazija had lost not only its physical location along the Miljacka River, but many of its students from Novo Sarajevo and Novi Grad municipalities to the west, along with its sense of identity. The shift in administrative responsibilities to the three local communities in Novo Sarajevo reflects the direction of Professor Avdagić back towards the home area that provided Treća Gimnazija with many of its students and that supported the school as "the gimnazija" for the newer western municipalities.

In this regard, the 1 April 1994 entry in the *School Annual* includes a letter sent to the Steering Board of Novo Sarajevo municipality that concerns this very issue. Following a detailed account of the state of the school buildings on Youth Promenade, the letter addresses the concerns of the dislocation of the school. A portion of the letter reads as follows:

> The Treća Gimnazija school building is on 16 Youth Promenade on the very frontline which brought it great damage. The building is now a function of defense. Turning to you at the start of the 1993/94 school year . . . the issue of the organization of work for the war schools within the local communities was the only thing solved. We are now in a situation where it is necessary to solve the issue of returning the work of Treća Gimnazija to Novo Sarajevo municipality, for the continuation of the normal work of the school as the only gimnazija in this municipality. Before the war this school, with a long tradition dating from 1948, satisfied the needs of schooling for a large population of this municipality, with a capacity of over one thousand students, and struggled to become one of the three most preeminent gimnazija of Sarajevo. The school is now in an extremely difficult situation. . . . Considering that the transfer of students from their war schools within the local communities to their main schools for normalizing life and work in the city, we are in a situation that we are literally out in the street because we are

not able to use the school building. That is why we turn to you with a request that you provide minimal working conditions, and that is working space. We suggest that you look at the possibility that we temporarily use the space of some primary school from the right side of the Miljacka River, because 90 percent of our students are there. . . . Considering that new gimnazija have been formed in Dobrinja and in Novi Grad municipality, . . . Novo Sarajevo is in a situation that it could be left without its gimnazija after almost half a century with it which would deprive it of one important component of development and the status of a city municipality. In these difficult times it is important that we react in time, because overnight you can lose year-long efforts. . . . This problem of ours should be solved as soon as possible, because at the start of the school year, the school and the municipality will be left without its students, because the students will enroll in the gimnazija of other municipalities. (*Školski Ljetopis*)

This request for space in a primary school building was to be solved for the 1994–1995 school year but, at this point late in the 1993–1994 school year, the letter clearly indicates the desire to return to Novo Sarajevo as the home territory for Treća Gimnazija. The initial September entry in the *School Annual* reflects this shift back to the local communities of Novo Sarajevo to begin the 1993–1994 school year. The entry reads that although "the students of Treća Gimnazija are attending classes in the war schools within their local communities in the four Sarajevo municipalities," the responsibilities of Treća Gimnazija to organize the instructional lectures for local communities in Novo Sarajevo municipality were now as follows:

> The obligation of Treća Gimnazija is for the operation of war schools within the local communities, Avdo Hodžić, Danilo Đokić, Kumrovec, and Bistrik (gimnazija section) in which general educational lectures are being realized and two punkts: (1) the Agricultural and Veterinarian and Food School Center; (2) Ivan Krndelj Hrasno for the theory and practicum lectures of the chemical–technological profession and of civil defense for the students of Treća Gimnazija. (*Školski ljetopis*)

Pursuant to the earlier discussion of the Bistrik Local Community War School in the previous section, this entry provides another indication of the complexity of the local community war school organization. Here again the distinction between the gimnazija and vocational–technical instructional programs is noted. In more specific terms, Treća Gimnazija has assumed administrative responsibility for: (1) the academic preparatory programs for the gimnazija at the four local community schools;

Table 4.4. Treća Gimnazija: Class Sections and Students, 1993–1994 School Year

School	Class Sections	Students
Treća Gimnazija	13	362

Source: Školski ljetopis.

Table 4.5. Treća Gimnazija: Class Sections and Students in the Local Community War Schools, 1993–1994 School Year

Local Community War School	Class Sections	Students
Avdo Hodžić	10	216
Danilo Đokić	9	184
Kumrovec	5	82
Bistrik	6	86
Total	30	568

Source: Školski ljetopis.

(2) the general educational instruction for those vocational–technical students at the four local community schools (note Bistrik here); and (3) the vocational–technical instruction at the two punkts. In other words, the entry makes clear that the responsibilities of Treća Gimnazija have expanded well beyond its traditional responsibilities of educating only gimnazija students in an academic preparatory program.

With the beginning of the 1993–1994 war school year, Treća Gimnazija assumed responsibilities for general education classes for vocational–technical students such as those enrolled in the Bistrik school during the previous year, as well as the vocational–technical instruction at two punkts for vocational–technical students. These roles and distinctions can be clearly seen in the breakdown of class sections and student numbers in tables 4.4 and 4.5. A comparison of these two tables indicates that the number of students and class sections of the local community war schools for which Treća Gimnazija assumed responsibility was well beyond the number of students who actually attended Treća Gimnazija classes. In other words, Emina Avdagić, the school director of Treća Gimnazija, assumed administrative responsibility for the organization of thirty class sections and the instruction of 568 students in the four local community war schools for which the school was responsible, not to mention the vocational–technical responsibilities at the punkts as well. If we remember the enrollment of students at the Bistrik Local Community

War School, for example, and the numbers registered at Treća Gimnazija, we see here in the four local community war schools a replication of the Bistrik school to a far greater degree. It becomes clear through closer examination of the *odjeljenska knjiga* (class section book) which, for the most part, has replaced the *dnevnik rada* (work journal) for the documentation of attendance and grades, and related documents of the local community war schools, that these schools educated not only Treća Gimnazija students but students registered at any one of the twenty-eight secondary schools trapped in these local communities. And even though they attended a war school in their local community of residence under the administration of Treća Gimnazija, they nevertheless maintained their enrollment in their school of register.

Viewed from another perspective, while Treća Gimnazija "received the obligation" to organize the instructional lectures for the areas of four local communities, the 362 Treća Gimnazija students attended not only these four local community schools but another fifty-one local community schools across the city. In other words, Treća Gimnazija students attended a total of fifty-five secondary schools including the local community schools under its administration, yet still maintained their enrollment in Treća Gimnazija as their school of register. Hence the entry in the *School Annual* reads that "the students of Treća Gimnazija are going to classes in war schools within local communities in four Sarajevo municipalities" organized by other secondary schools.

Thus Dino Ćatović, a student of Treca Gimnazija, attended classes in the basement of KUD Ivo Lola Ribar during the abbreviated 1992–1993 school year, and in the ground floor of the building of what was then Blagoja Parovića 4B during the 1993–1994 school year. Both classrooms were located within the local community of Blagoje Parović, which was under the administration not of Treća Gimnazija but of the Šumarski školski centar, the Forestry School Center. Just across what was then Braće Vujičić Street, today Malta Street leading down to the Malta Bridge, was the local community of Avdo Hodžic and the punkts of the Avdo Hodžić Local Community War School under the administration of Treća Gimnazija. In Dino's words, "KUD Lola was pretty close to my home. It takes maybe five minutes to get there." The classes on the ground floor of Blagoja Parovića 4B was the very building in which Dino lived. "It was my closest school ever," he said. "I could go in slippers" (2000).

Those school administrative forms that are the everyday bane of teachers and students alike are, in this case, historical documents that clearly indicate where those teachers and students fit within the organizational structure of schooling. For example, examination of the *potvrda* (certificate) of a Treća Gimnazija student indicates not only the grades received by subject area but, for example, the war school attended (Ratna škola Alispašino Polje) or local community (Miro Popara), as well as the school with administrative responsibility (Drvna tehnička škola, the Wood Technical School). Examination of the *izvještaj o uspjehu* (report of success or grade report) for a particular Treća Gimnazija student indicates not simply grades by subject area but the school with administrative responsibility (Gimnazija Dobrinja, for example) and local community (Dobrinja) as well. These individual grade reports comprised the *pregled* (review) of "student (academic) success and disciplinary (action)" (*uspjeha i vladanja učenika*) submitted by the school that organized instruction (*škola koja je organizovala nastavu*), the Drvna tehnička škola centar, for example, to the *matična škola* (the school of register), here Treća Gimnazija. These documents clearly indicate the complexity of school organization from the microlevel of the school itself and how that school fits into the larger organization of schooling across the city (Treća gimnazija, 1993–1994).

The listing of local community war schools attended by the 362 students of Treća Gimnazija, the school of register, and the schools of administrative responsibility, for the 1993–1994 war school year, offers some sense of the scale of the war school organization in the besieged city of Sarajevo. With the exception of the creation of the local communities of Alipašino Polje located in Novi Grad municipality, all other local communities appear consistent with those local communities previously cited in the Pedagogical Institute document for the 1992–1993 school year. Based upon personal interviews, entries in the *School Annual*, and Pedagogical Institute documents, table 4.6 contains the listing of local community schools attended by Treća Gimnazija students and the secondary schools that assumed administrative responsibility for these local community schools.

It is clear that the local community war schools did not operate in an isolated or independent vacuum divorced from connections with other secondary and local community schools. As we see here, Treća Gimnazija, as the school of register, was responsible for the academic progress of all 362 Treća Gimnazija students who were enrolled in a total of fifty-five local community war schools throughout the city, fifty-one of which were under the administration of other secondary schools. Indeed, Treća Gimnazija maintained academic records to that effect, and it was

Table 4.6. Local Community War Schools Attended by Students of Treća Gimnazija and Secondary Schools with Administrative Responsibility, 1993–1994 School Year

Local Community	School of Administrative Responsibility
Kumrovec	Treća Gimnazija
Avdo Hodžić	Treća Gimnazija
Danilo Đokić–Kvadrant	Treća Gimnazija
Bistrik	Treća Gimnazija
Trg Oslobođenja I	Prva gimnazija and
	Srednja škola primjenjenih umjetnosti
Staro Hrasno	Druga gimnazija
Koševsko Brdo	Četvrta gimnazija
Crni Vrh	Četvrta gimnazija
Gorica	Četvrta gimnazija
Otoka	Peta gimnazija
25 Novembar	Peta gimnazija
Jedinstvo	Peta gimnazija
(Alipašino Polje C)	Peta gimnazija
Švrakino Selo	Peta gimnazija
Dobrinja	Nastavni centar Dobrinja
Ivo Andrić (Alipašino Polje A)	Drvna tehnička škola
Miro Popara (Alipašino Polje B)	Drvna tehnička škola
6 April	Drvna tehnička škola
Olimpijsko Selo	Drvna tehnička škola
Adem Buć	Mješovita srednja elektrotehnička škola
Ragib Džindo	Mješovita srednja elektrotehnička škola
Sokolje	Mješovita srednja elektrotehnička škola
Marijin Dvor	Mješovita srednja građevinsko-geodetska škola
Skenderija	Mješovita srednja poljoprivredno veterinarska i prehrambena škola
Podtekija	Mješovita srednja poljoprivredno veterinarska i prehrambena škola
Mjednica	Mješovita srednja poljoprivredno veterinarska i prehrambena škola
Velešići	Mješovita srednja saobraćajna škola
Gornji Pofalići	Mješovita srednja škola za elektroenergetiku
Donji Pofalići	Mješovita srednja škola za elektroenergetiku
Hrastovi I	Mješovita srednja škola Hadžići
Logavina I	Srednja grafička tehnička škola
Logavina II	Srednja grafička tehnička škola
Medrese I	Srednja grafička tehnička škola

Table 4.6—Continued

Local Community	School of Administrative Responsibility
Medrese II	Srednja grafička tehnička škola
Sedrenik	Srednja grafička tehnička škola
Mladost	Srednja grafička tehnička škola
Koševo II	Srednja mašinska tehnička škola
Breka	Srednja mašinska tehnička škola
Bjelave	Srednja medicinska škola
Mejtaš I	Srednja medicinska škola
Mejtaš II	Srednja medicinska škola
Petar Dokić	Srednja škola metalskih zanimanja
Kovači	Srednja stručna trgovinska škola
Sumbuluša	Srednja stručna trgovinska škola
Trg Oslobođenja II	Srednja zubotehnička škola
Džidžikovac	Srednja zubotehnička škola
Koševo I	Srednja zubotehnićka škola
Omer Maslić	Šumarski školski centar
Blagoje Parović	Šumarski školski centar
Ivan Krndelj	Željeznički školski centar
Trg Heroja	Željeznički školski centar
Hrasno Brdo	Željeznički školski centar

Sources: Avdagić (1999); Pedagoški zavod (1993–1994 School Year); *Školski ljetopis.*

Emina Avdagić, as the school director, who signed the diplomas of these students upon their graduation. At the very same time, Treća Gimnazija was also responsible for all of those 568 students from secondary schools throughout Sarajevo who attended the four local community war schools under the administration of Treća Gimnazija. How the teachers managed these responsibilities during the 1993–1994 war school year is explored in the discussion that follows concerning the operation of *Ratna škola mjesne zajednice Avdo Hodžić* (Avdo Hodžić Local Community War School).

The Avdo Hodžić Local Community War School, 1993–1994 School Year

While Treća Gimnazija retained the responsibility for the Bistrik school at the beginning of the 1993–1994 school year, it also assumed responsibility for the local communities of Avdo Hodžić, Danilo Đokić, and Kumrovec in Novo Sarajevo as well. These three local communities were by and large comprised of large apartment complexes that merged into

each other on the north side of the Miljacka River. Avdo Hodžić and
Kumrovec rested dead on "Sniper Alley," or what was then Vojvode Radomira Putnika Street, and Kumrovec was located just behind Avdo
Hodžić to the back of the apartment buildings along the railroad tracks
below the hillside. The area in back of the three local communities was
dominated by Zuč hill, which rose 850 meters above the western end of
the city. In the words of Alen Gagula, writing in the Bosnian army newspaper, *Prva linija,* "Zuč hill. One of the dominant peaks over the city as
well as over Vogošća and Rajlovac. One has a perfect view over the entire Sarajevo valley. The strategic importance of this hill is known to the
aggressor as well" (1994:6). Whoever controlled Zuč controlled the
northern approaches to Sarajevo, and the defense of the hillsides around
Zuč by the Bosnian Army witnessed some of the most terrible and heroic
fighting of the defense of the city.

    Across the Miljacka River to the south, the western end of the city
was dominated by a ridgeline that ran to the slopes of Mount Trebević
and provided the Bosnian Serb forces that controlled the ridge with a
clear line of sight to the city below. From Hrasno hill along the ridgeline
to Mojmilo hill, the local communities in this area of the city were at the
mercy of enemy gunners and snipers. To organize schooling within this
setting could only have been something of a nightmare, yet this is precisely the area for which Treća Gimnazija assumed responsibility during
the 1993–1994 school year.

    The Avdo Hodžić Local Community War School served the neigh-
borhood generally known as Čengić Vila and, sometime during the renaming of Sarajevo places, Avdo Hodžić local community became Čengić Vila I, while the adjacent local community of Kumrovec became
Čengić Vila II. Danilo Đokić local community became known as Kvadrant local community sometime during the war, and the class books of
the local community school refer jointly to the Kvadrant–Danilo Đokić
Local Community War School. These class books also indicate that the
three local community schools, given their proximity, maintained approximately the same academic calendar and, in fact, coordinated their
class schedules while sharing their instructors. All the while, these three
local community schools, along with the Bistrik school, operated under
the guidance of Emina Avdagić, the school director, who was responsible
for their administration and operation.

    The boundaries of the Avdo Hodžić local community ran from Bla-
goja Parovića (Paromlinska) Street on the north and west to Džemala
Bijedića Street, then down and across what was then Vojvode Radomira
Putnika (Zmaja od Bosne) Street, or "Sniper Alley." On the south side of

the street, the boundary ran along the bend of the Miljacka River to the Malta Bridge to include a small area of Dolac Malta between the river and "the alley." The boundary line ran back along what was Ivana Krndelja (Azize Šaćirbegović) Street for about twenty meters and through the dangerous intersection at Sniper Alley to Braće Vujičić (Malta) Street. The line went up Braće Vujičic Street to the Željeznički školski centar, the Railway School Center, and over to Blagoja Parovića Street again. For several months during 1994, the lines were extended down Sniper Alley to include a storefront classroom that faced away from the frontline. The territory was in clear sight of the enemy on Hrasno hill and mortars and rockets pounded the local community with regularity. Those portions of the area closer to the river along Sniper Alley near the Malta Bridge were within range of enemy snipers located in the apartment buildings of Grbavica just up the river or those snipers with machine guns converted to sniper rifles on Hrasno hill. This was hardly the best place in which to conduct schooling, but Treća Gimnazija "received the obligation" to come forward and organize instructional lectures in these local communities and proceeded to do just that in the Avdo Hodžić Local Community War School.

Avdo Hajdo, today the deputy school director of Treća Gimnazija, was the coordinator of the Avdo Hodžić Local Community War School during the 1993–1994 school year. Like his counterpart, Mirko Marinović, at the Bistrik Local Community War School, Professor Hajdo went through the local community of Avdo Hodžić looking for empty rooms in relatively safe locations to turn into classrooms. And like Professor Marinović, his primary concern was the safety of his students:

> It was impossible. It was hard to imagine a school somewhere. We had to find a building, a location near the ground, because of the danger. We had students from both sides of the river, so it was very dangerous. It was dangerous to cross the bridge. The area was shelled all the time. It was dangerous everywhere, but it was really dangerous here. (1998)

The bridge to which Avdo Hajdo refers is the Malta Bridge across the Miljacka River near the end of Ivana Krndelja Street at the Dolac Malta intersection with Sniper Alley. Kemal Kurspahić, the editor of *Oslobodenje*, lived in the Hrasno area, and described the "geography of murder" in the following manner:

> Snipers practically had all of Hrasno in their sights and the number of dead and wounded rose daily. From positions in the high-rises of the shopping center and the hill of Hrasno, their gunfire raked the entire

area in front of our apartment complex and bullets streaked across the broad Ivana Krndelja Avenue up to the bridge at Dolac Malta intersection. Going out of the building, crossing the street, the bridge or the intersection was usually a hazardous operation. (1997:172)

As coordinator of the Avdo Hodžić Local Community War School, Avdo Hajdo had responsibilities similar to those of Professor Marinović the previous year with a few more added on. And like Professor Marinović who also taught chemistry, Professor Hajdo was a biology teacher as well, which added teaching assignments to his many responsibilities. In addition to securing classrooms for the school, Avdo Hajdo was responsible for the organization of class schedules and the supervision of teachers across the classroom punkts within the local community. He was responsible for the evaluation of the students and the transmission of student grade reports to their schools of register. He was also directly responsible to the parents for the safety of his students and for the cancellation of classes in the event of shelling or snipers. Because the enrollment of students gradually increased with the new school year, his responsibilities became more complex and more tenuous as the siege of the city lengthened. With the school year beginning at its usual time in September, coordinators like Avdo Hajdo had to face the realities of winter in rooms unequipped as regular classrooms with no electricity or heat and no running water or toilets.

If it was impossible to imagine a school in this area, Avdo Hajdo nevertheless created a war school where nothing had existed before. Indeed, the rooms or shelters he located within the local community became the war school punkts where students would attend classes. With the start of the school year on 6 September 1993, Professor Hajdo had found four classroom locations and, over the duration of the year, there were four or five or six punkts depending upon the time and the availability of space. The contemporary locations and original functions of five of the punkts are noted as follows: (1) a first-floor apartment on Jovana Cvijića (Nedima Filipovića) Street; (2) a basement shelter beneath a hairdressing salon on Džemala Bijedića Street; (3) a first-floor apartment on Sniper Alley; (4) a first-floor store now a pharmacy on Sniper Alley; and (5) a clothing store on Sniper Alley (Hajdo, 1998). Depending upon the time, these five punkts served as the classroom locations for the 216 students who comprised the ten class sections of the four secondary grade levels attending the Avdo Hodžić school. For the most part, these students resided within the boundaries of the Avdo Hodžić local community and, depending upon the location of their residence, they attended

The main classroom
building of Treća Gimnazija
showing the shell craters and
bullet holes in the west and
south walls. Photo courtesy
of Perry Lingman.

Apartment complexes of Novo Sarajevo municipality from Hrasno Hill, once in enemy
territory. Hrasno Elementary School can barely be seen between the burned-out highrise
apartments in Hrasno to the right of the photograph. Zuć Hill rises in the background above
the west end of the city. Photo by author.

Hrasno Elementary School and the concrete barriers erected by Dutch UNPROFOR troops during the siege that completely encircled the building. Photo courtesy of Perry Lingman.

The view from Hrasno Elementary School eastward toward the frontline. The apartment building seen between the poplar trees was occupied by enemy snipers just across the frontline in Grbavica. Photo by author.

School Director Emina Avdagić with Perry Lingman of the City of Stockholm, holding a certificate presented to him for his dedicated assistance in the reconstruction of the school. Photo courtesy of Perry Lingman.

Avdo Hajdo, associate director and biology teacher at Treća Gimnazija and coordinator of the Avdo Hodžić Local Community War School, and Edina Dmitrović, English teacher at Treća Gimnazija and Petar Dokic Elementary School. Photo by author.

Mirko Marinović, director, associate director, and chemistry teacher at Treća Gimnazija, and coordinator of the Bistrik Local Community War School. He is currently director of the Comprehensive Wood-Forestry Secondary School. Photo by author.

Treća Gimnazija welcomes U.S. President Bill Clinton to Sarajevo, 29 July 2000. Emina Avdagić, school director, is standing to the far right. Photo courtesy of Perry Lingman.

President Bill Clinton and Secretary of State Madeleine Albright, escorted by Emina Avdagić, view the interior of the main classroom building, 29 July 2000. Photo courtesy of Perry Lingman.

classes at the closest punkt within the local community boundaries (Hajdo, 1998).

In contrast to the usual accounting of numbers of teachers and students in the *School Annual* of Treća Gimnazija, for example, there is no record, to my knowledge, of the number of students or classes in the local community schools during the 1992–1993 school year. We know only from the Pedagogical Institute document cited previously that, as of 1 March 1993, there were 318 students registered at Treća Gimnazija for the beginning of the school year. To determine more information for the shortened school year, we must go to the work journals of the individual war schools to construct a picture of schooling and numbers of students and teachers involved. In contrast, for the start of the 1993–1994 school year, we not only have the *School Annual* that indicates 362 students registered for thirteen class sections, up 46 students from the previous school year, but we have the same information from the class books for each grade or class and each class section of the four local community war schools under the administration of Treća Gimnazija.

In the case of Avdo Hodžić, for example, the *School Annual* records that 216 students in four secondary classes attended ten class sections of the school as seen in table 4.7. The *School Annual* also records the same data for the other three local community war schools under its administration: Danilo Đokić, Kumrovec, and Bistrik, a portion of which appears in the previous section. However, examination of other school documents reveals the development of the Avdo Hodžić school in somewhat greater complexity and indicate the composition of each class section at the Avdo Hodžić school (Treća gimnazija, 1993–1994 School Year). Documents such as these, along with the individual class books and the *School Annual*, provide information on the organization and composition of the individual local community war schools under the administration of Treća Gimnazija.

In this regard, the number of students in each class section of the Avdo Hodžić Local Community War School, and their course of study, appears in table 4.8. It is clear that the teachers of Avdo Hodžić offered instruction to students in all instructional programs from schools all across the city. These 216 Avdo Hodžić students represented less than one-half the number of students who were taught in the four local community war schools under the administration of Treća Gimnazija. Given the 362 students registered at Treća Gimnazija, and that many of these students attended war schools under the administration of other secondary schools, it is clear that Treća Gimnazija assumed responsibility for the education of more students from other schools than from its own.

114   Chapter Four

Table 4.7. Avdo Hodžić Local Community War School: Class Setions and Students, 1993–1994 School Year

Class	Class Sections	Students
Class I	3	72
Class II	3	57
Class III	3	61
Class IV	1	26
Total	10	216

Source: Školski ljetopis.

Table 4.8. Avdo Hodžić Local Community War School: Class Setion, Course of Study, and Students, 1993–1994 School Year

Class/Class Section	Course of Study	Students
Class I		
I-1	gimnazija	21
I-2	technical	22
I-3	technical and professional	29
Class I Total		72
Class II		
II-1	gimnazija	14
II-2	other schools	22
II-3	other schools	21
Class II Total		57
Class III		
III-1	gimnazija	10
III-2	other schools	26
III-3	other schools	25
Class III Total		61
Class IV		
IV-1	gimnazija and other schools	26
Class IV Total		26
Avdo Hodžić Total		**216**

Source: Treća gimnazija, Ratna škola mjesne zajednice Avdo Hodžić, "Osnovni podaci o školi" (1993–1994 School Year).

Table 4.9. Avdo Hodžić Local Community War School: Gimnazija Students, Class Section, and School of Register, 1993–1994 School Year

Class Section	School of Register	Students
Class Section I-1	Prva gimnazija	1
	Druga gimnazija	7
	Treća Gimnazija	6
	Četvrta gimnazija	0
	Peta gimnazija	7
Class Section I-1 Total		21
Class Section II-1	Prva gimnazija	6
	Druga gimnazija	3
	Treća Gimnazija	5
	Četvrta gimnazija	0
	Peta gimnazija	0
Class Section II-1 Total		14
Class Section III-1	Prva gimnazija	0
	Druga gimnazija	3
	Treća Gimnazija	5
	Četvrta gimnazija	1
	Peta gimnazija	1
Class Section III-1 Total		10
Class Section IV-1 (gimnazija)	Prva gimnazija	2
	Druga gimnazija	1
	Treća Gimnazija	3
	Četvrta gimnazija	2
	Peta gimnazija	0
Class Section IV-1 (other schools)		18
Class Section IV-1 Total		26
Gimnazija Class Sections	Prva gimnazija	9
	Druga gimnazija	14
	Treća Gimnazija	19
	Četvrta gimnazija	3
	Peta gimnazija	8
Gimnazija Class Section Total		53

Source: Treća gimnazija, Ratna škola mjesne zajednice Avdo Hodžić, "Osnovni podaci o školi" (1993–1994 School Year).

Nevertheless, Treća Gimnazija was responsible for the administration and guidance of its own students as they attended their classes in the war schools of the city. In this regard, it is informative to break down the class sections of Avdo Hodžić to examine those students and their schools of register who attended the local community war school. The case of gimnazija students in particular indicates something of the complexity of the organization here, and in table 4.9, the gimnazija sections for each class of Avdo Hodžić are broken down by the student's school of register. Of the 216 students enrolled in the Avdo Hodžić school, only 53 were gimnazija students while the other 163 were classified as technical or professional students with the recognition that the others category appears interchangeable with the other two. Of these 53 students, Treća Gimnazija was the school of register for only 19 of them. In fact, Treća Gimnazija students were a distinct minority in the Avdo Hodžić school when viewed both in terms of all 216 students in the school and in terms of the 53 students in the gimnazija sections alone. In other words, students who were enrolled in each one of the twenty-eight secondary schools or school centers across the city, to include both gimnazija and vocational–technical schools, and who lived in the local community of Avdo Hodžić, attended the Avdo Hodžić Local Community War School under the administration of Treća Gimnazija while maintaining their enrollment in their schools of register, regardless of where those schools were located.

Student listings were compiled according to residence in the Avdo Hodžić local community and, based upon these listings, classes were organized for the students according to location of the nearest punkt. It is clear, however, that gimnazija and vocational sections were created in the interests of better instruction and the organization of instructional programs. The gimnazija students had their own intensive course of study directed towards the university examinations still required during the war for admission to one of the faculties of the University of Sarajevo. The vocational students were required to take general education subjects in a local community school and then attend their vocational classes at one of the punkts that offered such instruction. The students were then notified of their class schedules, by telephone if in service, whereupon they would attend the punkt closest to their residence or the closest nearby punkt for their particular course of study. The students would convene in one of the punkts of the Avdo Hodžić local community in the appropriate basement or building at the scheduled times to attend their classes organized by Avdo Hajdo and his teachers into the orderly sequence of a regular school day.

The teachers would organize their class schedules given their own neighborhood and local community of residence, circulating across the punkts of the Avdo Hodžić local community and Novo Sarajevo municipality on foot to teach a full class load, usually six classes each day, in the manner of itinerant teachers. The distances between these punkts varied anywhere from perhaps one to two kilometers but, given the demands upon the teachers to ensure a full schedule of classes for the students, many teachers had to teach outside Avdo Hodžić in the war schools of other local communities.

Thus Avdo Hajdo, the war school coordinator, taught biology in the school as well. According to Professor Hajdo, his teaching load before the war was approximately eighteen to twenty biology classes a week but, during the war, with the shortage of teachers, especially in subjects like biology, he taught perhaps twenty-eight classes each week. He not only had increased teaching responsibilities in the local community school, but his teaching responsibilities carried outside of the local community for which he was responsible and into the local communities of Kumrovec and Danilo Đokić next door, both under the administration of Treća Gimnazija. In addition to these teaching and administrative responsibilities, Professor Hajdo taught biology in Staro Hrasno local community, which was under the administration of Druga gimnazija. Professor Hajdo thus served as the coordinator of the local community war school, taught biology in the school, taught biology in two other local community schools under the administration of Treća Gimnazija, and taught biology in one other local community school under the administration of another gimnazija (Hajdo, 1998).

These demands of teaching under wartime conditions meant not only that many of the Treća Gimnazija teachers had to circulate across the local communities of Novo Sarajevo municipality, but many had to circulate across the local communities of other municipalities as well—on foot and under the range of enemy guns. The demands on teachers of specialized subjects, a teacher such as Gordana Roljić, the teacher of *informatika*, or information science, for example, were severe. In fact, Professor Roljić taught in the schools of local communities of three municipalities spread across an entire city that had no form of transportation for its citizens whatsoever. She taught in four local communities in the Mojmilo area of Novi Grad municipality where she lived, Kumrovec and Danilo Đokić local communities in Novo Sarajevo municipality under the administration of Treća Gimnazija, and the Bistrik local community also under Treća Gimnazija in Stari Grad municipality. Located at the opposite end of the city from her residence in Mojmilo, the journey to

Stari Grad was a two-hour walk one way and a four-hour round trip back home. "You never knew if you were going to return," she said, in recalling the difficulty and the exhaustion of her journey from home to classroom and then back again. To reach her assigned war school classrooms from her home in Mojmilo, she first had to cross what was then Prvomajska dio Street, which was controlled by snipers located across the frontline just down the street in Nedžarići. "Even when I go that way today," she told me as she recalled the trauma, "she fears crossing that street." Professor Roljić had two children, aged twelve and fifteen at the beginning of the siege, who "never knew if their mother would come back to them" (Roljić, 1998).

From discussions with teachers such as Professor Roljić, it is clear that the organization of classes and the selection of punkts were predicated upon minimizing the risks for the students by bringing the classroom to their neighborhoods. The teachers would face those risks, however, walking from classroom to classroom, from neighborhood to neighborhood, perhaps six to ten kilometers each day, under the range of enemy guns. After all, to reiterate the words of Professor Hajrija-Šahza Jahić, "Children didn't go to school, school came to them" (1996:15). According to the teachers, this arrangement was "the safest way for the students," and while Treća Gimnazija students were killed and wounded during the siege, the teachers proudly and gratefully point to the fact that no student was killed while attending classes at the Treća Gimnazija war schools. In the words of Emina Avdagić, the school director, "Students' lives are more precious than teachers' lives" (1998). And in the words of Edina Dmitrović, the English teacher, "Our agreement was, if there was danger, if somebody had to be killed, let it be us" (1996).

Demented City Shellings

By the summer of 1993, the Bosnian capital had become almost deaf to good news. Something had snapped; whatever it was that had enabled the city to endure, that had steeled its will to survive, had fractured. And what cracked it was not shells or sniper fire, but water and wattage. . . . Gordana Knežević, deputy editor of *Oslobođenje*, called it "a clear strategy: to strangle the city until it becomes so desperate, it commits suicide. They don't need to take Sarajevo, they just need us to kill ourselves with fear and prison psychosis." . . . At the grim mercy of the ultimatum, Sarajevo's End Game was under way. . . . But now the whole city was imploding, using up its last sparse reserves of drinking water. (Vulliamy, 1994:304–309)

If fear and psychosis were overtaking the city, the beginning of the new school year on time gave students and teachers the "hope and belief that peace and normal life would return" which, in the words of Mujo Musagić, "is equal to normal life itself" (1998). Thus the initial September entry in the *School Annual* for the 1993–1994 school year replicates those entries from the previous year that attest to the difficulty of schooling in wartime conditions. However, in the words of Mirko Marinović, the former school director, and the assistant school director at this time, who assumed responsibility for entries in the *School Annual*, at least "there is no uncertainty on the beginning of the new school year 1993/94." In fact, the new school year actually began on the scheduled date of 6 September 1993.

There was certainly no uncertainty for Professor Marinović since it was during August 1993 while in preparation for the beginning of the school year that he was mobilized into the Bosnian Army. Although blind in one eye, he served his tour of duty on Zuč hill where, after his regular day at school, he dug trenches from the very beginning of the 1993–1994 school year until the middle of the next school year in December 1994. After being relieved from his post during the night, he would return down the hillside to his home in the Marijin Dvor area of the city where he caught whatever sleep he could before waking for his regular school day. He then walked across the dangerous intersections in the center of town and crossed the Miljacka River to the Comprehensive Agricultural, Veterinarian, and Food High School on Dobrovoljačka Street where the school administrative offices were located, and to the Bistrik Local Community War School in Stari Grad, where he served as school coordinator.

With the beginning of the new school year, the autumn of 1993 proved an especially difficult time for schooling in Sarajevo as the siege continued into its second year. With the responsibilities of Treća Gimnazija having shifted primarily to the local communities of Novo Sarajevo, the dangers inherent in a city under siege came extremely close to the local community schools for which Treća Gimnazija was responsible. In this regard, the initial entry for the new school year in the *School Annual* reads:

> Life and work in the city are still extremely difficult. The war is not stopping even beside a number of signed ceasefires. Most frequently, there is no electricity, gas, fuel, water, telephone lines, communication, organized transport, and what is especially difficult is no food. Being out on the street is extremely dangerous because of the shelling of the

city and underhanded snipers. Everyday civilians are being killed and wounded.

The war continues and the work continues, and in such conditions a new, and that is second war school year. The entire work is being done with great effort and support of the employees and of the students, with great risk and exposure to danger. (*Školski ljetopis*)

Following this initial September entry, the majority of entries for September and October are nondescript and generally refer to matter-of-fact administrative pronouncements concerning day-to-day operations. These entries belie the extremity of conditions in Sarajevo during the fall of 1993, however, and it is not until 26 October that the world of the siege again enters the journal with the cryptic entry that "regular lectures stopped because of the city blockade."

The blockade of the city intensified the water crisis that had been strangling Sarajevo since the summer of 1992, previously noted in the 5 August 1992 *Oslobođenje* article, "Sarajevo Blackmailed with Water!" Indeed, the water supply to the city was a day-to-day occurrence since the spring of 1992 and the enemy occupation of the suburb of Ilidža to the west where the Sarajevo waterworks was located. The difficulties of basic water supply to the people is indicated in a 12 September 1993 *Oslobođenje* article:

> The aggressor is, intentionally, as a method of blackmail, depriving water for the citizens. A hurdle hard to overcome is to get this life dependent liquid. That is why Sarajevo citizens are constantly on duty in front of any kind of water sources. During the summertime, stolen hours of waiting in front of pumps or other water supply sites can somehow be endured, but the forthcoming winter days waiting in the lines for water will be far more difficult. (Banjanović, 1993:6)

At the same time, food supplies were problematic because, among other reasons, they were interconnected with, in Vuilliamy's terms, wattage. "Citizens of Sarajevo are getting more bread these days," stated a 16 October article in *Oslobođenje*:

> In the past two days bread was delivered to all priorities and most of the local communities in the city. The shortage in fuel is making bread distribution difficult. Many citizens are coming to the Velepekara [the Large (City) Bakery] and asking to buy flour. (Banjanović, 1993:11)

A 25 October article entitled "Bread Only for Priorities" provides some indication of the difficulties of supplying basic commodities to a city under siege:

> Because of oscillations in the supply of electric power and gas, the Velepekara yesterday has reduced the production of bread. In comparison to the previous ten days when most local communities of the city received bread, yesterday bread was available only to hospitals, collective centers, and public kitchens.
>
> The director of the Velepekara, Kemal Mešak, points out that bread will not be available for local communities until appropriate quantities of electricity and, of course, gas pressure is adequate.
>
> The production of bread is made difficult by the lack of fuel not only for transport but the occasional work of generators when production starts and is interrupted by the shortage of the electric energy supply. (1993:3)

In the third of a series of articles on "How to Survive," Mustafa Tvico, the assistant minister for the Department of Trade, Merchandise, and Tourism, answered questions about the supply and distribution of bread. Under the headline, "The People Need Bread," the assistant minister is asked, "How does your Ministry evaluate the situation of food in the Republic a minute before winter?" The response is as follows:

> Lousy. Catastrophic. People are standing in front of the bakery, intellectuals, professors, university workers, they don't have enough wheat flour even to make doughnuts. They cannot get a kilo of wheat flour! We are in a very difficult situation. The black market is booming. (Mrkić, 1993:5)

While the problem of bread production at the Velepekara, the large city bakery, affects the food supply throughout the entire city, the problem is of particular note to the Treća Gimnazija local communities. In this regard, the Velepekara was located in the Čengić Vila area, or to be more precise, in the Avdo Hodžić local community. The Velepekara was an especially prominent landmark, and its huge storage silos along Blagoja Parovića Street, which occupied much of the northern boundary of the local community, became principal targets for enemy gunners on the hills overlooking this area of the city. Indeed, the Velepekara was shelled on a regular basis as the enemy attempted to choke the food supply. Of course, this meant that the whole area became especially vulnerable as the shelling meant for the huge bakery reeked havoc throughout the area that surrounded the site. In fact, one of the punkts of the Avdo Hodžić

Local Community War School located in a first-floor apartment on Jovana Cvijića Street literally lay in the shadow of the Velepekara itself.
To repeat the words of Avdo Hajdo, "The area was shelled all the time. It
was dangerous everywhere, but it was really dangerous here" (1998).

While the early fall entries in the *School Annual* belie the extremity
of the situation as "the whole city was imploding," the shelling intensified during October as the city was being pounded into oblivion. The
newspaper accounts in *Oslobođenje* from mid-October on bear witness to
the assault. On 17 October, for example, the feature article, entitled, "152
MM Shells on Sarajevo," counted 122 shells fired by 152-millimeter
howitzers that fell on Centar and Stari Grad municipalities in just over an
hour early that morning. According to the article, UNPROFOR counted
517 shells that fell on Sarajevo the previous day killing six and wounding
fifty-five. On the following day, 18 October, the headline read, "New
Attack on Sarajevo," which cited shelling from enemy artillery throughout the whole city and the bombardment of the city center in particular.
The article could only note heavy casualties with some people killed and
many wounded. By 24 October, the headline read, "Over a Thousand
Shells on Sarajevo," and cited five dead and thirty-seven wounded, but
stated that "the defense line remains firm." The "Bulletin" of the Institute
of Public Health/Committee for Health and Social Security records 37
people killed in Sarajevo during the week with another 148 wounded
(Smajkić, 1993). By 26 October, the *School Annual* confirms the severity
of the situation with the entry that "regular lectures stopped because of
the city blockade."

In fact, the class section books of the Treća Gimnazija local community war schools record the interruption of schooling through the months
of October and November. With over a thousand shells falling on Sarajevo over the weekend of 23–24 October, for example, the entry in the
II-G Class Book of the Kvadrant–Danilo Đokić Local Community War
School for Saturday, 23 October reads, "*Opšta opasnost!*" or "General
danger!" and no classes were held. For the week beginning Monday, 25
October, through Saturday, 30 October, the entry reads, "*Nastava odgo-
đena zbog granatiranja i proglašene opšte opasnosti!*" or "Instruction
delayed because of shelling and proclamation of general danger!" (Treća
gimnazija, Ratna škola mjesne zajednice Kvadrant–Danilo Đokić, 1993–
1994 School Year). For the same week, the entry in the I-1 *Class Book* of
the Kumrovec Local Community War School reads, "*Nastava obustavljena zbog ratnih dejstava,*" or "Instruction Suspended Because of the
Effects of the War"(Treća gimnazija, Ratna škola mjesne zajednice
Kumrovec, 1993–1994 School Year).

Indeed, as the shelling continued into November, it was only a matter of time that schools were hit and schoolchildren became casualties while attending classes. With the Bosnian Army occupying many of the public buildings in the city, often located near the war school classrooms, the enemy had "two choices," in the words of Avdo Hajdo. "He could choose to kill soldiers or choose to kill students. It doesn't matter. With one shell, they could kill them both" (1998). It didn't take long for the new war school year to record student casualties. The 10 November issue of *Oslobođenje* read, "Massacre in Front of School," and the subheading read in the following terms:

Chetnik shells have once more massacred our fellow citizens, this time on Alipašino Polje, when deadly projectiles fell just in front of a school and wiped out the youngest. A great number of wounded were received in Sarajevo hospitals, and, unfortunately, there were some deceased

A selected portion of the article itself read as follows:

Another massacre in Sarajevo yesterday. The Alipašino Polje settlement was shaken around 11:00 by explosions. Screams, panic, escape, dead and wounded, puddles of blood, sirens. . . . Several dead, dozens wounded, at only one place. Automobiles were trying to transport the wounded and those who can were helped to hospitals. . . .

"The emergency ward of our hospital received 34 patients," says Dr. Čerkez, one of yesterday's surgery team on duty at the State Hospital. "Two of them came in dead . . . adults. One died later. Most of the wounded are children, 22 of them. The injuries are various, on practically all body parts. Six of them have very serious injuries. Eight are kept for further treatment."

At the time of our arrival all operation rooms in the State Hospital were working, five operations were going on.

"It hurts me, mother!"

"Between 11:00 and 1:00 we have admitted ten injured kids and 13 adult civilians," says Dr. Kemal Drnda, the main surgeon on duty in the reception area of the clinical center at Koševo. "The injuries are multiple, on various body parts. Two patients are extremely badly hurt. We also worked in all of our five operation rooms. There were no dead. The injured were given medical attention, transported to the Neurological and Childrens' Surgery Clinic, and those from ongoing operations will be located at another clinic." (1993:1)

124 Chapter Four

On the following day, 11 November, in a follow-up article, under the headline, "Massacre Again in Sarajevo," under a photograph of four dead children, "innocent victims of yesterday's shelling," the article read in further detail:

> Sarajevo is still mourning over the victims from the day before yesterday, and new deadly projectiles were flying from chetnik positions. In the shelling of the entire city, especially Otoka and Alipašino Polje, eight civilians were killed, 42 were wounded, unfortunately, mostly children.
>
> The duty doctor at the Surgical Clinic said yesterday, "From 12:00 to 3:00 only we admitted 20 children and five adults. All of them were wounded with shell fragments at Otoka and, unfortunately, among the admitted we had three dead kids."
>
> The report from the State Hospital was no better at all.
>
> "Among 35 injured, that were brought to our institution, were five dead persons including three kids. The most heavily wounded, 11 of them, were operated on instantly, others were forwarded to other clinics or upon treatment, sent to home care," says the doctor on duty in this hospital.
>
> Yesterday's tragic picture was unfortunately filled with the death of three more victims of a previous massacre when nine were killed and 70 persons injured. (1993:1)

The public health "Bulletin" cited 28 people killed in Sarajevo during the week with another 165 wounded, and "the children of Sarajevo once again were the target of the aggressor" (Smajkić, 1993).

While the 12–13 November entry in the *School Annual* concerns a variety of administrative pronouncements, it concludes with a single chilling sentence that brings the tragedy home to the Treća Gimnazija community. "In a demented city shelling, places where instruction was held were hit and nine children and a teacher were killed. The six-year-old son of Nura Huskić, mathematics teacher, was killed." The 15 November entry that followed noted that, "from 10 November to 15 November, instruction in the city was stopped because of the tragic events" (*Školski ljetopis*). The class books also record the cancellation of classes during the week of Monday, 9 November, through Saturday, 13 November. The *II-G Class Book* of the Kvadrant–Danilo Đokić Local Community War School records the cancellation of classes from Wednesday through Saturday of the week with the notation, "*Nastava obustavljena iz bezbjedonosnih razloga!*" or "Instruction suspended for security reasons!" with the warning again, "*Opšta opasnost!*" (General danger!) (Treća gimnazija, Ratna škola mjesne zajednice Kvadrant–Danilo Đokić,

1993–1994 School Year). As recorded in the *I-1 Class Book* for the Kumrovec Local Community War School, classes were cancelled for the entire week with the similar notation, *"Nastava obustavljena zbog ratnih dejstava,"* or "Instruction suspended because of the effects of the war." (Treća gimnazija, Ratna škola mjesne zajednice Kumrovec, 1993–1994 School Year). The *I-1 Class Book* for the Avdo Hodžić Local Community War School records that the only class day missed during this period was Tuesday, 26 October (Treća gimnazija, Ratna škola mjesne zajednice Avdo Hodžić, 1993–1994 School Year). Perhaps the reason for this discrepancy between the entries for the cancellation of classes was that the other two local community war schools were located adjacent to the local community of Otoka where this particular shelling occurred.

The reality is that virtually every teacher with whom I talked referred to similar situations in their local community schools, of shells just missing their punkts, of shelling to or from their classes and the wailing of sirens, of shelling just before or after the students had assembled. Most talk about how lucky they were that no students who attended the Treća Gimnazija war schools were killed going to or from their classes, and no students were killed at their classroom locations. Avdo Hajdo told me about a shelling at one of the punkts of the Avdo Hodžić Local Community War School at approximately the same time as the November shelling on Otoka and Alipašino Polje that just missed a group of his own students waiting to enter the building (1998). If schools were "to meet the requirements" for the adaptation of instruction to wartime conditions, the reality was that the every teacher was concerned for the safety of his students knowing full well that everyone took their lives in their hands in the game of Russian roulette on the streets of Sarajevo. To repeat the words of Emina Avdagić here, "Students' lives are more precious than teachers' lives" (1998). To repeat the words of Edina Dmitrović here, "Our agreement was, if there was danger, if somebody had to be killed, let it be us" (1996).

On 5 February 1994, a 120-millimeter mortar shell tore into the open-air market called the Markale on a busy Saturday morning. Another "66 massacred bodies of children and adults" were added to the death toll for 96 killed in Sarajevo that week, while another 195 were wounded (Smajkić, 7 February 1994; Softić 1996). An update recorded 67 deaths, although "some have not yet been identified because their bodies were horribly disfigured," wrote Elma Softić in her diary. "After all, you could see [on TV] headless torsos and a complete set of human entrails on a counter. A market of human meat" (1996:133). Three days before, dated 2 February 1994, Zlatko Dizdarević, an editor at *Oslobođenje*, wrote the following words about life and death in the dying city of Sarajevo, which he entitled, "We'll Die Together and in Love":

> In Sarajevo, we are spending our last reserves of hope in an effort to survive until the final act draws to a close. Even those who had been considered brave and optimistic, who refused to scurry in fear across the street but continued to stride nonchalantly, are now hanging on by a thread. Fear has entered every pore. We can no longer sleep. There is nowhere left to hide from the shells that have systematically narrowed the circle around every one of us. (1994:184–185)

Amidst this hopelessness, amidst the thirst and the hunger, the cold and rain, the shelling and the snipers, the resistance to the siege is seen in the work of the teachers and the organization and operation of the war schools of the city. If "the long-term siege was destroying in people the last spark of life, of hope for a possible solution, optimism," in the words of Mujo Musagić, then the war schools "offered strength and the belief that it is possible to survive the impossible conditions of hunger, thirst, constant wounding and dying." Thus, Musagić writes, "even the fighters with guns in their hands believed that there was a sense in fighting when they knew that their children were attending so-called classes" (1998). If the soldiers who were defending Sarajevo took heart from the war schools attended by their children, then perhaps this explains another more defiant view of the siege that appeared in a 15 April 1994 article in *Prva linija* entitled, "Unconquered City: Battle for Sarajevo." Here the history of the siege of the city is reviewed with an eye towards history and the mythology of the liberation struggle:

> Even if the battle for Sarajevo is not yet completely over, this defense represents one of the greatest epics of the BiH war of liberation. The history of this epic is yet to be written, and on this occasion we are writing some of the crucial events from the heroic defense of the capital city of Bosnia and Herzegovina. (Gagula, 1994:6)

Chapter Five

Treća Gimnazija as a Frontline School, July 1994–April 1996

The name of our country was unknown to a majority of people in the world until four years ago. Even today the picture they have about Bosnia is mainly superficial and to a large extent incorrect. The majority of them know only that Bosnia is somewhere in the Balkans and that there is a war going on there. They cannot or they do not want to know more.

In us Bosnians the word Bosnia brings out pride and defiance. We try to show and prove to the world that we are a part of it. We want to tell it that we are fighting for a righteous thing, and that we only want a free country. We are not in war because we are, as some call us "barbarians," but because we have to be. Because some want to take our country away from us. And, something in this way is approved by the world. They do not understand, however, that the whole world is being defended here. That here they are passing the exam of humanity, the exam of justice. Here in Bosnia on this piece of sparkling blue and white precious stone, justice is being defended.

—Amina Alispahić,
student of Treća Gimnazija

Welcome to Hell!

The 1993–1994 school year saw Treća Gimnazija return to its home territory of Novo Sarajevo municipality but, unable to use its buildings on Youth Promenade, the school was without a single and permanent location for classes. Although Treća Gimnazija had assumed the responsibility for education in three local communities of Novo Sarajevo, in addition to the Bistrik Local Community in Stari Grad, the administrative offices were still located in the Comprehensive Agricultural, Veterinarian, and Food Secondary School on Dobrovoljačka Street in Stari Grad. Thus, Emina Avdagić, as the school director, walked from her home in Buča Potok, located in Novi Grad municipality beyond Novo Sarajevo to the west, in the shadow of Zuč hill, across the city to the school administrative offices in Stari Grad, a distance of approximately five kilometers one way. How she walked across the city twice each day for two full years under enemy guns is beyond her own capacity to understand. In her own words, "I must be crazy—or I couldn't die" (1998).

The original school buildings of Treća Gimnazija were, for the most part, inaccessible to the teachers and certainly to the students, and they were in extremely poor condition for schooling after two years on the frontline. Considering that the army occupied the Hotel Bristol next door as well as the school, the whole area on both sides of the Miljacka River looked like the free-fire zone that it was. The difficulty of the situation is indicated by a 1 April 1994 entry entitled, "State of the Building of Treća Gimnazija," which notes a letter sent to the City Secretariat for Education requesting temporary space in Novo Sarajevo municipality until the location of the school was resolved. The state of the building is described, in part, as follows:

Treća Gimnazija consists of two buildings, an old one and a new one that are connected into a whole. The buildings are right on the first frontline at 16 Youth Promenade—between the Brotherhood and Unity bridge and the bridge near the Elektroprivreda building in the combat zone during the whole 24 months of the war, which is the reason for the state of the building, which now serves as the first defense line of the armed forces of the BiH Army, that resulted in new and heavier damage especially to the inside of the building—Among other things, activities to fortify the building for defending the line and to stop further penetration of the aggressor into the city.

The school building (both buildings) was hit with a number of shells and exposed to shrapnel and metal from which the second floor of the new part of the building was mainly damaged. Shells of a larger caliber had hit the physics cabinet on the second floor and had caused great damage in that part of the building. . . . There are no traces of fire in the building nor are there consequences that appear after larger detonations. The metal on both buildings has been totally destroyed from new damages during war activities. . . . Due to war activities practically all the equipment has been damaged, destroyed, or stolen. . . .

Access and stay in the school for now is inaccessible to civilians and you can only access the schools with a special approval form. The school building is used for military purposes. Because of the frontline very close to the aggressor, gathering and staying in the school is not permitted. The time when this will become possible is unknown. . . .

For the future of the school temporary rooms should be provided, adequate to the current development of the school (for approximately 20 classrooms, to use a primary school building or a high school building of some other school) if possible to be located in Novo Sarajevo municipality, or in some other part of the city, until the issue of the Treća Gimnazija buildings is resolved. (*Školski ljetopis*)

The letter to the City Secretariat for Education came towards the end of the 1993–1994 school year, approximately six months after an earlier request to the Steering Board of Novo Sarajevo municipality, dated 3 September 1993, cited in the previous chapter, for assistance to alleviate the situation. The concern of that request was the return of Treća Gimnazija to Novo Sarajevo "as the only gimnazija in this municipality." A portion of the request is reiterated here since the resolution of this request for the 1994–1995 school year marked a new direction for the school:

We are in a situation that we are literally out in the street because we are not able to use our school building. That is why we turn to you with a request that you provide minimal working conditions, and that is working space. We suggest that you look at the possibility that we temporarily use the space of some primary school on the right side of the Miljacka River, because 90 percent of our students are there. (*Školski ljetopis*)

In fact, on 18 July 1994, two years and four months after the shelling of her buildings, Treća Gimnazija found a new home using "the space of some primary school on the right side of the Miljacka River." Several of the July entries in the *School Annual* note the impending move along with the parties involved, including the City Secretariat for Education, the Pedagogical Institute, and the Hrasno Elementary School (Osnovna škola Hrasno), represented by its school director, Krešimir Krznarić. Under a headline dated 18 July 1994, the entry records the move:

Treća Gimnazija Sarajevo, has continued operation in the new temporary spaces of Hrasno Elementary School (formerly Ivan Goran Kovačić Elementary School). The school is located on Heroes' Square (formerly Pere Kosorića Square) on Braće Ribar Street Number 2. Treća Gimnazija was given the annex of the school to use. There are five classrooms on the first floor and there is a room that can be adapted and made into a teaching staff room, one smaller room, and the possibility to get one or two smaller classrooms. On the ground floor there are four classrooms and two of them are being used for distributing humanitarian aid. (*Školski ljetopis*)

A small newspaper clipping at the bottom of the entry, under the headline, "Treća Gimnazija Changes Residence," reads in similar fashion:

Treća Gimnazija Sarajevo changes residence to the rooms of Hrasno Elementary School—formerly Ivan Goran Kovačić Elementary School, in the Novo Sarajevo settlement of Hrasno, the director of Treća Gimnazija Professor Emina Avdagić said to BiH Press.

Work in the new whitewashed rooms begins on Monday, 18 July, of this year. New students will be brought about and registered in this place by announcement, reception, and examination. (*Školski ljetopis*)

The initial teacher reaction upon moving into the elementary building annex was "the sense of being in school again . . . after those basements, after the running, it felt like . . . Florida" (Avdagić et al., 1996).

It is clear from the entries in the *School Annual* that the direction for Treća Gimnazija set by Emina Avdagić was toward the acquisition of classrooms in a more permanent location in Novo Sarajevo. However, there is no discussion in these entries of the demise of the local community war school organization so painstakingly constructed over the previous two years. From my conversations with school administrators, they noted there was general agreement on the part of educators across the city that the local community war schools had served their purpose by providing an organizational structure for schooling to adapt to the new conditions created by the siege. Now that they had the experience of two years under siege, it was time for schools, and especially schools like Treća Gimnazija, to create a greater sense of stability for students in more permanent educational settings. For schools like Prva gimnazija that had retained their buildings, and offered instruction in these buildings in addition to classes in war school locations, the transition was not so great, but for schools like Treća Gimnazija, the effort to secure buildings for schooling was a more difficult process. With no sense of an end to the siege of the city, but with a sense to create greater stability for students, the local community war schools were phased out during the summer of 1994, and with the 1994–1995 war school year, students attended classes at their schools of register. Unfortunately, I have been unable to acquire the relevant documents concerning this period from the Ministry of Education of Sarajevo Canton, and so will leave it to a future researcher to provide the documentation to clarify this transition.

The elementary school buildings were located directly on what was formerly called Pere Kosorića Square, named after a World War II *partizan* executed by the Nazis on the site. Sometime during the war, Pere Kosorića Square was renamed Heroes' Square in honor of the defenders of Hrasno, who fought the enemy to a standstill in the streets around the square in deadly urban warfare. Referring to the heroic defense of the Dobrinja settlement, *Prva linija* also makes reference to the defense of Hrasno settlement as well. "Besides Pere Kosorića Square, Dobrinja is surely one of the best examples of an 'urban war campaign,' a campaign in places of dense population" (Gagula, 1994:6). Kemal Kurspahić, the editor of *Oslobođenje*, who lived in the Hrasno area, described the "urban war campaign" and the life and death struggle for the Hrasno neighborhoods:

> Over the following months of the siege, the Serbian forces attempted, often with tank reinforcement, to occupy the neighborhood. Almost every night I could hear the sounds of fierce infantry fighting and see the flashes of incendiary bullets and exploding shells aimed at the buildings, but I knew the young men from the neighborhood who had taken on the job of defending Hrasno, and was no longer worried. I knew that they were defending their own families and homes, and that they would fight to the death rather than yield. (1997:7)

The urban warfare that raged across Hrasno was played out among the apartment buildings that surrounded the square itself. This setting added what can only be described as a surreal dimension to the siege as these apartment buildings were heavily shelled and then burned in the night sky, and the residents leaped from the windows. Kurspahić writes:

> And some distance from us, in the Pere Kosorića Square, now called the "Heroes' Square," dozens of people were killed or wounded. Two of the five 21-story apartment blocks on the square had been completely gutted in the fire started by artillery attacks. . . . While the buildings burned through the night, we could see silhouettes of people in a desperate struggle to stop the fire, and then watched a huge fireball rolling down from the upper to the lower floors, spreading the fire, until the entire building was a terrifying mass of red flames—the intensity of the light and the heat from the fire was so great that it even filled our apartment. All night I watched people leaving that place in tears, with not a shred remaining of what constituted their lives to carry away with them. (1997:174–175)

Some of the heaviest fighting occurred during the fall of 1992 when many of the apartment buildings were battered by shelling from Grbavica just across the frontline to the east. In her diary of the siege, Elma Softić recalled her view of the area at that time:

> Pero Kosorića Square at that time looked ghostly. Charred high-rises and destroyed buildings, punctured by shells like old, rust-eaten tin cans' on a cold, murky, rainy late autumn day, they resembled a region devastated by an ancient cataclysm in a long extinct galaxy. There were no people, no automobiles, no sign of life, yet there were still people there, huddled behind the precarious walls of their demolished apartments, and life flowed on there nevertheless. (1995:150)

In her personal diary, dated 5 October 1992, Jelena Andrić, the student who attended Prva gimnazija, and who lived in the Ciglane district of Centar municipality, witnessed the fighting on makeshift television:

> The attack that everyone was talking about started on Monday and it is very bad. Novo Sarajevo, or more specifically Pere Kosorića Square, is gone. All the apartments have burned down and Elektroprivreda is destroyed. We saw people jumping out the windows to get saved and firefighters helped them. The car battery that we use for TV is good for 45 minutes every night, just for us to watch the news. I saw cats eating human brains on the street a couple of days ago. What are they doing to us? God, for the first time in my life, I am very scared that I will die. I am too young to die, for Christ's sake. I am very scared and cold. It is blistering cold in Sarajevo, so my fingers get blue sometimes. It is sad but I do not even feel the pain anymore. I guess that means that I am getting used to it. Well, it is good then. (1992)

This deadly urban warfare began when Bosnian Serb forces that occupied Grbavica down to the banks of the Miljacka River sought to expand their territory into the adjacent Hrasno settlement just down river to the west. In order to do this, they had to cross a wide street known then as Milutina Đurašковića, and the apartment buildings on both sides of the street became the "first battle line" as Bosnian Serb forces attacked and Bosnian Army forces fought to hold the line.

Within this setting, Treća Gimnazija became a "frontline school" located immediately along the Hrasno frontline, the confrontation line between Bosnian Serb and Bosnian Army forces. These "front-line schools" were not simply near the frontline—they were literally on the frontline within sight and sound of the fighting that raged along what *Sarajlije* called the "first battle line." Here in the Hrasno settlement, Heroes' Square was located in the shadow of the apartment buildings held by the Bosnian army forces on the west side of Milutina Đuraškovića Street facing the Bosnian Serb forces in Grbavica just across the street. Indeed, the school took on the appearance of a fortress simply to function under wartime conditions. Trench lines led from the school to the apartment buildings in the immediate area around the square to provide, in relative terms, safer access for students and teachers.

From the Grbavica area on the east side of Milutina Đuraškovića Street, Bosnian Serb forces lay in wait in a gutted, yellow, high-rise apartment building from where Hrasno Elementary School and Treća Gimnazija located on the square below were clearly visible. Conditions were such that by the spring of 1994, several months prior to the move of Treća Gimnazija into the elementary school, Dutch UNPROFOR troops erected concrete barriers forming a series of three, concentric rings that completely surrounded the school to protect it from snipers. Turned vertically, these barriers were approximately twelve to fifteen feet in height, but only two to three feet in width, and, with three concentric layers around the school, completely covered the first-floor classrooms, yet still left the second floor classrooms partially exposed. "The lower part of the school was completely protected by cement blocks," wrote Dino Ćatović, a third-year student at Treća Gimnazija during that first year in Hrasno Elementary School, "so that part was very dark and cold; it was almost impossible to write and read in the wintertime. The few classrooms on the upper floor were on the opposite side from the direction of the snipers, so they were relatively safe." When the shooting started, students would move from the second floor classrooms down to the first floor hallway. "In the case of general alarm or danger, we would go down in the hall and stay there until they would give the signal it's over" (1999). Thus the 10 November 1994 entry in the *School Annual* reads:

> At the end of the second shift shooting was repeated near the school, same as the last time. Due to that we took the students down to the ground floor, kept them there for awhile and then we sent them home in small groups. Everything ended well without consequences. (*Školski ljetopis*)

In the words of Avdo Hajdo, "It was dark. It was cold. But we were protected. You could hear the bullets hit the blocks from the inside" (Avdagić et al., 1996).

Artillery and tanks shelled the apartment buildings of Hrasno into ruin and created the surrealistic devastation of the urban battle zone, but snipers from the apartment buildings of Grbavica and the heights of

Hrasno hill put fear into the hearts of the residents with the cold precision of their executions. Kemal Kurspahić, also cited in the previous chapter for his description of the Dolac Malta intersection, is cited again here for the same description of the "geography of murder" in Hrasno:

> Snipers practically had all of Hrasno in their sights and the number of dead and wounded rose daily. From positions in the high-rises of the shopping center [of Grbavica] and the hill of Hrasno, their gunfire raked the entire area in front of our apartment complex and bullets streaked across the broad Ivana Krndelja Avenue up to the bridge at Dolac Malta intersection. Going out of the building, crossing the street, the bridge or the intersection was usually a hazardous operation. (1997:172)

According to the residents, some seventy civilians were killed on Malta Bridge alone, the bridge at the Dolac Malta intersection, by enemy snipers, yet these residents were often left with no choice but to cross the bridge for any number of reasons (Avdagić et al., 1996). Residents had to cross the bridge to get water at the base of Hrasno hill itself, teachers had to cross the bridge to get to their classrooms on both sides of the Miljacka, and students had to cross the bridge to attend their war school classrooms as well. "When I went to school there," wrote Dino Ćatović, "I tried to avoid open spaces as much as possible using concrete barriers or metal screens at the crossroads for protection from the snipers. Malta Bridge was a very dangerous intersection so you had to be very careful. Using shortcuts was never a good idea, because even when it seemed very quiet (no sniper bullets whistling), snipers could surprise you" (1999). Just off the Malta Bridge, there was an epitaph, noted in an earlier chapter, etched on the wall of a small building at the intersection with Sniper Alley, that read, in English, "Welcome to hell!"

The cold precision of Grbavica snipers is related in an article in *Oslobođenje* entitled, "Grbavica Violinists (one story about snipers from Grbavica)":

> There were—Grbavica snipers—many kinds of them.
> There was one in Grbavica, young, pretty, with short and heavy butt cheeks which ruined the entire artistic perspective. With pride she went to work in the Vemex skylight, sharp like a Swiss watch from 7 until 3. She carried her gun in a case, so she looked like a violinist. A Serbian violinist on a shiny Serbian roof. . . .
> She would go to work, in deep thought and like a duck would shake her ass. They say she was a nice wife, gentle mother and hard

worker. I don't know if a bullet from our side caught up with her, but people say that she especially loved—kids! . . .

Like any job, even at the workplace of Grbavica, there are many kinds of violinists. The professional swears maybe once, and with a knife makes a mark on his belt, who like a seducer takes his trophy into a museum of memories, collects his money, and looks for a nice Muslim apartment where he could celebrate with his buddies by watching the evening Muslim news that reports the biographical information of his victims. . . .

Another joker was shooting at people's canisters, which is not an insignificant war crime to an individual to whom that happens in front of his door steps after coming back from the brewery. In that situation, a man would forgive blood easier than he would water. When a small caliber bullet hits the canister filled with nice, cold water, that priceless liquid flows through the hole in a perfect thin line going into an arc, so that line reminds me of a stone-peeing Venetian boy's fountain. . . .

It is not easy for one man to kill another, until he reaches that point where some sense that tells the difference between right and wrong, slowly but surely disappears. The type of victim, the distance and movement, all depend on the usage of appropriate instruments. A man chooses his subject . . . takes his instrument, places it on his shoulder, takes a deep breath and stops it like before diving, closes one of his eyes . . . and even for a moment feels like . . . God. (Topčić, 1996:2)

The weapon of choice for the Grbavica sniper was the Yugoslavian Peoples' Army M76 *PASP, poluautomatska snajperska puška* (semi-automatic sniper rifle), which fired a 7.9-millimeter bullet over a maximum range of approximately 800 to 1,000 meters. A good shooter, however, according to friends who served in the Bosnian Army, preferred an optimum distance of 400 to 600 meters, which was the approximate range from the Grbavica high-rise apartments along the Miljacka River down to the Malta Bridge. But as residents began dying on the bridge with greater frequency, it became apparent that snipers were operating on Hrasno hill with an even more deadly weapon, the M84 *Mitraljez*, the M84 machine gun converted into a sniper rifle with a 5X80 scope attached. The *mitraljez* fired 7.62-millimeter ammunition over a maximum range of approximately 1,500 meters, but the optimum range was somewhere between 800 to 1,000 meters or the approximate distance from Hrasno hill down to the Malta Bridge. With a maximum firing speed between 650 and 700 rounds a minute on automatic, the mitraljez was referred to as the *sijač smrta*, or, in American terms, the deathmaker.

In the words of Edina Dmitrović, the English teacher at Treća Gimnazija as of the second semester of the 1994–1995 school year, and a teacher at Petar Dokić Elementary School in Otoka prior to that time, walking the streets under the eye of the Grbavica violinist or the death-maker on Hrasno hill:

> The snipers, that was everyday. I don't know whether you can imagine this. . . . You have the feeling of being watched—And then he chooses. In a second you can hear his decision. . . . At first, you're afraid. Then you play tricks with him—three fingers [the Serbian salute] "Hi!" I don't know if it's pride or something else that makes you mad. He's up there. He can see. "Look! Here I am! Do what you want!" You become angry. . . . Snipers! . . . When you see, when you choose. . . . That I can't understand. When you shoot, why don't you shoot a soldier? I'm sorry for the soldier, but he's a soldier. And this is war. But not civil-ians, not children. That's what I can't understand. . . . I was always afraid for children, my students, and my own children because I knew— (1996).

The Third War School Year, 1994–1995: 47th Student Generation of This School

The third war school year is beginning. The war continues, and the work for Treća Gimnazija continues as well, but in new conditions. The entire work continues with a lot more effort and with support of em-ployees and students. Due to the war situation, the employees did not have a right to an annual leave this year as well.

However, there is no uncertainty for the start of the new school year. The necessary number of students have been enrolled into the I class year, and the II, III, and IV class years of the Gymnasium an ap-propriate number of students have been enrolled for the normal classes to be conducted. The uncertainty as to whether the school would lose a part of the students because it would move to a new location was re-moved, and the school enrolled a sufficient number of students.

The school opened up the gates for the start of the new school year. The work schedule was defined, classrooms and class-masters were also defined, and all other preparations for the start of the new school year. The students received all the necessary information and an-nouncements. The school director, Emina Avdagić, greeted the students of certain classes with appropriate words. (*Školski ljetopis*)

Five years later, on 2 November 1999, Emina Avdagić recalled her words to the students on that September day at the very beginning of the 1994–1995 third war school year. With the recognition that Treća Gim-nazija would now have a temporary home, she could look with foresight to the day that the school would be back in its original home on the banks of the Miljacka River. She first asked the students if they could be happy going to school under these temporary conditions. She then asked, "Do you know what it means to be back home?" There were two primary concerns in her "appropriate greetings" to the students. First, she told them to take care of their own lives, that their lives were more important than their classes, and not to come to school if it was too dangerous. She told them to talk to their parents if there were any questions of whether or not to come to school. Hrasno was a dangerous area, she said, and there were still enemy tanks next door in Grbavica. Second, she said that the elementary school was not their own place and that they would eventually have to leave their temporary location. She told the students that they would have to be very disciplined in this setting because they were attending school in the same building as elementary school students. In this regard, the students of Treća Gimnazija were also responsible for the care of the elementary students. When younger students asked for their help, they were to respond to them in the appropriate manner. She also indicated that when the elementary school asked for their help as teachers, they would respond as well, in the case of teaching obligations, the sharing of teachers for specialized subjects, for example. And so the students and teachers of Treća Gimnazija would assist the students and teachers of Hrasno Elementary School as part of their responsibility to their neighbors, with the recognition that they would eventually return to their original home on the banks of the Miljacka River just upstream.

At the start of the 1994–1995 school year, the *School Annual* recorded the number of students by class and class section, and these numbers indicate that student enrollment at Treća Gimnazija had significantly improved from previous years. The breakdown of these numbers appears in table 5.1. It is clear from these numbers that, while Treća Gimnazija was hardly back to its prewar total of 1,297 students as of 1 April 1992, its numbers were significantly improved when compared to the two previous war school years. The lowest point for student enrollment was 1 March 1993, the beginning of the abbreviated 1992–1993 school year, when 318 students were registered at the school. As of the beginning of the 1993–1994 school year, there were 13 class sections with 362 registered students attending classes in the local community war schools.

For the beginning of the third war school year, 1994–1995, Treća Gimnazija had 50 more registered students than the previous year and 94 more registered students from the first war school year. Furthermore, with four sections of 118 students, registration in the first-year class was

Table 5.1. Treća Gimnazija: Class Sections and Students, 1994–1995 School Year

Class	Class Sections	Students
Class I	4	118
Class II	5	136
Class III	3	88
Class IV	2	70
Total	14	412

Source: *Školski ljetopis.*

strong indicating two straight years of improved student enrollment. These numbers appear to indicate that, although Treća Gimnazija had spent the last two war school years "out in the street," the school had temporarily solved its immediate problems of physical space and student enrollment. In fact, the school had found space in its home municipality of Novo Sarajevo so that, to paraphrase the *School Annual*, neither the school would be left without students nor the municipality would be left without a gimnazija because the students would enroll in the gimnazija of other municipalities.

There were now twenty-three teachers employed full-time at Treća Gimnazija with another seven also employed in one capacity or another, for a total of thirty teachers actually providing instruction to the students. The school indicated specific needs for instructors in the Bosnian language, German, mathematics, and physics. There were individual situations where, for example, classes in the German language did not begin until 11 October because the permanent instructor was out of the country for personal reasons, and the temporary instructor was teaching in four different schools. These thirty teachers taught the 412 gimnazija students in the seven classrooms of the Hrasno Elementary School annex that were available to them. The classrooms of the annex were organized in the following manner: one classroom for foreign language classes, one assembly hall room for the school administration, one room for pedagogues or counselors along with the Russian language classes, and two wide hallways on the ground floor to be used for classes as well. The elementary school had approximately two hundred more students and retained the main classroom building and the majority of classrooms, approximately two-thirds of the physical space, indeed the better space since the library and gymnasium were reserved for the elementary students. Nevertheless, when compared to the basement and hallway classrooms of the local community war schools, there was at least a sense of stability for both teachers and students with a permanent school location.

The lack of classroom space required the school to adapt instruction to the conditions by shortening classes to thirty-five-minute sessions and by organizing two shifts of students for instructional purposes. The 412 students were roughly divided into two groups who attended classes in morning and afternoon shifts. The initial group attended a regular class schedule from 8:00 A.M. to 1:00 P.M., while the second shift arrived at 1:00 P.M. and attended a regular class schedule until 7:00 P.M. The longer afternoon session was designed to accommodate student clubs for one hour during the late afternoon. The teachers, of course, taught both shifts of students and, for the most part, stayed the whole school day, teaching from 8:00 A.M. until 7:00 P.M., arriving home late in a city that seldom had electricity to light their way, which only made them easier targets for snipers anyway. They then had to attend to the chores of caring for their own families. In the words of Edina Dmitrović speaking on behalf of many of the teachers of Treća Gimnazija at the end of the 1995–1996 school year, "we have been working for four years without a day of rest" (Avdagić et al., 1996).

While Treća Gimnazija had found a sense of stability and order in the elementary school building on Heroes' Square, the difficulty of conditions in Sarajevo during the fall of the third war school year is indicated by the 7 October 1994 entry in the *School Annual*:

> Sarajevo was without electricity, water, and gas. The first snow could be seen on top of the surrounding hills. Conditions for work and for life are extremely difficult, but as of up till now—we are not giving up and we will still keep going. (*Školski ljetopis*)

Yet in spite of these conditions, the *School Annual* records the attempts of Treća Gimnazija to operate in as normal manner as was possible, "to normalize the lives of children living in totally impossible circumstances" (Jahić, 1996:11). Thus the entries record the business of schooling, the resignations, firings, employment, reassignments, leaves, and class schedules of teachers, meetings attended by teachers and administrators, communications with the Pedagogical Institute and the City Secretariat for Education, and entries that record the welfare and safety of the school community. The 10 October entry, for example, notes the firing of Slavica Bašić, the physics teacher, who failed to return from family leave in Germany and the firing of a maintenance worker for not calling in to the school. One notation above the October entries notes that

Emina Avdagić would assume responsibility for the entries in the *School Annual* in place of Mirko Marinović, the assistant school director, as of the beginning of the month. A 22 February entry records the appointment of Avdo Hajdo, the biology teacher, as the new assistant school director, replacing Professor Marinović who was appointed the new school director of what was then the Drvna tehnička škola, the Wood Technical School. The entry noted that "the employees of Treća Gimnazija are very sorry for Mirko's departure."

The resumption of classes in the elementary school buildings allowed a semblance of more normal activities for the students as well. A school basketball tournament was held in September, a new school club called "Amicus" was formed in October to improve communication between students, along with a new journalism club that saw thirty students attend the first meeting, many of whom already worked for radio stations in Sarajevo: Radio BiH, Radio 99, and Radio "Zid." One student, Seid Fazlagić, was granted leave from 30 October to 10 December to compete in the European Champions Volleyball Cup for Club Bosnia Sarajevo, the Bosnian champion for 1994. On 29 October, over fifty students attended the second meeting of the journalism club when specific assignments were designated. On 3 November, Amira Rustempašić, the health and physical education teacher, attended a meeting of her colleagues at the Pedagogical Institute where she signed Treća Gimnazija up for the city table tennis competition. On 23 December, Gordana Roljić, the computer science teacher, brought students to the Skenderija Sports Center, where they participated in technical games and won a prize for their competition.

The 4 November entry in the *School Annual* refers to the regular meeting of secondary school directors at the City Secretariat for Education. Amidst the usual business of schooling discussed at the meeting, there is a reference to the textbook situation for Sarajevo schools which reflects both the attempt at normality for schooling as well as the surrealism of the siege, and reads as follows:

> Schools need to prepare for the distribution of new textbooks which have entered the city through the tunnel under the airport runway with the help of the Army. For months now we wait for UNPROFOR and UNHCR to reach an agreement with the aggressor on using the "Blue Route" to bring textbooks into the city. Such an agreement has never been reached. (*Školski ljetopis*)

With the declaration of independence of the Republic of Bosnia and Herzegovina from the Socialist Federal Republic of Yugoslavia, a whole new set of textbooks was in order, and these textbooks were almost completely rewritten by Bosnian authors for an audience of Bosnian students. These new textbooks were published in Ljubljana, Slovenia, two years into the war, through the efforts of the Soros Foundation's Open Society Fund of Bosnia and Herzegovina, whose efforts in the field of education at all levels were beyond measure. These textbooks then had to be sent back to the Ministry of Education in Sarajevo for distribution to schools throughout Bosnia. With the closing of the "Blue Route," the makeshift road that ran over Mount Igman, and then around the eastern end of the airport runway, the textbooks could not be brought into the city by vehicle. Instead, they had to be unloaded from trucks near the tunnel entrance in Butmir on the southwest side of the airport. They were then carried through the tunnel that ran some eight hundred meters in length under the airport runway to Dobrinja on the city side of the airport to the northeast. Indeed, the tunnel was constructed, controlled, and defended by the Bosnian Army and provided the city a lifeline to the outside as soldiers and supplies were transported in and out of the city. As the *School Annual* indicates, the distribution of these textbooks to the schools of Sarajevo occurred during the latter months of 1994 "with the help of the Army."

Several days after the initial reference for schools to prepare for the distribution of new textbooks, the 9 November entry indicates which of the textbooks have arrived:

> The distribution of the textbooks received for all our students began. The students are obliged to return the textbooks at the end of the school year and the same textbooks will be given to the next generation [of students]. The textbooks are produced in accordance with the curriculum.
>
> The first class received: a reader, a grammar book, a computer science textbook, a history textbook and a geography textbook.
>
> The second class received: a reader, a grammar book, a computer science textbook, a history textbook and a geography textbook.
>
> The third class received: a grammar book and a geography textbook.
>
> The fourth class received: a reader, a grammar book, and a geography textbook.
>
> Students who came on the second shift were sent home due to firing near the school (snipers and heavy detonations). (*Školski ljetopis*)

The normality of textbook distribution to students in schools and the surrealism of the tunnel passage by which the textbooks entered the city suggest something of the disjunction of schooling in wartime conditions.

Of course, on the same day the textbooks were distributed, the second shift of students was sent home because of the fighting, suggesting something of the insanity as well. The distribution of new textbooks continued, nevertheless, with their arrival in the city through the tunnel passage under the airport runway. Over a month later, on 26 December, the entry records that the school received another textbook:

> The school received a new textbook—*History* for class IV of the gimnazija (authors: Mustafa Imamović and Muhida Pelesić). The distribution of the textbook to all the graduating students began.
>
> Due to the siege of the city by the aggressor, the history textbook for class III of the gimnazija and the music culture textbook (class II) have not been delivered.
>
> Preparations for marking 1,000 days of the siege have begun. Negotiations for war activities and hostilities in the entire Republic to stop are in progress. There are implications that an agreement could be signed by the end of the month. (*Školski ljetopis*)

The *History IV: Razred Gimnazije* textbook was distributed to students of the senior class who would soon graduate and attend one of the faculties of the university. It is worth noting that this history textbook begins with the First World War and continues through the last two chapters on "the World after the Second World War" and "Bosnia and Herzegovina after the Second World War." The last substantive section of the last chapter on Bosnia after World War II concerns "Crisis politics and constitutional reforms 1971–1974." The concluding section, entitled "BiH [Bosnia and Herzegovina] as an independent and sovereign country" ("BiH kao samostalna i suverena država"), contains only a single reference to the Bosnian war and no reference to the siege of Sarajevo. In minimal fashion, this section reads:

> After the independence of Slovenia and Croatia, by the logic of politics taking place BiH had to set off on the same path. On the observance of the referendum of 29 February 1992, the citizens of Bosnia and Herzegovina declared themselves for independence, for an independent and sovereign country. Precisely at the start of the day of Serbian-Montenegrin aggression on BiH, 6 April 1992, the European community recognized the legal government of the subjects of the Republic of Bosnia and Herzegovina. Finally, on 21 May 1992 the Republic of Bosnia and Herzegovina applied to the United Nations. (Imamović and Pelesić, 1994:121)

The rationale for the publication of new textbooks by the newly independent country and the surrealism of a history textbook passage that makes no substantive attempt to confront the war that threatened the country suggests something of the disjunction of schooling during this time. How does the history teacher, for example, well into the third war school year, make sense out of the siege of the city when the new history textbook fails to mention the siege of the capital of the country?

The surrealistic scenario of school textbooks entering a city under siege by tunnel passage, and a new history textbook that makes no reference to the siege, is also reflected in the entries of the *School Annual* that document the attempt to continue with schooling under siege conditions. Indeed, from the very beginning of the fall semester of the third war school year, the siege is omnipresent as classes were interrupted by the shelling and the snipers and casualties of the Treća Gimnazija community enter the pages of the *School Annual*. On 13 September, for example, the school supplied information on sixteen students of the school for the scholarship and education of the children of soldiers who were casualties of war and of civilian victims of the war. This task was often quite difficult since the school had lost contact with many of its students from the prewar era who no longer attended the school, approximately two-thirds of the 1991–1992 student population. Some of these students and their families simply fled the city as refugees to other countries, some went to "the other side" in Bosnian Serb-controlled territory, and some simply disappeared. There was minimal information available and almost solely in regard to students who were registered at that time. The 3 October 1994 entry in the *School Annual* indicates something of the difficulty of keeping track of people, even registered students, during the war. The entry reads:

> Incidentally, while talking to Ms. Hafija Kudić, counselor of Hrasno Elementary School, we found out that our student, Vanja Vuk, was killed in her apartment (address: Porodice Ribar 6) [formerly Braće Ribar on Heroes' Square]. She enrolled in our school in the 1992–1993 school year and was registered under the number: 51/I-92-93 [a first-year student during the abbreviated 1992–1993 school year]. She finished her first year with a 4 (very good) and with exemplary behavior. We did not receive this information on time because instruction was held at the punkts within the local communities. (*Školski ljetopis*)

Siege conditions were only intensified for the Treća Gimnazija community by the location of the school on Heroes' Square where Vanja Vuk was killed in her own apartment. The 7 November entry relates to the location of the school near the frontline and concerns for the safety of the students and, in the process, provides a sense of the wartime setting:

> The school was visited by the representatives of the war council of the Heroes' Square Local Community. They turned our attention to the seriousness and our responsibility due to the increase of attacks from the aggressor on the city of Sarajevo and, due to possible revenge because of the offensive of the RBiH Army. They could not help concretely, they claim that the situation is extremely complex, and that it is risky that a great number of students are in the school at the same time (elementary and our school, since we share the same building). (*Školski ljetopis*)

Such concerns become a regular feature of the entries in the *School Annual* during the 1994–1995 academic year. While these concerns were due to the location of the school on Heroes' Square in the shadow of Grbavica and Hrasno hill, the Bosnian Army offensive around the Bihać enclave to the northwest, followed by the assault on Bosnian Serb positions on Mount Igman, also prompted "the increase of attacks from the aggressor." Snipers from Grbavica were particularly active during this time and the 9 November entry that describes the textbook situation, cited above, makes a brief reference to the students of the second shift who were sent home because of "snipers and heavy detonations." On the next day, the 10 November entry, also cited in the previous section, noted that students on the second shift were moved down to the ground floor for protection during the shooting and then sent home for their own safety. On 11 November, another meeting was held to address safety concerns:

> A meeting was held of the directors of Hrasno Elementary School, Treća Gimnazija, and the commander of the civil defense of the local communities of Heroes' Square, Ivan Krndelj, and Staro Hrasno. At that meeting, it was agreed that lessons will continue to be held. There are no indicators that would result in lessons to be stopped. The weather is rather warm for this time of the year and it would be a shame not to work. If the heating problem of the school isn't solved with the coming of colder days, the lessons will have to be stopped. (*Školski ljetopis*)

The 11 November entry points to two important concerns for Treća Gimnazija, in addition to instruction, the physical safety of the students who attended the school and the basic welfare of these students attending classes in school buildings without the basic necessities: running water, sanitary facilities, electricity, and, as a result, heat for the winter months. Against the backdrop of shelling and firefights that were increasing in intensity, the immediate question concerned the operation of school during the relatively warm fall weather in order to accumulate school days prior to the cold of the forthcoming winter. The 14 November entry reflects this very dilemma:

> Sarajevo is shelled again today. The tramway was hit by mortars and because of that the trams are not working. School is on and we are trying to gain as many working days as possible. The weather is sunny and warm. Too nice for this time of year. (*Školski ljetopis*)

Three days later, on 17 November, the city was shelled again by Bosnian Serb forces firing 82-millimeter, wire-guided missiles at the Presidency building on Maršala Tita Street in the very heart of the city. The entry in the *School Annual* cites another state of general danger and the cancellation of classes over concerns for student safety:

> Sarajevo is shelled again. Before noon, three shells hit the building of the Presidency of RBiH, and one shell went astray in the office of U.S. Ambassador to RBiH, Mr. Victor Jackovich. General danger has been declared in the city. The afternoon was peaceful and we had regular classes. Thanks to that we are gaining working days and doing everything in order for the school year to appear as the real thing.
>
> A chetnik offensive continues on Bihać and Cazinska Krajina, and the chetniks around Sarajevo shell the city on a daily basis. In the afternoon general danger was declared again. Because of that we stopped work on the second shift.
>
> Faruk Isaković, Secretary of the Secretariat for Education, Science, Culture and Physical Culture, informed the school that all schools in Sarajevo will stop work until 28 November 1994. The city is exposed to constant shelling and sniper fire, and students are not to gather together. . . . Today the commander for civil defense of the Heroes' Square Local Community delivered guidance for procedures during attacks. In the guidelines there is a note to the person working on the work plan for Treća Gimnazija in regard to its updating and functioning. (*Školski ljetopis*)

By 28 November, regular classes began once again, which marked the twelfth working week for the 1994–1995 school year. "Taking into account the safety and health of the students," read the 12 December entry, Treća Gimnazija decided to continue with classes through 16 December and include fourteen weeks of school prior to the winter break. The intent was to have a first semester of fifteen weeks with the last week of the semester beginning with the resumption of classes after the break on 15 February. The second semester would then follow and continue into the warmer weather of the spring and summer months. In fact, after a break of almost nine weeks for the cold winter weather, classes for the last week of the first semester began again on 20 February with the following entry:

> The fifteenth working week started, regular classes for Treća Gimnazija students. There isn't an official order for this but there is a recommendation for work to begin. It is cold in the school, there is no heating, but these days of armistice are used to do as much work as possible. The aggressor violates the armistice daily but to a smaller extent (*Školski ljetopis*).

The dilemma of schooling in a wartime winter is reflected in the 20 February entry once again, but this time there is the opportunity "to do as much work as possible" even during the cold because a cease-fire agreement, referred to here as an armistice, was now in effect. The cease-fire, brokered by former American President Jimmy Carter, was announced on 21 December, designed to go into effect on 23 December, and extend for a four-month period during which time peace negotiations would begin between the warring parties. On 22 December, two mortar rounds tore into the flea market across from the market area known as the Markale, killing two people and wounding seven. The next day, 23 December, representatives of the Republika Bosna, the Bosnian Republic, and the Republika Srpska, the Serbian Republic, signed the cease-fire agreement to go into effect at noon, 24 December, for an initial period of seven days until the end of December, and then extend another four months. The agreement would thus end on 1 May 1995 unless renewed (Cohen, 1994).

In the very first issue of the new year, dated 2 January 1995, at the onset of the cease-fire agreement designed to halt the killing, the "Bulletin" of the Institute of Public Health/Committee for Health and Social Welfare, began by wishing everyone "Seasons Greetings" and a "Happy New Year." It then proceeded to chart the chronology of casualties from 1992 through 1994 and provided casualty figures after one thousand days of the siege. The death toll throughout Bosnia was recorded as 144,235 and in Sarajevo as 10,068. The wounded toll in Sarajevo alone was recorded as 58,741 with 19,116 recorded as severely wounded (Smajkić, 1995).

There is no particular reference to the new year in the *School Annual* of Treća Gimnazija, but the 26 December entry that noted the new fourth-year history textbook also noted the beginning of preparations to mark one thousand days of the siege. Amidst the cold winter months of the winter break and the purgatory of the cease-fire agreement, and as a follow-up to the 26 December 1994 entry, the *School Annual* records the following entry for 26 January 1995 concerning the commemoration of this event:

> Mayors of many cities of Europe and the World have arrived in the city to mark with their presence—the sad 1,000 days of resistance to the siege of Sarajevo. They will be in the city from 26 to 29 January 1995. (*Školski ljetopis*)

Like the textbooks, the mayors of Europe and the world arrived in the city through the tunnel passage since the airport and the Blue Route were still closed. Once inside the siege lines, they were greeted with a petition signed by 179,700 citizens calling for Sarajevo to remain an undivided city (Cohen, 1995). Zlatko Dizdarević could never have envisioned, when writing his essay of 13 July 1992, entitled "One Hundred Days of Solitude," that he would write another essay nine hundred days later entitled, "One Thousand Days of Solitude," to mark the occasion. In his later essay, Dizdarević writes something about the loss of hope after one thousand days under siege and the feeling that Sarajevo had been abandoned to its fate by the international community:

> It is cold in Sarajevo, and people are hungry again. During the summer, after two months of having a road open to the outside world, we had the feeling that things might turn around. Then, at least, there was some hope; now all hope has been buried. We hear people say, "Sarajevo is abandoned, left alone." It's remarkable how people who say such things really don't have a clue. The world—at least that part that makes decisions—was never with Sarajevo or Bosnia to begin with. To say we've been abandoned now only adds insult to injury. Come Jan. 1, Sarajevo will have been under siege for 1,000 days—1,000 days of solitude. How can anyone say that it is only now that we've been abandoned? (1994:33)

Amidst one thousand days of solitude, Treća Gimnazija continued with the business of schooling. Amidst a cease-fire agreement that was falling apart as well, the entries in the *School Annual* continue to document the security situation in the area around Heroes' Square as well as around

Sarajevo city. Several of these entries were previously noted in the first chapter in the context of the discussion of my very first visit to Sarajevo during March 1995, and similar entries continue through the remainder of the year. Interspersed with these references are several entries that refer to the politics and the patriotism that shaped the birth of the new republic during its struggle for survival. Thus, on 1 March 1995, the entry reads:

> It is the first time that 1 March was celebrated as the Independence Day of RBiH, in a correct manner also. That is the greatest holiday in the history of the people of Bosnia and Herzegovina. On that day in 1992, the people of RBiH declared at the referendum for a whole, sovereign and independent Bosnia and Herzegovina. The representatives of the school were guests at the central ceremony that was held at the Hrasno Elementary School, where Treća Gimnazija is situated in a part of the building. All the official representatives of Novo Sarajevo municipality, the Army, the Heroes' Square Local Community, the schools, and the Pedagogical Institute were invited to attend. (*Školski ljetopis*)

The 1 March reference to "the greatest holiday in the history of the people of Bosnia and Herzegovina" refers to the 1 March 1992 referendum in which the majority of voters in Bosnia except most of the Bosnian Serbs voted for independence from Yugoslavia. It was just over a month later, on 6 April 1992, when the European Community recognized Bosnia's independence, that Suada Dilberović became the first casualty of the siege of Sarajevo while walking across the Vrbanja Bridge. By this time, at least 1,300 people had already been killed throughout the hinterlands (Donia and Fine, 1994).

Although the cease-fire agreement negotiated by former President Carter was still in effect until 1 May, the attacks on the city began to intensify during early March, and the security situation continued to present an issue for the school. To repeat here the 12 March entry cited in the first chapter of the book:

> So the armistice is still on in Sarajevo. The snipers still fire and have killed more people. Near the school one child was shot to death, and on Darovalaca Krvi Street, the mother of our student, Naida Podić, II/1, was shot to death. At the very end of the session of the Teachers' Council, a state of general danger was declared in Sarajevo. The night before that Stari Grad was shelled. (*Školski ljetopis*)

The newspaper account in *Oslobođenje* read, "Bloody Weekend in Sarajevo: Snipers Again Sow Death," and noted the killing of at least four people. Sarajevo was shelled by 82- and 120-millimeter mortars as well killing another five people and wounding another two (1995). The airport was closed once again, the Blue Route was also closed, and a state of general danger was again in force throughout Sarajevo. The ticker tape message that ran across the television screen read, *Opasno/Opasnost u Sarajevu* (Danger/Dangerous in Sarajevo). On the very next day, Monday, 13 March, the entry in the *School Annual* read:

> In agreement with the civil defense, the local community, and the Army, regular classes were stopped until Thursday, 16 March 1995, due to the difficult situation in the city and at Heroes' Square, where the school is located (*Školski ljetopis*).

With the cease-fire falling apart, and the four-month deadline of 1 May fast approaching, the expectations were that the war would resume with an even greater intensity. With a 20 March dateline, Roger Cohen wrote that, according to UN officials, "Bosnian government forces began an offensive today, shattering a cease-fire six weeks before it was scheduled to expire." With the Bosnian Army's preemptive strike in central and northern Bosnia, the talk was now of a full-scale resumption of the war around Sarajevo as well. By firing at UN planes and effectively closing the airport, and closing the Blue Route over Mount Igman, Cohen wrote, "the Serbs have made clear that they intend to tighten their noose on the city once more" (1995:1).

At a 7 April meeting of all secondary school directors organized by the City Secretariat for Education, the 1994–1995 school year was officially shortened from a regular thirty-six-week school year to a thirty-week year, and the curriculum obligations were reduced as well. At this meeting, the official date for the start of the 1995–1996 school year was set for 1 August 1995 to take advantage of the warm summer days for classes. The 8 April entry the next day begins with a reference to a school physics competition to be followed by a city competition at the Pedagogical Academy but continues with another reference to the shelling of the city and the difficulty of working under such conditions:

> Shells started falling on Sarajevo again. In the city itself two people were killed and five wounded. Working conditions are difficult. The state of general danger is frequently on. It is extremely cold for this time of the year. Many teachers and students are sick, but we are putting in a lot of effort because we still have work to complete the third quarter. (*Školski ljetopis*)

By 14 April, workers were painting the classrooms, and the UNHCR plastic foil that covered the windows in place of the glass was being replaced. "We are happy that our working conditions will improve," stated the entry in the *School Annual*. Yet the entry for 22 April, while referring to the range of passing grades for the third quarter, also cites the teachers for their efforts to complete their school obligations under the most difficult of conditions and the effects of these conditions upon their health:

> Certain teachers have seriously damaged their health while doing this hard work in cold offices and under the fear of a declaration of general danger. Every day in Sarajevo somebody is injured or killed. The humanitarian situation is difficult, the city is closed, the airport doesn't work, and food cannot enter the city. It is almost the end of April, and there are still no November salaries. (*Školski ljetopis*)

The entry for 25 April indicates the "work on the school has been completed today and everything is nice and smells beautiful." By 27 April, however, the tone of the entries becomes serious once again:

> With the decision of the Ministry of Education, Science, Culture, and Physical Culture [of the Republic located] in Sarajevo, instruction is being stopped in all elementary and secondary schools until 8 May 1995 due to an extremely complex security situation. On 30 April, the four-month long armistice and the halt of all hostilities is coming to an end. Sarajevo is being shelled and the state of general danger is very frequently in force. (*Školski ljetopis*)

This entry notes the official end of the four-month, cease-fire agreement negotiated by former President Carter, although Sarajevo was, in fact, being shelled on a regular basis from mid-March onward. The expectations in Sarajevo as well as on the diplomatic front were that all hell would soon break loose around the city. With the end of the cease-fire just two days away, the 28 April headline in *USA Today* read, "'Full-scale' war around the corner in Bosnia," citing UN spokesman, Alexander Ivanko, who stated, "We can assess the pattern as basically a slippage toward full-scale war" (Squitieri, 1995:10A).

Many of the entries in the *School Annual* during May and June refer to the renewal of the fighting and its impact on schooling in the city. The 6 May entry, for example, refers to the closing of the airport once again along with the closing of the Blue Route over the mountains and into the city. On 7 May, five 82-millimeter mortar shells hit the entrance to the tunnel in Butmir killing eleven people and wounding at least forty

(Cohen, 1995). On 8 May, when school was supposed to reopen, the entry reads that "regular instruction has not continued today and has been stopped until further notice, until safe working conditions are reached." By 17 May, the headline in the *New York Times* read, "Bitter Fighting Rages Around Sarajevo," while the article stated that "shelling of front lines and Sarajevo's outskirts this morning escalated into a major battle between Government and Serbian troops" (1995:4). On 25 May, the entry refers to another massacre of students, this time in Tuzla, where two shells landed precisely at 7:20 P.M. at an outdoor café where teenagers gathered killing 71 and wounding 140, while in Sarajevo, another five people were killed and another 31 wounded. On the same day, NATO aircraft began bombing Serb positions around Pale, the capital of the Republika Srpska, just up the road from Sarajevo.

On 26 May, representatives of the Ministry of Education, the Pedagogical Institute, the City Secretariat for Education, and all elementary and secondary school directors met to discuss the security situation. Reports were presented on safety preparations for students, teachers, and documents, the direction of work as regular classes were interrupted under "the new difficult conditions," and the reduction of the school curriculum as an instructional adaptation to these conditions. The discussion of the business of this meeting comprises the first half of the entry in the *School Annual*. The second half of the entry, written by Emina Avdagić, reads as follows:

> TODAY THE CITY IS WITHOUT ELECTRICITY, WATER, GAS, BREAD (the Velepekara is unable to work) AND NO FOOD ENTERS THE CITY. These days every citizen received ½ kilogram of macaroni, 300 grams of dried peas and 0.33 liters of oil. That is what we received in the tenth round of humanitarian aid and this should feed one citizen for the next 15 days or more. That is absurd and I do not know whether anyone will know how the citizens of Sarajevo have suffered. The chetniks are firing at other cities, they threaten, they took away all the heavy artillery from UNPROFOR, they took members of the international peacekeeping forces as hostages (over 300 of them), and the situation in the city and the country is difficult. A few days ago we celebrated three years of recognition and acceptance of RBiH as a member of the UN. (*Školski ljetopis*)

The reference to the taking of heavy artillery from UNPROFOR is to the Serb raid on nine UN-monitored weapons collection sites around Sarajevo where they seized at least 250 heavy weapons. The reference to hostages is to the taking of at least 325 UNPROFOR soldiers or "peacekeepers" to be held at "potential air strike targets," to cite the words of Lieutenant Colonel Milovan Milutinović, a Bosnian Serb officer (Cohen, 1995). On 2 June, Roger Cohen wrote, in reiteration of the entry by Emina Avdagić in the *School Annual*, that "the situation became more critical for the almost 300,000 people in Sarajevo, with water and electricity cut, bakeries running out of flour, and the main streets deserted because of intermittent sniping. The Bosnian Serbs' noose around the city tightened to the point where no international aid is getting in" (1995:1). In fact, aid flights had been unable to land for over two months, while the airport had been closed to all flights for over a week.

The entry of 5–15 June notes that instruction has sometimes been broken down into smaller groups, and that the lectures for both larger and smaller groups are underway, dependent upon the security situation. By mid-June, Bosnian Army forces were massing on several fronts to break the siege. On 16 June, the *School Annual* records the beginning of the Bosnian Army offensive to break the siege "for the de-blockade" of Sarajevo.

> At 4:00 this morning, intense battles began for the de-blockade of Sarajevo. You could hear detonations from Ilijaš, Vogošća, Igman. There are many members of the Army and the Croatian Defense Council around Sarajevo. All movements are limited for the security of the citizens. They are saying that the chetniks are losing and that they might shell Sarajevo. The curfew is in force from 9:00 P.M. to 6:00 in the morning in the whole Republic. The school is without students. Today is the 1,143rd day of the siege of Sarajevo by the chetniks. (*Školski ljetopis*)

While fighting raged in the northern suburbs of Ilijaš and Vogošća, and on the slopes of Mount Igman to the southwest, the Bosnian Serb response was to shell the city itself which, along with the snipers, killed at least eleven people that day. With relatively minor gains, but with heavy casualties, the offensive stalled and, in Dobrinja, another seven civilians were killed and ten others were wounded while standing in line for water. On 21 June, another entry in the *School Annual* refers to the intensity of the fighting as the school year comes to a close:

> Today is the first summer day of the fourth war school year. Detonations can be heard throughout the city and the state of general danger is in force all the time. The soldiers of the RBiH Army have had great success on the Igman–Trnovo battlefield and Semizovac. The students come to school individually and have exams and often teachers go to

the students' homes. The school year is slowly being brought to an end. (*Školski ljetopis*)

The hopelessness of the *Sarajlije* upon the failure of the army to break the siege is reflected by Roger Cohen in a special report to the *New York Times* entitled, "Where Hope Has Withered." Under a headline that reads, "As Lull in the War Ends, Sarajevo is Shellshocked," Cohen wrote:

> Always, the stomach contracts. When, through the still air, there comes the flat boom of rending and fracture that is the sound of another shell's impact, indifference can only be feigned. Even the war-hardened of this city feel the familiar knife in the gut. . . .
> The hope that accompanied a brief lull last year, when streetcars ran and water actually flowed from taps and that deafening sound of destruction did not reverberate in the valley, has also disappeared. All that is left today is a shattered people confronted by the renewed slide of Sarajevo into the abyss. (1995:1)

On 28 June, another eight people were killed and at least thirty-eight wounded in the shelling of the city when rockets tore into an apartment building and the television center.

The July entries primarily concern the final examinations at the end of the school year and include an explanation of the senior examinations and the performance of the graduating seniors. Some forty-eight students passed their examinations, while one senior student did not take the exam leaving at the end of the year for Australia. This senior class was comprised of those students who began their first year of secondary school with the 1991–1992 school year, completed their four years of secondary school during the war school years, and graduated at the end of the 1994–1994 school year, the fourth war school year. These students were referred to as the *ratna generacija* (war generation) of Treća Gimnazija.

Amidst the frenetic pace of exams and the coming and going of students during the state of general danger, the 8 July entry records yet another student casualty in bold capital letters:

> TODAY IN FRONT OF HIS BUILDING OUR STUDENT ELVEDIN (NEZIR) HASANBEGOVIĆ WAS KILLED AT 18 YEARS OF AGE.
> A day earlier, at the session of the section council, his performance was established—the third class (III/2) year completed with a very good performance. (*Školski ljetopis*)

While playing soccer with friends in front of his apartment building, El-vedin Hasanbegović was killed by shrapnel that tore through his body as he was attempting to escape from the shelling through a gate near his building. A student such as Vanja Vuk could get killed inside her own home in the shelling of her apartment building, or a student such as El-vedin Hasanbegović could get killed outside his own home in the shelling outside his apartment building. Or students and teachers could get killed by "the snipers, that was everyday," on their way to or from school, where "you have the feeling of being watched—And then he chooses. In a second you can hear his decision" (Dmitrović, 1996).

To conclude the 1994–1995 war school year, a war school prom (*ratno matursko veče*) was held on the night of 12 August at the HRS Club located near the intersection of Maršala Tita and Kranjčevićeva streets just down from the Presidency building. The Red Rose band played to the sixty or so students and the five or six teachers crammed into the little club where they danced the siege away perspiring in the madness until the early hours of the morning. They were sent on their way sometime around 3:00 A.M. to ensure they arrived home safely by avoiding the snipers who would have a clear view of the city with the sunrise. The girls wore high-heel shoes for one of the few times during the siege and, as they left the club, they took off their shoes and walked home in their stocking feet on the sidewalk pavement (Avdagić, 2000).

One of the concluding entries for the 1994–1995 school year is dated 28 August 1995 and records yet another marketplace massacre on the sidewalks of Sarajevo. It was the bloody scene of this massacre on television that finally galvanized the international community into action that came to fruition with the intensified NATO bombing of Bosnian Serb targets and created the conditions for the negotiations at Dayton. The entry in the *School Annual* records the massacre in the following manner that reflects something of the pathos of the time:

> Today in Sarajevo a new massacre happened in front of the Markale [the open-air market]. At 11:15 A.M., a 120-mm shell was fired and killed 35 civilians and wounded 90. That is one of the blackest days in Sarajevo. The same day ten more shells were fired and at 6:00 P.M. one was fired at Koševo Hospital where three patients were wounded. Everything is so sad and disgusting, and the world is silent or is afraid to react. (*Školski ljetopis*)

The Fourth War School Year, 1995–1996:
48th Student Generation of Treća Gimnazija

It is the start of the fourth war school year. All the work is still being done in very difficult conditions, in the building of the Hrasno Elementary School, Porodice Ribar No. 2 [formerly Braće Ribar]. We started the school year with painted classrooms, painted windows and doors, but we still have foil instead of window glass. Like in many schools in Sarajevo, the heating problem has not been solved. That might cause the regular lectures to stop in the winter months. The employees have not had their annual leave this year either. The reason for that is that the 1994/95 school year ended in July, and in August enrollment into the first class and all other classes started. In accordance with the plan of enrollment, we took four first-year class sections, and for the first time, two general gimnazija sections, and two sections of the natural sciences-mathematics gimnazija. The school enrolled a sufficient number of students, regardless of the opening of the Bosniac Gymnasium and the Catholic School Center. The work will start with 14 class sections (4 first class, 3 second class, 4 third class, and 3 fourth class). Emina Avdagić, the school director, welcomed all first class students and visited all the others, wished them better days, and organized for textbooks to be distributed as well as notebooks and pens. (*Školski ljetopis*)

Following the introduction, the first entry, dated 1 September, for the 1995–1996 school year in the *School Annual* of Treća Gimnazija reads simply: "THE SCHOOL STARTED WITH WORK!" The time is September 1995, and "it is the start of the fourth war school year" since the beginning of the siege in April 1992. For Treća Gimnazija, the new school year would be the second year of schooling in the annex building of Hrasno Elementary School, which rests below the apartment buildings on Heroes' Square in one of the most dangerous areas of the city. After the intensity of the war during the spring and summer months of 1995, however, that saw its climax with the 28 August marketplace massacre, the NATO air campaign that followed created a reprieve in the mindless assault on Sarajevo and some breathing room for its inhabitants. Within just over a month, by 12 October, offensive actions came to a halt, and by 17 October, the fighting finally stopped across most of the country (Dizdar, 1996). Within but a short time, peace negotiations to end the Bosnian war would begin in Dayton, Ohio.

The registration period for enrollment of new students into the first class of secondary school for the 1995–1996 school year was the subject of a 2 August meeting at the City Secretariat for Education. Dates for

Table 5.2. Treća Gimnazija: Class Sections and Students, 1995–1996 School Year

Class	Class Sections	Students
Class I	4	92
Class II	3	83
Class III	4	90
Class IV	3	76
Total	14	341

Source: *Školski ljetopis.*

enrollment in the first term were set for 8–18 August, while the dates for the second-term enrollment were from 18 August until 1 September. Thus the 8 August entry in the *School Annual* read, "The enrollment into the first class of the 1995/96 school year has started and will be on every day until 18 August 1995 except for Sunday." Enrollments were down in many schools, however, since "there are fewer and fewer students in the city. They are leaving the city in many ways. It is known that there are 1,000 fewer candidates for enrollment into the secondary schools and everybody is concerned" (*Školski ljetopis*). During the madness of the summer months that culminated in the 28 August marketplace massacre, it is a wonder that anyone even went outside to register for school during the August registration period. For the 1995–1996 school year, student enrollment at Treća Gimnazija had dropped by seventy-one students just below the numbers for the 1993–1994 school year. However, the first-year class of Treća Gimnazija had a "sufficient" enrollment and the numbers for all four classes had begun to even out as had the number of class sections. The numbers of class sections and students for the 1995–1996 school year appear in table 5.2 above.

The opening paragraphs that mark the first entries for the 1995–1996 school year in the *School Annual* contain references to several developments of particular note in regard to schools, programs, and student enrollment. On the one hand, the enrollment of students is cited with specific reference to the opening of two other private schools in Sarajevo, both of which were classified as gimnazija: the Bosniac Gymnasium, today the First Bosniac Gymnasium, Prva Bošnjačka gimnazija, and the Catholic School Center, or as it is referred to today, the Catholic School Center (Gymnasium), Katolički školski centar (Gimnazija). In other words, two private gimnazija designed to prepare students for the university, and organized on the basis of religious affiliation, opened up during the fourth year of the war. The Bosniac Gymnasium was opened specifically for Bosnian Muslim students who wanted an academic preparatory school with a religious character. Indeed, the designation of "Bosniacs" (Bošnjaci) for Bosnian Muslims marked their identification as a people analogous to but distinct from Serbs who were Eastern Orthodox, or Croats who were Roman Catholic, each of whom were identified with their own homeland. Thus Bosniacs referred to Muslims whose homeland was to be Bosnia itself. These two private gimnazija were created during the war in addition to the public Gimnazija Dobrinja, which served the Dobrinja settlement, and the reorganization of Peta (Fifth) gimnazija. With the increasing number of gimnazija in a city where student numbers had significantly decreased, the fears of Emina Avdagić that Treća Gimnazija "will be left without its students, because the students will enroll in the gimnazija of other muncipalities," were not unfounded (*Školski ljetopis*). Since her letter of 1 April 1994, Treća Gimnazija had moved into the elementary school and operated from a position of greater stability, but now had increased competition for gimnazija students in a city with fewer students whose movements were restricted by the siege. The entry in the *School Annual* indicates student enrollment under these conditions is still a major concern.

The other item of note refers to the general gimnazija and natural sciences–mathematics gimnazija class sections. As early as 6 December 1994, Treća Gimnazija had indicated an interest in expanding its traditional curriculum "since we as a school are interested in educating certain sections in accordance with such programs." The specific reference concerns the development of a curriculum for what was referred to as the natural sciences–mathematics gimnazija (*prirodno–matematička gimnazija*) in order to accommodate gimnazija students who were interested in a natural sciences or mathematics specialization in preparation for the university. In fact, there were five different curricular models for the gimnazija: (1) the *opća* (general) *gimnazija*; (2) the *filološka gimnazija* (philology or languages); (3) *priorodno–matematička gimnazija*; (4) *matematičko–informatička gimnazija* (mathematics–information science); and (5) *sportska* (sports) *gimnazija*. The school curriculum of Treća Gimnazija had traditionally been organized on the general gimnazija curricular model, which involved instruction in all major subject areas, as did the other types of curricular organization. The difference between the natural sciences–mathematics curriculum and the general gimnazija curriculum was not in the subject areas themselves but in the instructional hours devoted to those subjects across all four secondary classes (Pedagoški zavod, 1994; 1995). It was clear that an expansion of the Treća Gimnazija curriculum from the general gimnazija to also in-

clude the natural sciences–mathematics gimnazija was an attempt to expand course offerings for students and thereby attract more students to
the school. Thus the school wrote the 6 December letter to the Pedagogical Institute under the City Secretariat for Education, which was responsible for curriculum organization in Sarajevo schools.

On 6 January 1995, Treća Gimnazija, in conjunction with the Pedagogical Institute, had come to terms with the new curricular organization.
The entry for that day reads:

> A meeting with the director of the Pedagogical Institute of the Ministry
> of RBiH was held. On behalf of the school, Emina Avdagić, school di-
> rector, Mirko Marinović, deputy director, and Azemina Osmanagić,
> secretary, attended this meeting. It was agreed that the school will have
> permission for a couple of class sections of the natural sciences and
> mathematics gimnazija enroll for the 1995/96 school year. In regard to
> that, the creation of programs and norms will start immediately. In such
> creation the teachers of Treća Gimnazija will participate as well, under
> the management of the advisors of the Pedagogical Institute of the
> Ministry (chemistry–Professor Biserka Miošić, biology–Professor
> Avdo Hajdo, physics–Professor Mersa Šalaka, and mathematics–Pro-
> fessor Emina Avdagić). (*Skolski ljetopis*)

Four months later, there is another entry for 4 May 1995 that refers to the
reorganization of the school curriculum and the implications for the enrollment of students in Treća Gimnazija:

> The City Secretariat for Education, Science, Culture and Physical Cul-
> ture organized a meeting of all secondary school directors in Sarajevo
> (28). At the meeting the issue of enrollment of students into the first
> year of secondary schools in the 1995/96 school year was discussed.
> All the gimnazija in Sarajevo (First, Second, Third, Fourth, Dobrinja,
> and Fifth), plan to enroll four class sections (4 x 30 = 120), and most
> probably the Catholic Gymnasium, which started work this school year.
> It is planned for a Bosniac Gymnasium to be opened and to start work
> in the 1995/96 school year. There are too many gimnazija in one Sara-
> jevo, more than before the war, and the number of children in the city is
> lower. Treća Gimnazija will try to admit one class section of the
> mathematics gimnazija. All preparations have been completed in regard
> to the created curriculum and standards into the current one with the
> Pedagogical Institute of the RBiH Ministry. If the city (district) ap-
> proves it for the 1995/96 school year that would mean a lot in the
> struggle of our gimnazija for survival among so many gimnazija. (*Škol-
> ski ljetopis*)

The 2 August 1995 entry noted the enrollment period of 8–18 August for first-year students and that, "in accordance with the plan of enrollment, Treća Gimnazija can enroll four first-year class sections out of which are two general (60 students) and two mathematics (60 students)." By the end of the enrollment period on 18 August, "Fifty-one students enrolled into the general major, and 24 enrolled into the mathematics major. Due to that, enrollment is extended until 1 September 1995." To repeat a portion of the very first entry in the *School Annual* for September of the 1995–1996 school year, "In accordance with the plan of enrollment, we took four first-year class sections, and for the first time, two general gimnazija sections and two sections of the natural sciences–mathematics gimnazija. The school enrolled a sufficient number of students," regardless of the fact that two new private gimnazija that had been created.

Although September was the beginning of the fourth war school year, it was, in a sense, an anticlimax in terms of the war itself. The NATO bombing that began after the 28 August marketplace massacre set "the aggressors," as the *Saralije* would say, back on their heels and forced them to move their heavy weapons twenty kilometers back from the hills around the city by mid-September. Although fighting would rage to the northwest of Sarajevo, and while there were incidents during the early fall months, the intense shelling of the spring and summer had been effectively terminated. In fact, there are no entries in the *School Annual* that directly refer to the siege until 5 October when, after a reference to a regular meeting at the City Secretariat for Education, the entry reads, "It was stated that the school year began somewhat 'normally.' There is no shelling but the schools are without heat, electricity, and lacking in staff (foreign languages, mathematics, history)." With the cessation of the assault on the city, the people and the schools were nevertheless left with all the problems for which the siege had been responsible, some of which are noted in the pages of the *School Annual*. One month later, there is an entry on 1 November that reads:

> Salary was handed out to all employees. An average salary is 8000 dinars (80 DM) for the month of September. Lists of all employees were delivered to the Finance Department of the Ministry of Education, Science, Culture and Physical Culture for distribution of food for the winter (30 kilograms of onions, 10 kilograms of cabbage, etc.). The days are nice and warm and that enables us to work well since there is no heat in the school. It is peaceful in the city. The armistice is being respected. In America, in the state of Ohio, discussions started about the countries created with the fall of the SFRJ [Socialist Federal Republic of Yugoslavia]. This could be the last chance for ending the war. The

Presidents of RBiH, the Republic of Croatia and Serbia and Montenegro (with delegations) will attend the negotiations. (*Školski ljetopis*)

Several entries follow that, for the first time in several years during the
months of the fall, refer not to the shelling and the snipers, but to acquisition of the basic necessities for the teachers. Several of the November
entries, for example, read:

> *4 November:* Food for the winter has been distributed to all the em-
> ployees (30 kg of potatoes, 10 kg of cabbage, 1 kg of honey, 1 kg of
> jam, 1 kg of pickles, 1 kg of nuts).
> *5 November:* All employees received a warm meal allowance for July,
> August, September, and October (1,500 + 1,500 + 2,500 + 2,500 di-
> nars).
> *10 November:* All employees received a warm meal allowance for Feb-
> ruary 1995 (2,100 dinars).
> *18-23 November:* We are working in extremely difficult conditions. It
> is cold (below 0) and the school does not have a solution for heating.
> (*Školski ljetopis*)

Amidst the regular entries in the *School Annual* for the month of December were entries concerning the political situation:

> *14 December:* Peace was signed today in Paris. Mr. Alija Izetbegović,
> Franjo Tudjman, and Slobodan Milošević were present at the peace
> signing. The final words were given by the President of the USA
> Clinton.
> *20 December:* UN forces handed everything to IFOR [Implementation
> Force] today. The mandate of the UN forces ended today and every-
> thing is taken over by NATO. It is peaceful in the city, there is no great
> astonishment, but there is some humble hope for a better tomorrow.
> (*Školski ljetopis*)

The peace negotiations that began on 1 November in Dayton, Ohio, resulted in the signing of the peace agreement in Paris, but for Treća Gimnazija, the entries through the remainder of the winter continually refer to
the cold, the lack of heat, and the severely damaged heating system
eventually fixed with assistance from the Swedish Embassy. The final
casualty of the war for Treća Gimnazija occurred on 8 January, when
Mensur Zahiragić, fifteen years old, a second-year student, fell to his
death down an elevator shaft damaged by shelling from the twelfth floor
of his apartment building on Ivana Krndelja Street, just around the corner
from the school.

Irretrievably Lost Years

I first saw the epitaph in March 1995 upon our return from Pale with the UNICEF Program Officer. We had just traveled from Pale down Mount Trebević and back around the airport runway and through checkpoints into Dobrinja and the siege. We were racing down Sniper Alley when Ryan slammed on the brakes and pulled over to show us the epitaph on the wall in Hrasno, which read, "Welcome to hell!" Just over a year later, in May 1996, I walked by the building again on a visit to Treća Gimnazija located in the Hrasno Elementary School building on Heroes' Square. The names of the streets had changed, but the epitaph was still there to remind us of the siege of the city. I was with Safija Rašidović, of what was then the City Secretariat for Education, and I would have missed the story of Treća Gimnazija had she not hustled me on a bus to Hrasno for a visit to the school in what was once the fires of hell.

The Dayton Peace Agreement had been signed, the shelling and the shooting had stopped, and the siege of the city had been lifted. You could walk along the Miljacka River today on what was now Wilson Promenade to the old Treća Gimnazija school buildings just across from Grbavica. The second semester of the 1995–1996 school year had begun on 5 February 1996, and the routine of school would continue during peacetime. The entry that day noted it was extremely cold, and the boiler room was not working. Between 12–15 February, workers in the boiler room were "putting in impossible efforts to repair the heating network—severely damaged during the war." Emina Avdagić managed to get the Swedish Embassy to give 300 DM to the workers for their efforts in repairing the heating system. By 15 February, the entry read:

> All classrooms and hallways are warm. The heating has started. In the last couple of days glass was placed in all the windows. Due to that the working conditions increasingly improved. Now it is warm, bright, and comfortable. (*Školski ljetopis*)

Dated 20–29 February 1996, the last entry of the month noted that the school was receiving new students, many of whom were refugees, and offered the following commentary:

> The city is opening up and refugees and displaced persons are coming in (from Žepa, Srebrenica, Vlasenica, Hadžići, etc.). They all bring with them a sad story. We try to receive them and help them, even though our working conditions are difficult. As of 1 February 1996, Professor Ekrem Baraković, history (teaching half a norm) and Osman

Tabaković, janitor, who were in the Army of RBiH, returned to the school. (*Školski ljetopis*)

The March entries were very much routine noting visitations, meetings, competitions, and that, from 22–26 March, "the radiators were being fixed and the valves were changed." The 31 March entry referred again to these new students as follows:

> The school received around 30 new students in the last month. All the new students brought with them very difficult life stories. For them these war years were harder than could be imagined. (*Školski ljetopis*)

I first heard about these new students from places like Žepa and Srebrenica during my visit to the school in May 1996 when I first began the process of interviewing the teachers. Emina Avdagić had indicated to me that new students were now registering for school from all over the country and that a number of these students were Serbian kids who attended the school during the prewar era. What I do remember is the realization that all of these students had stories to tell. I remember sitting in the office of Safija Rašidović at the City Secretariat for Education and hearing the story of one young refugee girl who had witnessed firsthand as her father's throat was sliced open in front of her during the fall of Srebrenica. One year later, she had come with an uncle to register for elementary school in Vogošća where many of the refugees from Srebrenica were resettled. All of these new students had stories to tell, and these stories serve to both continue and enhance the story of Treća Gimnazija as a school under the gun during the siege. In this regard, the 31 March entry continues in the following manner:

> One of them [new students] is Jasmin Kulovac who is attending first-year classes at 18 years of age. "I want to go to the gimnazija. I want a quality education. I will catch up with everything in life," he says. (*Školski ljetopis*)

Entitled "Life after Žepa," the story of Jasmin Kulovac appeared in *Oslobođenje* that very same day and concludes the March entries in the *School Annual*. I will offer Jasmin's story here as both a continuation and conclusion of the story of the students and teachers of Treća Gimnazija of which Jasmin became a part late during the fourth war school year. Jasmin's story would, of course, stand on its own, but as one of those new students who brought with him a "very difficult life story," these war years were indeed "harder than could be imagined." In one sense,

Jasmin's story, the idea of "irretrievably lost years," becomes the story of all young adolescents who lost the most precious years of their lives during the Bosnian war and, in particular, during the siege of Sarajevo. I offer it here as the story of one new student from the besieged eastern enclave of Žepa who became part of the unfolding story of the teachers and students of Treća Gimnazija in the aftermath of the siege:

Life after Žepa:
Irretrievably Lost Years

An eighteen-year old from Žepa, prisoner at a camp in Rogatica, says that because of everything he lived through he will never return to his hometown.

Jasmin Kulovac is eighteen years old and has just entered into the first year of the gimnazija. The Sarajevo Third. In Žepa where he was born, all schools for him have been violently closed. They almost closed his eyes.

At the start of the war, Jasmin was still a child, confused by all that was happening, petrified by all the shelling and attacks on the town. Surrounded and lacking in food, forced him to start working to feed his family: father, mother, brother and sister. He received a UNHCR card, which will later after his capturing and being shot at by the firing squad, save his life. At the beginning of 1994 he completed his military training, and in 1995 when the heavy fighting began in the town in which he was born, he joined the units of the Bosnian Army. He says how he was dying of fear but was ashamed to run away, to leave his comrades. He hadn't run away, even at the point when they asked Sarajevo for help but in vain; even when the fall of Žepa was certain.

Death by Firing Squad

"I was handcuffed to Azmir Sulejmanović, a boy of my age when they took us out to the firing squad in Višegrad. I didn't think of anything. I was waiting for the shot. I wasn't directing my thoughts anymore. Everyone fell down and I was standing, although Azmir who was dead pulled me down to the ground. The day after I came around in a cell," Jasmin says quietly, making a stop after every sentence and remembering all what happened after the Serb forces had entered into Žepa.

Together with Jasmin Kulovac, the following were taken to be shot by the firing squad: Šemsudin Aruković and his sons Fadil and Sendin, Agonja Omerspahić and his son Belmir, Ramiz Cocalić and Hazim Sulejmanović with his son Azmir.

"I know they were all killed by Milan Lukić. No one knows why he spared me," says Jasmin.

Days of Prison

"The majority of us headed towards Serbia, thinking as they had promised, we would be accepted over there. However, my group was arrested at the border crossing near Višegrad. Many of them ended up in camps in Serbia, some were killed by the road, in the forests. . . . Everything was contrary to what was promised at the negotiations to our commander Avdo Palić. Even for him every trace of finding him is lost."

Jasmin doesn't like to talk about his days in prison in Rogatica, where he was transferred on 8 August until his release in January this year. He couldn't make contact with other prisoners. They hid him and others from Žepa from the Red Cross and other prisoners. Only by very poor light that broke through blankets on the windows he knew whether it was day or night, tortured by loneliness and despair, hunger, beatings.

"I was afraid of that isolation. I couldn't figure out why I was so important for them to hide me and not for anyone to see me. Once I got courage and asked the commander of the camp Rajko Kušić about my hiding. He said how I was supposed to be killed, since I was the only one who saw the killing of the six from Žepa, but that they decided to let me live since I was young. He also had said that this time they would release me," says Jasmin, stressing that he thinks that they were just playing with him and were waiting for a "better chance."

After six months of imprisonment, on 11 January the Red Cross registers Jasmin. His hope returned and he thought that he might not be killed so easy after all. And if they kill him, someone will know, someone will look for his number, look for his body he says. (The same words, completely irrational, I heard from many former camp inmates).

Without Return

Eight days upon registering Jasmin was released and met with his mother Hasena, brother Ramiz and sister Jasna. His father called from the United States, where he had been deported with others from Žepa held at the Serbian camp Šljivovica. He says his father called him to join him in the States, to start a life there.

"I often thought how I was young and that time had no importance; how I was to make up for everything; the school, the missed parties, socializing. When I enrolled into the first year with fifteen year olds, even with young *Sarajlije*, I realized how much I had lost. "I cannot make up for the lost time, not even in America," says Jasmin convincing me with other arguments as well as to how right the decision he had made is.

He plans to study languages, find an apartment. Six of them live in his cousin's one room apartment. He wants to earn something aside from school, to help his family. He received 50 DM from his municipality. He knows that from others he can't receive even that. With determination he says:

"No, I am never going back to Žepa. Why? Everything that I had is burnt. I don't even look back to those days, I am happy that they will not repeat. The doctor that I am seeing tells me that the images will come to my memory less and less. (Rudić, 1996:9)

I was introduced to Jasmin one day by Emina Avdagić and Avdo Hajdo during the fall of 1999 towards the end of my research while Treća Gimnazija still occupied the annex of Hrasno Elementary School. Over the next several weeks, Jasmin and I would spend time on the second floor of a small pizza place on what was once Sniper Alley just down the street from Malta Bridge. We first talked about life after Žepa, about going to school at Treća Gimnazija, and about his studies at the Faculty of Criminal Studies of the University of Sarajevo. After some time, we began to talk about those four irretrievably lost years in the eastern enclave of Žepa, just across the hills from Srebrenica, about another siege in another place at another time with somewhat less notoriety than Sarajevo. I finally asked Jasmin what he might say if he were to write his story in his own words for an American audience. Here is a fraction of the story of Jasmin Kulovac, one of the new returning students at Treća Gimnazija, who began high school in the immediate aftermath of the siege, one week after his release from captivity, written in his own words. Perhaps it might serve as a fitting ending to the story of "the heroes of Treća Gimnazija" who, in a school where there were no makeup exams, fought their own war for sanity and survival:

My name is Jasmin Kulovac. Twenty-two years ago, I was born in a little town called Žepa. That is the place where I lived and spent the dearest days of my life, my childhood. I went to elementary school there. Then . . . the year 1992 came. That year I should have started my freshman year in high school but instead of holding a pencil, in my hands I held a gun. That was the end of my innocent childhood. The war took its toll on me. At sixteen years of age, I became a grown man. I had to fight for my parents, brother, and sister. For me, a smile on a child's face was nothing but a faded memory. I knew only about the grim reality which was the explosion of shells, the buzzing of bullets, and the screams of my wounded friends. That reality replaced my high school years. I still wanted to be a kid, a teenager. Instead, I had to fight for my life.

:

Despite all of the suffering, not once did I lose hope that better days will come my way. Days in which I will hold a pencil instead of a gun. Many of my friends never lived to see those days. They are: *Rifet Omanović, Emir Torlak, Nezir Ćesko, Adil Zimić, Ahmet Ramić*. It was like yesterday that we sat and laughed in the same classrooms, and now they are gone. They left this world like legends, heroes, while not living to see their eighteenth birthdays. Unlike many kids their age in various countries all over the world, they did not live to see what it is like being a high school student. War took that away from them. They have lost their lives in combat fighting like heroes, like men. At sixteen and seventeen years of age, they fought for their mothers, fathers, brothers, and sisters. Sometimes I ask myself, "Was this our destiny?" I have survived this horrible war and even when I was captured and placed in a Serbian prison, I still had hope for better days. I was in that concentration camp from August 1995 until January 1996. I survived an onsite execution. Eight of my friends did not. When I was freed in January, I realized that a man has so much strength in him that he has to fight and have faith even if all seems lost. And that is when I decided: "I am going back to finish what I was prevented from starting in 1992, high school." I was eighteen. I turned eighteen in a concentration camp, and I still wanted to go back to school. Soon, I enrolled in Treća Gimnazija in Sarajevo. Everyone was telling me that I would not be able to handle it. Not even a week had passed after regaining freedom that I was sitting in a classroom. That is how I continued my education that was halted in 1992. I did not want to give up during the horrendous times of war, and now when the war is over, everything else looks better. I graduated from my high school with honors. I have a job, and I am also going to college majoring in Criminal Justice. . . .

I am a fighter by nature and will continue to be. I will continue to fight for a rightful return to my hometown from which I was forced to leave by the Serbian criminals. I will also contribute toward the development of my country, and I am not intending to give up. Maybe I do not have same living conditions like my friends in Sarajevo or Germany, Australia or America, but one thing is for sure: I won't give up! Because, life is a fight and if a man is not a fighter, soon life will overcome him. He will lose that fight and will become useless. I won't be a man of such fate. Even though I am only twenty-two years old, the experiences that I have can be attributed toward a much older man. War itself is a type of school, except in this school, there aren't any makeup exams. If one has failed, he has failed. I have passed that school and now everything else is easier.

—Jasmin Kulovac,
Sarajevo,
7 November 1999.

Epilogue

Pedagogical Patriotism:
The Aftermath

What can one say about teachers in wartime? We hope that history will devote both space and time to them and their efforts, because it is thanks to their merit that such a fundamental segment of the new state has been preserved and continues to thrive. None of this could have ever functioned without the teachers, who were thus in the frontline in the fight against the aggressor . . . [and] in the fight to preserve the schools and the educational system as a whole. . . . However much is written, it will never be enough, because each pupil and each teacher, each parent, represents an individual history, a drama and an inspiration. Therefore I dedicate these lines to *THE TEACHER*, the warrior and pedagogical patriot of our land.

—Hajrija-Šahza Jahić,
"The War Schools of Sarajevo"

The Most Difficult Decision Ever

"You have to live," said Avdo Hajdo to me, in explanation of why teachers did what they did during the war. Such decisions to live, such decisions to survive, were not easy decisions, however, in the midst of the degradation and the suffering. You could have easily become one of the *podrumski ljudi* (cellar people) in the words of Hajrija-Šahza Jahić, who remained in their basements while others fought the war in frontline trenches or in basement classrooms. "Anybody who wanted to could give up," said Edina Dmitrović to me with a certain defiance. "It was really exhausting for us, but something kept us going. Now when I think about it, I don't know what it was . . . Was it just an instinct for survival, for doing something, or not to surrender?" (1996).

"Conditions of extremity compel one to choose what is most important," wrote Anna Pawełczyńska (1979:140). In this regard, the decisions to survive, and to teach, and to go to school, amidst the conditions of the siege, were conscious and courageous decisions that required a certain mindset, "a certain kind of psychology that is not easy to understand" (Drakulić, 1994:14). Living in the besieged capital city of a country in a war for its very survival, within the high mountain walls that surrounded the city, within "a closed system," the *Sarajlije* developed their own inimitable mindset and their own patterns of behavior in order to survive the extremity of wartime conditions. That's how we come to the "Miss Besieged Sarajevo" competition, and "that's how we come to 'war schools,'" wrote Mujo Musagić, because these schools placed a "value on the significance of life" as a means of surviving the siege (1998).

It is clear that these war schools were an educational adaptation to the siege or, in the words of the *Oslobođenje* article, dated 10 September 1992, an adaptation of instruction to wartime conditions. In this regard, the directives set forth by the Ministry of Education during the early months of the war instructed educational administrative units at the local level "who are responsible for the security of students and teachers to insure conditions for the normal progression of instruction" in order to begin the 1992–1993 school year. Such a directive "obliges each school to work," in the words of Abdulah Jabučar, "without regard to conditions—it is necessary to adapt to conditions and organize the work of schools" (1994:5). In response, the City Secretariat for Education took approximately eleven months to implement these directives "to insure conditions," in other words, to adapt instruction for wartime conditions, in order to initiate the abbreviated eighteen-week, 1992–1993 school year, on 1 March 1993.

It was, of course, left to the local educational administration, and the teachers themselves, to adapt instruction to local conditions and to organize the work of schools. From conversations with Sarajevo educators, it appears that people simply could not believe what was happening to them and their city and, once they did comprehend the situation, they thought the madness that had descended upon them from hell and beyond would soon be over. Someone would sort through the situation, someone would come to their rescue, the idiots would come to their senses. Thus wrote Lejla Polimac, the high school student at the onset of the siege, "Something has changed but we cannot believe it. We don't want to believe. We don't want to accept the fact that war is here. My parents are confused. I never saw them looking like that. They don't know what to say, how to react, how to behave. The only thing they are saying is, 'Everything will be fine in a couple of days,' and they kept saying that for four years" (1996).

So the teachers and administrators were faced with the problem of adapting the instructional process to wartime conditions as, not simply a short-term fix for a couple of months but as a long-term adaptation over almost four years of the siege. "Is it better for students to go to school— or not to go?" asked Avdo Hajdo. "We were in a dilemma—a decision to teach or not to teach. They thought the war would be finished soon," he said in reference to those who issued the directives that required each school to work, "but it wasn't. So there was the decision to go to school" (1998). With an eye towards the future in the aftermath of the siege, Azra Belkić noted the importance of schooling to the next generation of the country. "It was important," she said, "that students didn't lose those years during the war" (1998). However, this decision for students to go to school was hardly unanimous for the consequences were unforgiving. What teacher in her right mind could accept the blood of her students on her hands. This was, in the words of Edina Dmitrović, "the most difficult decision ever" (1996).

Indeed, it was one thing to say that schools must "meet the requirements" or that each school "received the obligation" to organize instruction, but what do you do if you have no school, if your school was shelled into ruin, or if your school is dead center on the frontline? Who in their right minds thought about surrealistic conditions such as these, about how teachers and students would adapt to conditions where there was simply no school and classes were organized and taught in basements or shelters below the ground? Thus Avdo Hajdo wondered, when he looked back on his own personal creation, the Avdo Hodžić Local Community War School, about what it was like then at the beginning. "It was impossible," he said as we stood near the Malta Bridge just off Sniper Alley and gazed out across Čengić Vila. "It was hard to imagine a school somewhere" (1998).

Just as the teachers thought about somehow doing the impossible, the parents also thought about the impossibilities, refusing to send their children to school with the city under siege. Why would any parents in their right mind send their kids off to school, allow them to walk the streets and sidewalks to school, while rockets and mortars were tearing into the city and snipers on Hrasno hill and in Grbavica apartments were killing people on those very streets? "When I went to school there" in Hrasno, wrote Dino Ćatović, one of the students, "I tried to avoid open spaces as

much as possible." Dino walked the streets behind sniper screens of concrete barriers or sheet metal placed at critical intersections for protection
from the snipers. "Even when it seemed like it was very quiet (no sniper
bullets whistling)," he said, "snipers could surprise you" (1999). Thus in
the process of creating the Kvadrant–Danilo Đokic Local Community
War School, Azra Belkić was one of those teachers who went door-to-
door to talk with parents, indeed to persuade these parents to send their
children to school amidst the shelling and the snipers (1998). The teachers did not take this task lightly for it was these very teachers who would
assume responsibility for the safety of their students, for the safety of the
children of the parents whom they persuaded to send their kids to their
schools. Thus said Edina Dmitrović, an elementary teacher during the
early years of the war, and a parent:

> We were frightened. We were frightened because it was too much re-
> sponsibility. We were frightened for ourselves, for our families. But to
> be involved in such a risk, to invite other people's children and get
> them killed, that was too high a risk for most of us. . . . two–three
> weeks thinking, meetings, talking. Most women teachers were against
> it. We said, "to hell with school, let them be alive." I don't want to be
> responsible. I don't want somebody's mother to look at me and say,
> "You killed him." (1996)

"Why did they do this?" I would ask the teachers, and the answer, striking in its simplicity, came from Avdo Hajdo, "You have to live." You
could have been a "cellar person," one of the *podrumski ljudi*, but then,
of course, you couldn't have been a teacher. "OK, we have to survive,"
said Edina Dmitrović. "Let's go and do it."

So, "that's how we come to 'war schools.'" If the psychology of
people in the besieged city was trying to establish "a normal life . . . to
form a more ordinary environment that resembled a normal way of life,"
then schools were indeed a reflection of the ordinary, of the normality, of
life before and the hope of life in the aftermath of the siege. On the sur-
face, schooling during the siege suggests a certain abnormality, sending
kids to war schools amidst a war for survival, surely the abnormal for
those of us living our lives in normal conditions. But then the siege itself
was abnormal, and what schools represent here is, instead, a normal adaptation to the abnormal conditions of biblical siege warfare utilizing
modern military technology in the last decade of the twentieth century.
Only by creating the illusion of normality, suggests Mujo Musagić, could
the people of Sarajevo maintain the desire to survive the madness of
siege conditions. "The war schools offered an additional sense of normal

life to children and adults; they offered strength and the belief that it is possible to survive the impossible conditions of hunger, thirst, wounding, and dying" (1998). Amidst the shelling and the snipers, "our inner compulsion [was] to organize a school, as quickly as possible and *whatever the cost*, to normalize the lives of children living in totally impossible circumstances." In the words of Hajrija-Šahza Jahić:

> We realized that school was the only institutional structure, which could offer continuity from the pre-war life to the current life of refugees and war. . . . School makes us look ahead to the next lesson, to an activity we have to prepare for.
> We knew that school is a stabilizing factor in a life where the future is unclear, where no one knows what the next day will bring. The elements which stabilize life and make it predictable are of enormous importance to the psychological well-being of a child. (1996:11)

Thus, in the process of adapting instruction for wartime conditions in the war schools of Sarajevo, the teachers and students in their basement and corridor classrooms developed a common bond of teaching and learning under the gun while sharing a common danger. "In those days," wrote Dino Ćatović of this common bond, "students and teachers were like a family. We all shared the same danger and troubles of war. . . . Maybe it is unusual that a student says all the best about his school, but I still think that Treća Gimnazija had the best teachers, maybe not in the academic sense, but they were good people who always cared for the students even in the hardest times" (1999). And those teachers with whom I talked thought that the students were good people as well, who always cared for the teachers, even in the hardest times.

Once a local school was organized at one of the punkts, the idea was then to organize another such punkt, and then to connect these points to each other within the local community, and develop a systematic network of local community schools. "The idea was to connect the small points, the micro-environments, which, at the beginning, operated independently," to reiterate Professor Jahić, "to develop a scheme, to develop a kind of organized system of war schools" (1998). While teachers such as Azra Belkić in Kvadrant–Danilo Đokic, Avdo Hajdo in Avdo Hodžić, and Behija Jakić in Dobrinja, organized schooling in the micro-environments of the local communities, educators such as Hajrija-Šahza Jahić and Melita Sultanović at the Pedagogical Institute developed the scheme of an organized system of schooling across the city. It was the organization of the war schools in the local communities systematically organized across the four municipalities of "free Sarajevo" that implemented the directives of the Ministry of Education. The organization of the war schools of Sarajevo forged the "structural conditions" of schooling that had to "undergo transformation resulting from pressures for adaptive efficiency" in order to survive the siege (Shimahara, 1979:2).

To the teachers then, the organization of war schools during the early years of the siege represented an opportunity to normalize life, or at least to create the illusion of normality, for the children of Sarajevo who were living in totally impossible circumstances. Indeed, these circumstances were brought on by a ruthless enemy from the hills above who sought to physically destroy the city and to psychologically destroy its people. "By October 1992," wrote Ed Vuilliamy, "Sarajevo was not just under siege . . . it was on the rack." Vuilliamy's words provide some of the most powerful images of the psychological effect of the siege. He wrote, "The shelling was cynical and calculated to terrify as well as to kill. . . . People looked out as though the air itself was menacing them and could tear their bodies to shreds, their faces vitrified in the frozen effort of concentration and fear" (1994:186–187). Indeed, to strive for normality, or even the illusion of normality, or even to adapt to the abnormality, became a battle in itself, "a battle of the mind," in the words of Robert King Hall, "that most intangible yet fundamental of battlegrounds" (1948:59). Should there be any doubt about this "battle of the mind," we need only to recall the words of Ratko Mladić ordering the shelling of Sarajevo neighborhoods that he couldn't pronounce. "*Razvućite im pamet*," said General Mladić to his artillery commander in no uncertain terms. "Stretch their brains."

If you were not carrying a rifle then, and you had made the decision to live, the decision to survive, you fought the battle of Sarajevo, the battle of the mind, in whatever way you could. In this regard, the teachers of Sarajevo fought their battle in the basement classrooms of the war schools in their local communities and in the frontline schools on the "first battle line" in the shadow of the enemy. Thus the struggle to normalize the lives of children living under the totally impossible conditions of the siege became a struggle of the adaptation of instruction for wartime conditions by Sarajevo educators, viewed here through the lens of the war schools and the frontline schools of the city. "For sure, the war schools in Bosnia and Herzegovina played a part in defending this country and its people," writes Mujo Musagic, who is able to locate the place of war schools within the larger context of the war for the country itself. Indeed, Hajrija-Šahza Jahić offers this vision of the battle of Sarajevo as a battle of the mind fought by the teacher as "the warrior and pedagogical patriot" of the country. "What can one say about teachers in wartime?" she asked, only to answer that it was "the teachers who were thus in the front line in the fight against the aggressor." Professor Jahić then offers the hope for their place in history, that history will recognize their sacrifice during the war for the independence of the country:

> We hope that history will devote both space and time to them and their efforts, because it is thanks to their efforts that such a basic part of the new state has been preserved and continues to thrive. . . .
>
> The work of teachers and school inspectors with pupils and the way in which pupils and parents slowly accepted this work, and how they all burned with a desire to build up education and fought a common battle—all this will form an inexhaustible source of inspiration for writers and artists. But however much is written, it will never be enough, because each pupil and each teacher, each parent, represents an individual history, a drama, and an inspiration.
>
> Therefore I dedicate these lines to *THE TEACHER*, the warrior and pedagogical patriot of our land. (1996:27)

In this regard, I dedicate this book to the teachers, and to the students, of Treća Gimnazija who fought the battle of Sarajevo in the war schools of the local communities and in the frontline school dead on Heroes' Square. Their story has served as a source of inspiration for this writer, and I know very well that this book will never be enough to represent their individual histories, their own personal battles of the mind, and their courage and defiance during the siege of Sarajevo.

Postscript

On 25 March 2000, on a warm Saturday evening almost eight years to the day of the initial assault on Sarajevo, Treća Gimnazija celebrated the return of the school community to the original school buildings under the linden trees on Wilson Promenade just by the Miljacka River. With flags hanging from the rafters in the new auditorium, representatives from the Bosnian government, from Sarajevo city, as well as from the United States and Sweden, the two countries that provided reconstruction assistance monies, were in attendance to celebrate the occasion. The honored guests included: United States ambassador to Bosnia and Herzegovina, Thomas Miller, and USAID officials, Edward Kadunc and Merrit Broady, the ambassador of Sweden, Nils Eliasson, and the mayor of the City of Stockholm, Carl Cederschiold. Perry Lingman, the rector of the Stockholm Office of Educational Administration, perhaps the single most prominent figure in the reconstruction assistance program, was unable to attend because of the grave illness of his wife.

Eight months before, on 30 July 1999, in the aftermath of the NATO bombing of Yugoslavia, the president of the United States, Bill Clinton, used his speech at Treća Gimnazija, referred to by the *Washington Post* as "an ethnically diverse high school in Sarajevo," to remind the people of Yugoslavia that they could expect no reconstruction monies until Milošević was removed from power (Babington, 1999). In the process, Clinton stated his wishes for the future of Treća Gimnazija in the following manner. "I want this school—this school rebuilt—to be the symbol of all of our tomorrows," he said. "And I will do my best to see that the United States is your partner and your friend" (USIA, 1999). Indeed, within the year, the school was completely rebuilt, and USAID monies provided the basis for reconstruction and repair of the buildings. Monies from the City of Stockholm and the government of Sweden provided the basis for reconstruction and repair of the interior structure.

The honored Bosnian guests included Alija Izetbegović, the president of Bosnia and Herzegovina, Mustafa Mujezinović, the governor of Sarajevo Canton, and Sven Alkalaj, the Bosnian ambassador to the United States, who wrote a foreword for this book, and who was instrumental in obtaining American assistance for the reconstruction of the school. The first day of spring, 21 March, was selected as the new school day to replace the original school day of 6 April, Sarajevo Liberation Day, but which also happened to mark the first day of the assault on the city. On Monday, 27 March, the teachers returned to the school for their first day of inservice and were given a tour of the new buildings for the very first time. On Tuesday, 28 March, the students returned to the school where they were given their own tour of the new classrooms by the teachers and administrators. Wednesday, 29 March, was a regular school day, the first full day of classes in the original school buildings since the beginning of the siege of Sarajevo on 6 April 1992. The program to honor the occasion of the return of the Treća Gimnazija community back to its original school buildings read as follows:

> In the period from 1992–1995, the school premises were badly damaged and the entire school property was destroyed as the school was located on the frontline. The school clock was silenced completely, life was frozen and there was a foreboding that life would never come back to the school. The defenders of the city entered [and occupied] the school premises [on the frontline] and we are proud of it. The school did an honorable service for the defense of the city. (Treća Gimnazija, 2000)

References

Alispahić, Amina. 1995. "M. Selimović: Bosna je moja velika i stalna ljubav" [M. Selimović: Bosnia is My Great and Permanent Love]. Unpublished Paper, Treća gimnazija (27 July).

Andrić, Jelena. n.d. Personal correspondence to author.

Avdagić, Emina. 2000. Personal communication to author, Sarajevo (28 March).

———. 1998. Personal interview by author, Sarajevo (26 May).

Avdagić, Emina, and Avdo Hajdo. 1999. Personal interview by author, Sarajevo (2 November).

Avdagić, Emina, Edina Dmitrović, and Avdo Hajdo. 1996. Personal interview by author, Sarajevo (10 June).

Avdić, Avdo. 1995. Personal communication to author, Zenica (6 March).

Babington, Charles. 1999. "West to Bolster Balkans." *Washington Post* (31 July): A15–16.

Banjanović, N. 1993. "Voda iz novih izvorišta" [Water from New Springs]. *Oslobođenje* (12 September): 6.

———. 1993. "'Velepekara' ne krčmi brašno" ['Velepekara' Does Not Sell Flour]. *Oslobođenje* (16 October): 11.

Baudrillard, Jean. 1996. "No Pity for Sarajevo"; "The West's Serbianization"; "When the West Stands in for the Dead." In *This Time We Knew: Western Responses to Genocide in Bosnia*, ed. Thomas Cushman and Stjepan G. Meštrović. New York: New York University Press. 79–89.

Belkić, Azra. 1998. Personal interview by author, Sarajevo (26 May).

Berman, David M. 1995. "In the City of Lost Souls." *The Social Studies* 86:5 (September/October): 197–204.

————. 1997. "The Heroes of Treća Gimnazija: A War School in Sarajevo." *School of Education Newsletter*. University of Pittsburgh (Winter): 6–9.

Bešlija, Hajrija, Atija Fako, Hajrija Jahić, and Melita Sultanović. 1995. "Pedagoški patriotizam" [Pedagogical Patriotism]. *Bosansko-hercegovački školski glasnik* 1:2 (February): 22–23.

Bogdanović, Bogdan. 1995. "The City and Death." In *Balkan Blues: Writing out of Yugoslavia*, ed. Joanna Labon. Evanston, Illinois: Northwestern University Press. 36–73.

Bulja, Seniha. 1994 (1993). "Haustorska škola: model vaspitno-obrazovnog rada na Dobrinji" [The Stairway School: A Model of Educational Work in Dobrinja]. Paper presented at *Školstvo u ratnim uslovima* Symposium, Sarajevo (18 April).

Burns, John. 1992. "Intense Fighting in Sarajevo Traps 350 from U.N. Staff." *New York Times*. (15 May): 12.

————. 1992. "The Death of a City: Elegy for Sarajevo—A Special Report; A People under Artillery Fire Manage to Retain Humanity." *New York Times* (8 June): 1.

————. "Taped Order Loud and Clear: 'Burn It All.'" *New York Times* (9 June): 10.

Castra. 1995. www.damir@cip.e-technik.uni-erlangen.de, message posted on Bosnet list: bosnet@doc.ic.ac.uk, "Voices from Sarajevo" (10 April).

Ćatović, Dino. 1996. "Što za mene znači mir" [What Peace Means to Me]. Unpublished Paper, Treća gimnazija.

————. 1999. Personal correspondence to author (26 December).

————. 2000. Personal correspondence to author (18 January).

Cohen, Roger. 1994. "Bosnia Foes Agree to a Four-Month Truce, Carter Reports." *New York Times* (21 December): 1.

————. 1994. "A Cease-Fire Called Winter Settles over Bosnia." *New York Times* (22 December): 12.

————. 1994. "Two Die as Blasts Rip a Market in Sarajevo." *New York Times* (23 December): 3.

————. 1994. "Foes in Bosnia Sign Cease-Fire Accord, but Pitfalls Remain. *New York Times* (24 December): 1.

————. 1995. "Under Its Calm, Sarajevo Hides Deep Bitterness." *New York Times* (28 January): 1.

————. 1995. "Bosnian Army on the Attack, Breaking Truce." *New York Times* (21 March): 1.

————. 1995. "Serb Shells Kill 8 in a Sarajevo Suburb." *New York Times* (8 May): 3.

————. 1995. "In Sarajevo, Victims of a 'Postmodern' War." *New York Times* (21 May): 1–8.

————. 1995. "Serbs Kill Bosnian Leader and Take More Hostages: Copter Downed—33 Britons are Seized." *New York Times* (29 May): 1, 5.

————. 1995. "Fighting in Bosnia Flares over Posts Abandoned by U.N." *New York Times* (2 June): 1.

————. 1995. "Where Hope Has Withered: A Special Report." *New York Times* (28 June): 1, 6.

Conić, Nada. 1996. "Translator's Preface: Parallel Lives." In *Sarajevo Days, Sarajevo Nights*, by Elma Softić. Saint Paul, Minnesota: Hungry Mind Press. 1–9.

Čustović, Emin. 1994 (1993). "Organizovanje i izvođenje nastave u ratnim uslovima" [Organizing and Conducting Instruction in War Conditions]. Paper presented at *Školstvo u ratnim uslovima* Symposium, Sarajevo (18 April).

Dizdar, Srebren. 1996. "Prospects for Peace: The Reconstruction of Bosnia and Herzegovina." Paper presented at University of Pittsburgh, Pittsburgh, Pennsylvania (6 November).

Dizdarević, Zlatko.1994. "One Thousand Days of Solitude." *Time* (12 December): 33.

————. 1994. *Portraits of Sarajevo*. New York: Henry Holt.

————. 1994. "We'll Die Together and in Love," In *Sarajevo: A War Journal*, ed. Zlatko Dizdarević. New York: Henry Holt. 184–187.

Dmitrović, Edina. 1996. Personal interview by author, Sarajevo (7 June).

————. 1996. Personal interview by author, Sarajevo (19 June).

Dnevni avaz. 1998. "Ovo je naših pet minuta" [This is Our Five Minutes]. (18 May): 12.

Donia, Robert J., and John V.A. Fine, Jr. 1994. *Bosnia & Herzegovina: A Tradition Betrayed*. New York: Columbia University Press.

Drakulić, Slavenka. 1994. "Afterword." In *Sarajevo: Exodus of a City*, by Dževad Karahasan. New York: Kodansha International. 113–123.

Ensar, Zgodić. 1996. "Šta za mene znači mir" [What Peace Means to Me]. Unpublished Paper, Treća gimnazija.

Gagula, Alen. 1994. "Nepokoreni grad" [Unconquered City]. *Prva linija* 3:14 (15 April): 6–7.

Glenny, Misha. 1994. *The Fall of Yugoslavia: The Third Balkan War*. New York: Penguin Books.

Grossberg, Lawrence. 1989. "Pedagogy in the Present: Politics, Postmodernity, and the Popular." In *Popular Culture, Schooling, and Everyday Life*, ed. Henry A. Giroux, Roger I. Simon, and

Contributors. Granby, Massachusetts: Bergin & Harvey Publishers. 91–115.

Hadžić, Jasna. 1995. "Rat je velika čekaonica nasilne smrti u koju je pretvoren svijet" [War is a Large Waiting Room of Violent Death into Which the World Has Turned]. Unpublished Paper, Treća gimnazija (27 July).

Hajdo, Avdo. 1998. Personal interview by author, Sarajevo (6 May).

———. 1998. Personal interview by author, Sarajevo (12 May).

Halimić, Azra. 1994 (1993). In *"Muzej školstva u ratnim uslovima"* [Museum of Schooling in War Conditions], by Božana Sakal et al. Paper presented at the *Školstvo u ratnim uslovima* Symposium, Sarajevo, (18 April).

Hall, Robert King. 1948. "The Battle of the Mind: American Educational Policy in Germany and Japan." *Columbia Journal of International Affairs* 2:1 (Winter): 59–70.

Hoang Thi Mai Huong. 1992. Personal communication to author, Ho Chi Minh City, Viet Nam (9 July).

Hrapović, Ehlimana. 1994. "The Wounded Youth of My Town." Unpublished Paper, Treća gimnazija (June).

Hromadžić, Mehmed. 1993. "Školska godina nije izgubljena" [The School Year is not Lost]. *Prosvjetni list* 48:831 (June): 3.

Huskić, Belma. 1995. "Rat je velika čekaonica nasilne smrti u koju je pretvoren svijet" [War is a Large Waiting Room of Violent Death into Which the World Has Turned]. Unpublished Paper, Treća gimnazija (27 July).

Imamović, Mustafa, and Muhidin Pelesić. 1994. *Historija: IV Razred Gimnazije* [History: IV Class Gimnazija]. Sarajevo: Ministarstvo Obrazovanja, Nauke i Kulture.

Isaković, Fahrudin. 1993. "Uslovi za odvijanje nastave u srednjim školama" [Conditions for Organizing Instruction in Secondary Schools]. Unpublished Document (6 September).

Jabučar, Abdulah. 1994. "Organizacija škola u ratu" [Organizing Schools in the War]. *Bosankso-hercegovački školski glasnik* 1:1 (August): 4–5.

———.1997. *Zbirka propisa iz oblasti obrazovanja* [Collection of Regulations from the Field of Education]. Fojnica: Svjetlost—Fojnica.

Jahić, Hajrija-Šahza. 1996. "The War Schools of Sarajevo." In *Schools War Children: Sarajevo*, ed. Kirsten Wangebo. Copenhagen: Royal Danish School of Educational Studies. 11–27.

————. 1997. "Ratne škole Sarajeva" [The War Schools of Sarajevo]. *Naša škola* 50:2: 101–107.

————. 1998. Personal interview by author, Sarajevo (20 May).

————. 1999. Personal communication to author, Sarajevo (21 October).

Jakić, Behija. 1998. Personal interview by author, Sarajevo (19 May).

Jevdević, Karmela. 1996. Personal interview by author, Sarajevo (7 June).

Kovačević, Tatjana. 1996. "How Did I Survive the War?" Personal correspondence to author (19 June).

Kulovac, Jasmin. 1999. "Zovem se Kulovac Jasmin" [My Name is Jasmin Kulovac]. Personal correspondence to author (7 November).

Kurspahić, Kemal. 1997. *As Long As Sarajevo Exists*. Translated by Colleen London. Stony Creek, Connecticut: The Pamphleteer's Press.

Maas, Peter. 1996. *Love Thy Neighbor: A Story of War*. New York: Alfred A. Knopf.

Marinović, Mirko. 1998. Personal interview by author, Sarajevo (20 May).

Memišević, Mirzeta. 1998. In *Almanah Treće gimnazije, 50 godina, 1948-1998*. 43.

Miković, Milanka. 1998. "Djeca sa teškoćama u razvoju—briga društvene zajednice" [Children with Difficulties in Development—Community Social Responsibility]. Paper presented at the *Djeca sa specijalnim potrebama* [Children with Special Needs] Ombudsman Roundtable, Sarajevo (7 May).

Ministarstvo obrazovanja, nauke, kulture i sporta, Republika Bosna i Herzegovina, and Sekretarijat za obrazovanje, nauku, kulturu i fizičku kulturu, Grada Sarajeva. 1993. "Organizacija i rad srednjih škola u mjesnim zajednicama" [Organization and Operation of Secondary Schools by Local Communities]. Unpublished Document (25 January).

Mrkić, V. 1993. "Narodu treba hljeba" [The People Need Bread]. *Oslobođenje* (18 October): 5.

Musagić, Mujo. 1998. "Ratne škole u Bosni i Hercegovini" [War Schools in Bosnia and Herzegovina]. Personal correspondence to author (24 August).

New York Times. 1995. "Bitter Fighting Rages Around Sarajevo" (18 May): 4.

Oslobođenje. 1992. "Sarajevo se branilo napadom" [Sarajevo Defended Itself from Attack]. (14 May): 1.

————. 1992. "Slike užasa u Hrasnom" [Pictures of Horror in Hrasno]. (14 May): 3.

————. 1992. "Nesalomljivo Sarajevo" [Unbreakable Sarajevo]. (1 August): 1.

————. 1992. "Sarajevo ucijenjeno vodom!" [Sarajevo Blackmailed with Water!]. (5 August): 1.

————. 1992. "Mrak po planu agresora" [Darkness by Aggressor's Plans]. (17 August): 1.

————. 1992. "Baščaršija u plamenu" [Baščaršija in Flames]. (18 August): 1.

————. 1992. "Nove rane na duši Sarajeva" [New Wounds on the Soul of Sarajevo]. (24 August): 1.

————. 1992. "Osmero mrtvih" [Eight Dead] (31 August): 1.

————. 1992. "Rat određuje termin" [War Determines the Term]. (8 September): 4.

————. 1992. "Nastavu prilagoditi ratnim uslovima" [Instruction to be Adapted to Wartime Conditions]. (10 September): 8.

————. 1992. "Bakir (Šemsudina) Hrapović" (10 December): 3.

————. 1993. "'Školsko zvono' za srednjoškolce" ["School Bells" for Secondary Schools]. (8 February): 4.

————. 1993. "Srednje škole: produžen upisni rok" [Secondary Schools: Term of Enrollment Extended]. (16 February): 8.

————. 1993. "Granatama od 152 MM po Sarajevu" [(With) 152 mm Shells on Sarajevo]. (17 October): 1.

————. 1993. "Novi napad na Sarajevo" [New Attack on Sarajevo]. (19 October): 1.

————. 1993. "Preko hiljadu granata na Sarajevo" [Over a Thousand Shells on Sarajevo]. (24 October): 1.

————. 1993. "Hljeb samo za prioritete" [Bread Only for Priorities]. (25 October): 3.

————. 1993. "Masakr pred školom" [Massacre in Front of School]. (10 November: 1.

————. 1993. "Opet masakr u Sarajevu" [Massacre Again in Sarajevo]. (11 November): 1.

————. 1995. "Granatirano Sarajevo" [Sarajevo Shelled]. (13 March): 1.

————. 1995. "Krvavi vikend u Sarajevu: snajperisti ponovo siju smrt" [Bloody Weekend in Sarajevo: Snipers Again Sow Death]. (13 March): 11.

Pawełczyńska, Anna. 1979. *Values and Violence in Auschwitz: A Sociological Analysis*, trans. Catherine S. Leach. Berkeley: University of California Press.

Pedagoški zavod. 1992. "Program rada u ratnim uslovima za 1992 godinu" [Operational Program in War Conditions for 1992]. Unpublished Document (September).

————. 1993. "Informacija o početku nastave u srednjim školama, 92–93 godine" [Information on the Beginning of Instruction in Secondary Schools, 92–93]. Unpublished Document (April).

————. 1993–1994 School Year. "Zaduženja škola po mjesnim zajednicama (šk. 93/94 godine)" [Assignment of Schools by Local Community (93/94 School Year]. Unpublished Document.

————. 1994. *Nastavni planovi i programi: 1994/95* [Instructional Plans and Programs: 1994/95]. Sarajevo: Ministarstvo obrazovanja, nauke, kulture i sporta, Republika Bosna i Hercegovina.

————. 1995. *Nastavni planovi i programi 2: 1995/1996* [Instructional Plans and Programs 2: 1995/1996]. Sarajevo: Ministarstvo obrazovanja, nauke, kulture i sporta, Republika Bosna i Hercegovina.

Polimac, Lejla. 1996. Personal correspondence to author (19 June).

Prcić, Amira. 1996. "My Experiences in the War," Personal correspondence to author (19 June).

Prstojević, Miroslav. 1993. *Sarajevo Survival Guide*. Translated by Aleksandra Wagner with Ellen Elias-Bursac. FAMA.

Prva linija. 1993. "Obruč oko Sarajeva" [Noose around Sarajevo]. 2:2 (1 February): 2–3.

Rieff, David. 1996. *Slaughterhouse: Bosnia and the Failure of the West*. New York: Touchstone.

Roljić, Gordana. 1998. Personal interview with author, Sarajevo (5 May).

————. 1998. Personal interview with author, Sarajevo (19 May).

Rudić, Borka. 1996. "Nepovratno izgubljene godine" [Irretrievably Lost Years]. *Oslobođenje* (31 March): 9.

Sakal, Božana, Nadija Hadžimehmedagić, Senada Nakaš, Azemina Osmanagić, Nada Hrasnica, and Mirko Marinović. 1994 (1993). "Muzej školstva u ratnim uslovima" [Museum of Schooling in War Conditions]. Paper presented at *Školstvo u ratnim uslovima* Symposium, Sarajevo (18 April).

Silber, Laura, and Allan Little. 1996. *Yugoslavia: Death of a Nation*. New York: TV Books, Inc.

Shimahara, Nobuo K. 1979. *Adaptation and Education in Japan*. New York: Praeger Publishers.

Službeni list RBiH [Official Gazette of the Republic of Bosnia and Herzegovina]. 1992. "Odluka o zavođenju radne obaveze" [Decision on Establishing a Work Obligation]. 1:92 (9 April).

————. 1992. "Odluka o upisu učenika u osnovne i srednje škole i o početku nastave u školskoj 1992/1993 godini" [Decision on the Registration of Students in Elementary and Secondary Schools and the Beginning of Instruction in the 1992/1993 School Year]. 4:92 (18 September).

Smail, Vesnić. 1994. "Ratni nastavni centar Dobrinja" [The Dobrinja War School Center]. *Glasnik* 1:1 (August): 17–20.

Smajkić, Arif. 1992. "Bilten," Republički zavod za zdravstvenu zaštitu–Republički krizni štab za zdravstvenu i socijalnu bezbjednost 21 (6 September).

————. 1993. "Bilten," Republički zavod za zdravstvenu zaštitu–Republički krizni štab za zdravstvenu i socijalnu bezbjednost 68 (2 August).

————. 1993. "Bilten," Republički zavod za zdravstvenu zaštitu–Republički krizni štab za zdravstvenu i socijalnu bezbjednost 80 (25 October).

————. 1993. "Bilten," Republički zavod za zdravstvenu zaštitu–Republički krizni štab za zdravstvenu i socijalnu bezbjednost 83 (15 November).

————. 1994. "Bilten," Republički zavod za zdravstvenu zaštitu–Republički krizni štab za zdravstvenu i socijalnu bezbjednost 95 (7 February).

————. 1995. "Bilten," Republički zavod za zdravstvenu zaštitu–Republički krizni štab za zdravstvenu i socijalnu bezbjednost 142 (2 January).

Softić, Elma. 1996. *Sarajevo Days, Sarajevo Nights*. Translated by Nada Conić. Saint Paul, Minnesota: Hungry Mind Press.

Spaho, Fehim. 1993. "Organizacija i rad srednjih škola u mjesnim zajednicama" [The Organization and Operation of Secondary Schools in Local Communities]. Unpublished Document (2 March).

Squitieri, Tom. 1995. "'Full-Scale War' Around the Corner in Bosnia." *USA Today* (28 April): 10A.

Sudetic, Chuck. 1998. *Blood and Vengeance: One Family's Story of the War in Bosnia*. New York: W.W. Norton.

————. 1999. Personal correspondence to author (30 June).

Sultanović, Melita. 1993. "Prva 'ratna škola'—na Bjelavama" [The First War School—in Bjelave]. *Prosvjetni list* 831:48 (June): 4.

————. 1996. "Organization and Maintenance of the School System during the Civil War in Sarajevo 1992–1993." In *Schools War Children: Sarajevo*, ed. Kirsten Wangebo. Copenhagen: Royal Danish School of Educational Studies. 7–10.

————. 1998. Personal interview by author, Sarajevo (1 June).

Topčić, Zlatko. 1996. "Grbavički violinisti" [Grbavica Violinists]. *Oslobođenje*. (6 June): 2.

Treća gimnazija. 1992–1993 School Year. *Dnevnik rada, punkt: Ivan Krndelj* [Work Journal, Punkt: Ivan Krndelj]. Unpublished Document.

————. 1992–1993 School Year. *Dnevnik rada, Ratne škole na području mjesne zajednice Bistrik* [Work Journal, War Schools on the Territory of Bistrik Local Community]. Unpublished Document.

————. 1992–1993 School Year. *Dnevnik rada, Ratne škole na području mjesne zajednice Kovači* [Work Journal, War Schools on the Territory of Kovači Local Community]. Unpublished Document.

————. 1992–1996. *Školski ljetopis* [School Annual]. Unpublished Document.

————. 1993–1994 School Year. *Ratna škola mjesne zajednice Avdo Hodžić*, "Osnovni podaci o školi" [Avdo Hodžić Local Community War School, Primary Data about the School]. Unpublished Document.

————. 1993–1994 School Year. *Ratna škola mjesne zajednice Avdo Hodžić, Odjeljenska knjiga, Razred prvi I, Odjeljenje I* [Avdo Hodžić Local Community War School, Class Section Book, Class I, Class Section 1]. Unpublished Document.

————. 1993–1994 School Year. *Ratna škola mjesne zajednice Kumrovec, Odjeljenksa knjiga, Razred I, Odjeljene I* [Kumrovec Local Community War School, Class Section Book, Class I, Class Section I]. Unpublished Document.

————. 1993–1994 School Year. *Ratna škola mjesne zajednice Kvadrant–Danilo Đokić, Odjeljenska knjiga, Razred II, Odjeljenje G* [Kvadrant–Danilo Đokić Local Community War School, Class Section Book, Class II, Class Section G]. Unpublished Document.

————. 1993–1994. Unpublished School Documents.

————. 1998. *Almanah Treće gimnazije: 50 godina 1948–1998* [Almanac of the Third Gymnasium: 50 Years, 1948–1998]. Sarajevo: Grafičko-Izdavačka kuća d.d.).

————. 2000. School Program. Unpublished Document (25 March).

————. n.d. Letter. Unpublished Document.

UNICEF. 1994. *Children and Women in Bosnia and Herzegovina: A Situation Analysis.*

————. 1997. *Bosnia and Herzegovina, Women & Children: Situation Analysis.*

USIA. 1999. "Transcript: Clinton Remarks at Sarajevo Secondary School July 30" (30 July).

USIS. 1999. "US Assistance to the Third Gymnasium" (2 July).

Van Creveld, Martin. 1991. *The Transformation of War*. New York: Free Press.

Videopress. 1993. *Children under Seige: Sarajevo*. Milan Trivic, Producer (June).

Videoteka "Vankee," n.d.

Višnjić, Miodrag. 1979. *Mesna zajednica u političkom sistemu sociajalističkog samoupravljana* [The Local Community in a Political System of Socialistic Self-Governance]. Belgrade: "KOSMOS," 1979.

Vuilliamy, Ed. 1994. *Seasons in Hell: Understanding Bosnia's War*. New York: St. Martin's Press.

Winterbottom, Michael, Director. 1998. *Welcome to Sarajevo*. Miramax Films and Channel Four Films, A Dragon Pictures Production.

Zuković, Ljubomir. 1995. Personal communication to author, Pale, Republika Srpska (10 March).

Index

188   *Index*

194

Index

About the Author

David M. Berman is an associate professor in the department of instruction and learning, School of Education, University of Pittsburgh, where he is an affiliated faculty member of the Russian and East European Studies (REES) Program. He has been a visiting scholar on the faculty of philosophy at the University of Sarajevo on two occasions: in 1996 in the department of English language and literature, and in 1998 in the department of pedagogy. In 2001 he returned to Bosnia as a Fulbright scholar, continuing his research on war schools at both the University of Sarajevo and the University of Banja Luka.